WHALEHUNTERS

WHALEHUNTERS
DUNDEE AND THE ARCTIC WHALERS

Malcolm Archibald

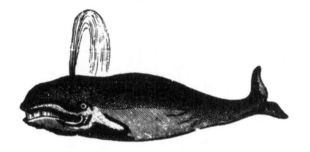

mercatpress
www.mercatpress.com

First published in 2004 by
Mercat Press, 10 Coates Crescent, Edinburgh EH3 7AL
www.mercatpress.com

ISBN: 184183 0658

For Cathy

Set in Korinna and Galliard at Mercat Press

Printed and bound in Great Britain by
Bell & Bain Ltd

CONTENTS

ILLUSTRATIONS

ACKNOWLEDGEMENTS

I would like to thank the following people for their help in the making of this book. Mr Fred Payne, Scoresby Curator, Whitby Museum; D. Sweeney and Eileen Moran, Local Studies Department, Central Library, Dundee; Elspeth Alexander, McManus Galleries, Dundee; Meic Pierce Owen, Special Collections, University of St Andrews; Arthur Credland, Humberside Libraries, Kingston upon Hull; Mr Edward Nicoll, Kinmont Court, Leamington Spa; Mr Angus Johnson, Shetland Archives; Mr Peter Holt, Muri, Switzerland; Mr Iain Flett, Richard Cullen, Angela Lockie and Angela Defede, City of Dundee Archives; Sheila Campbell, reference and Local Studies Department, War Memorial Gardens, Kirkcaldy; Jenny Tait and Michael Bolik, University of Dundee Archives; Mrs Pauline Smeed, historian, East Lothian Council; Mr Alexander Alison of Berwick upon Tweed, for permission to quote his great grandfather's account of his whaling experience; Mr James B. M. Gibson, of Ontario, Canada, for information on his great-great-grandfather, Robert Edgar, harpoonist and preacher. Lastly, I would like to thank my wife, Catherine, and children Alexander and Hannah, for their patience while I was researching and writing.

SOURCE NOTES

The copyright for all the Customs and Excise (CE) records used in this book belong to the National Archives of Scotland (NAS), but are held in Dundee under the 'Charge and Superintendence' scheme. For reference purposes they are recorded as 'Dundee City Archives, held on behalf of the Keeper of the Records of Scotland', followed by the AF (Agriculture and Fisheries) or CE number. In this book that has been shortened to DCA/KRS/CE, followed by the reference number and, where applicable, the date.

Copyright for the Alexander Alison material rests with the family.

University of Dundee material is referenced as 'Archive Services, University of Dundee'. That has been shorted to ASUOD/.

Material from the McManus Galleries, Dundee, is referenced as 'McManus Galleries, Dundee City Council Leisure and Arts'. That has been shortened to MDCLA/.

Material from Dundee Central Library is referenced as 'Central Library, Dundee City Council Neighbourhood Resources and Development'. That has been shortened to CLDCRD/.

Abbreviations

AUL—Aberdeen University Library, Dept of Manuscripts and Archives
CLDCRD—Central Library, Dundee City Council Neighbourhood Resources and Development
FCKDM—Fife Council, Kirkcaldy District Museums
NAS—National Archives of Scotland
SA—Shetland Archives
SA/SC—Shetland Archives Sheriff Court
SA/AD—Shetland Archives, Procurator Fiscal records
SAUSC—St Andrews University Special Collections
SPRI—Scott Polar Research Institute

INTRODUCTION

*'The Whale went to the bottom. It remained there some time, came up—
as soon as she appeared the fast Boat threw a lance which mortally
wounded her. The fish blew blood and nearly sunk the boat with the
quantity... the Boat I was in got right on the top of her back. She raised
herself, shuddered, upset the Boat, went down to the bottom and died...
the ice began to close in upon us, the Ship could not get near us. The wind
shifted, increased the intensity of the cold. For want of exertion my
circulation flagged. I soon became useless. Laid down in the bottom of the
Boat for dead.'*

A fourteen-year-old Scottish seaman named Alexander Alison wrote the
above lines. He was only one of many youngsters who signed on the
whaling ships that sailed annually to the Arctic, but unlike most others
he left some sort of record of his voyaging. As it is the purpose of this
small book to record the whaling industry as it affected the seamen and
their families, memoirs such as Alison's are invaluable. However it is the
distillation of the experiences of all sections of the ship's company, together with that of the wives and families they left behind and of the
land-based people with whom they came in contact that creates the narrative of the whalers. For this reason logbooks and journals as well as
custom records, company records and newspapers have been consulted.

Shipmasters, mates or the surgeon that every whaling vessel was
obliged to carry wrote the vast majority of the journals that survive, in
Dundee as elsewhere. They provided a literate view of the whaling industry. Although many of the men who served before the mast could
write, few would be able to write a coherent piece of writing of any
length. Other evidence must therefore be sought to create a picture of
them. The opinions of their more socially fortunate contemporaries may
not always be unbiased, but do offer clues about the lives and characters
of whaling men.

Arctic whaling was a brutal business both for the men and the animals involved. The experience of sailing to the north, of hunting and of
killing the whales was intense and personal, but it was also a business
that was viewed as essential to the economy of the nation. The Scottish
Arctic whaling industry was based in a number of ports along the East

Coast. Peterhead, Aberdeen, Montrose, Dundee, Fraserburgh, Kirkcaldy, Burntisland, Bo'ness, Leith and Dunbar, all, at one time or another, had whaling companies, while many of the smaller ports contributed men, expertise and finance to the industry.

Of all these ports, Dundee had perhaps the largest interest, with the first known successful ship sailing north in 1754 and the last in 1913. For a period of some decades, Dundee was Britain's largest whaling port, and a city that built some of the finest and strongest vessels in the world. Captain Scott's *Discovery*, which still sits proud on the waterfront of Dundee, was built using skills perfected in the city's whaling fleet, while *Terra Nova*, the ship that rescued her from the Antarctic ice, was built in Dundee and manned by Dundee whalers. Although it is nearly nine decades since a Dundee ship last caught a whale, there are still reminders. East Whale Lane lies a long harpoon cast from the docks where whaling ships once berthed, Baffin Street recalls the great bay that lies between Canada and Greenland, and the Arctic Bar sits square in the centre of the city.

Obviously there can be no single portrait of a whaling man. Whaling ships carried large crews, many of whom were recruited in Dundee and the small ports of Angus and Fife. Others came from the Orkney and Shetland Islands. There are a recorded 820 whaling voyages from Dundee between 1815 and 1912,[1] giving an average of 8.45 whaling ship voyages a year. If every vessel carried around 45 crew, that would mean there were 36,900 separate experiences of a whaling voyage, in one city, in one century, mostly by before-the-mast seamen. Yet there are only a handful of accounts by these men, which makes those that do survive, such as the few pages of Alexander Alison, all the more important. The ordinary members of the crew, known variously as 'the people' or 'the hands' are the neglected men of whaling. They appear in the occasional photograph, huddled behind furs or looking suitably tough as they clutch harpoon or lance, but the lack of documentary evidence ensures that they are not really known. What sort of men would willingly sail to one of the most inhospitable areas of the world? What were their experiences? How did the world view them and how did they view themselves? Where did they come from and how did they behave?

Possibly because of the lack of written accounts, the world seems to have viewed whaling men less than favourably. The few influential men who did write of whalers appear to have seen them as drunken, boisterous and even mildly dangerous; they wrote of whalers as they perceived them. Almost invariably, the writers saw them on shore, when they had either returned from the ice, or were about to sail northward into danger. Any British seamen of the eighteenth or nineteenth century were at their worst at this time; whalers were no different. They got drunk, they sang, they caroused and brawled. Witnessing this behaviour, and knowing or caring nothing of the reasons behind it, respectable men affected to be appalled. They wrote of the whalers as 'the worst of people',[2] and the reputation stuck.

Even more recent writers have tended to categorise whaling men as wild, drunken and riotous. Perhaps more weight is given to this characterisation by the current interest in conservation. As whale hunting is now no longer necessary, so, by association, earlier whale hunters must have been unpleasant. But that is to impose modern perceptions onto the past. In the eighteenth and nineteenth centuries whaling was regarded as an economically essential industry, while whaling skippers were as respectable as any Master Mariners in the British merchant fleet.

There have been many excellent books written about the whaling industry, some about the adventures of the whalers, but few, if any, about the actual day-to-day life of the whaling men. It is the purpose of this small book to investigate the reality of whaling as experienced by the men themselves. By taking Dundee as the focal point, no slur was intended on any of the other whaling ports; many are mentioned throughout the text. Rather, the intention is to focus on one leading centre, so that it may be used as an example for all the other one-time whaling ports of Scotland, and, indeed, Britain.

The book is divided into thematic chapters that will draw a picture of whaling as experienced by the men who were there. Their background, beliefs, pastimes and behaviour will be examined so that what emerges is, hopefully, a rounded portrait of whaling. There is no intention of arguing the moral rights and wrongs of whaling as an industry: it would be unfair to put a twenty-first century question to an eighteenth or nineteenth century man. The question asked was *what:* what these men did, and what kind of people they were.

1

THE HISTORICAL BACKGROUND

'They that go down to the sea in ships, that do business in great waters;
these see the works of the Lord, and his wonders in the deep'
Psalms 107:23–24

Man has always hunted. He has hunted for food, for protection, for sport and for whatever commodity he believes can enhance his lifestyle. Sometimes the quarry is live, such as a whale, at other times it may be inanimate, such as the crystallised carbon known as diamonds. Hunting for living prey may be a compulsion, a vestige of the prehistoric instinct for survival, or part of the same competitive urge that powers top business and sports professionals. However, in many cases hunting was seen as necessary, either for food or for reasons that were perceived as economically sound at the time. In every form of hunting, for sport, food or business, there are three elements, the hunter, the quarry and the environment. Often the latter has a great influence on the outcome. Nowhere is that more evident than in Arctic whaling.

In whaling, as in other types of hunting, men were pitted against nature, but what was different was the constant presence of danger. While forms of hunting such as tiger stalking had moments of extreme danger when hunter and quarry were in close proximity, whaling men were in danger from the minute their ship sailed out of port. Rather than the quarry, their danger came from the environment, and increased the closer they came to the hunting grounds and the longer they remained there. Many more whalers died of shipwreck and exposure than ever were killed by the flailing flukes of a whale's tail.

It is natural that the hunter should take every advantage in hunting his quarry, whether that means using the most modern equipment possible or waiting for favourable weather. Whaling men were no exception. They used the most ingenious tools that civilisation could devise: harpoon guns, steam-powered vessels and the accumulated skills of centuries of experience, but even so they often lost the contest. In the eighteenth and nineteenth centuries, British whalers hunted in far northern or far southern waters on or beyond the edge of the polar ice. Seamen of the southern ocean had a saying to describe these high latitudes:

South of the 40s there is no Law,
South of the 50s there is no God.

The situation was little better in the north. The whaling men operated always in the natural element of the whale, where savage storms, fog and the presence or the threat of ice tended to equalise the odds. Frequently the margin between success and failure, between life and death, was no more than the width and substance of an ice floe. Whaling may be seen as a slaughter of the innocents, but the hunters were never supermen immune from danger. Nor were they hunting for fun, but to pursue an economic commodity. Whaling ships were expensive to build and run, the crews had to be paid, and the ship owners still required to make a profit. Whaling was commercial.

Today it would be extremely difficult to buy whale meat in Europe, and a post-war attempt to push it from shop shelves into the baskets of housewives was not a success. However, in the sixteenth century it was popular in England, for those who could afford it, but before the meat could be eaten, man had to catch his whale.

In the beginning, European whaling was a casual affair where coastal peoples pounced on whales that lay stranded on shore. Whalebone and stone harpoons dating from the Neolithic period have been found, but it is unlikely that Stone-Age man actively went to sea to hunt whales. Nonetheless, historians believe that around 1000 BC the Phoenicians, those fascinating Biblical mariners who sailed their black ships from Tyre to the 'Ocean Sea' beyond the Straits of Heracles, hunted whales in the Eastern Mediterranean. Perhaps the great fish that swallowed Jonah was seeking revenge for some unrecorded earlier attack.

Despite the harpoons and legends, there was an ambiguity about whaling among the ancient seamen of the Mediterranean. Dolphins, the smallest of the whale family, were particularly highly regarded, with the Greeks believing that their god Apollo disguised himself as a dolphin to swim the Central Sea. Perhaps that divine connection explains why the oracle at Delphi was named after the dolphin, with the perceived wisdom of that animal supposedly easing the passage of those who sought counsel. Greek law also imposed a death penalty for anybody who killed a dolphin, which they believed were men who had withdrawn to the sea, which, given the current beliefs about evolution, may not be too far from the truth. Even Pliny the Elder wrote of the friendliness of dolphins to man. There were other beliefs concerning whales; for instance to find a stranded whale was a sign that a member of the family would die.

Outwith the Mediterranean, mariners who probed the rougher waters of more hostile seas also knew and wrote about whales. There was the Norseman named Ohthere who, in 890 AD, sailed to the White Sea that lay beyond the North Cape. There he claimed to have seen a whale of 48 ells, or about 60 metres, in length. There is no reason to doubt his sighting, as large whales were more common before the spread of commercial whaling. Compare his account to that of William Scoresby, the whaling master and scientist who wrote that a respectable *mysticetus*—whale—would be from 80 to 100 feet (25–30 m) in length. Scoresby also wrote that when the animals reached maturity they could be 150 to 200 feet (45–60 m) long. As one of the most successful whaling captains of the early nineteenth century, Scoresby's words cannot be discounted and his book on Arctic whaling can be considered a classic.

Organised whaling in Western Europe seems to have begun around the Bay of Biscay, perhaps in the twelfth century or a little before. The Basques erected watchtowers along their coasts, from where a lookout gave warning when a whale was seen. These early whalers targeted the Right Whale, *Balaena Glacialis*, a slow-moving animal that was prolific in the bay at that time. Because *Balaena Glacialis* floated when it was killed, it was the right whale to kill and the hunters could tow it ashore for dismemberment. Even at that period, Europeans could find use for the whalebone, or baleen, that was in the mouth of the whale. A knight clad in anonymous grey armour required as many means of identification as possible while in battle, and strips of tough and flexible baleen made excellent plumes for his helmet.

The Basques were so successful that they virtually exterminated the once teeming whale population in the Bay and had to extend their operations. Having learned their seamanship in one of the stormiest areas of sea in Europe, there was no hardship in sailing into the open Atlantic, particularly as they had benefited from the advances in seamanship and ship design of the later Middle Ages.

One major innovation was the introduction of the stern-rudder for the side-rudder. The stern-rudder remained in the water even in bad weather, whereas a side-rudder would leave the sea with the heeling of the ship. In the Mediterranean the stern-rudder was named the 'Bayonnese rudder' in honour of the Basques. However, the side-rudder is remembered in the steering-board, or starboard side of the vessel.

Until the early fifteenth century, most vessels had a single mast and a square sail; thereafter the number of masts increased, while the pump, possibly an English invention, helped keep the vessel drier. The style of shipbuilding was also changing as carvel building spread from the Mediterranean. In carvel building the planks that form a ship's hull meet edge to edge over the load-bearing frame of the vessel, as opposed to the northern European style of clinker-build where the planks overlap each other. The invention of a sounding lead for taking measurement of depth, a primitive compass for determining north, and an hourglass for keeping time, all helped allow ships to sail further and with relatively greater safety.

When a Genoese captain named John Cabot sailed out of Bristol with an English ship and an English crew and discovered Newfoundland, whalers and fishermen headed west. The Newfoundland Banks were a happy hunting ground, spoiled only by the fogs that became notorious and weather that could veer from atrocious to the merely insufferable. The Basques seem to have hunted in the Gulf of St Lawrence and along the coast of Newfoundland, where again they were the pioneers of whaling. In the sixteenth century they established what has been called the whaling capital of the world at Red Bay in Labrador, with perhaps twenty ships a year battering across the mighty Atlantic to hunt the bowhead and right whales. It was a hard, bitterly cold life for the whalers from France and Spain who came here, and some 140 of their graves have been discovered around Red Bay, a sobering reminder that not only whales suffered because Europe desired whale oil. Port aux Basques, on the south-western tip of Newfoundland Island, was another Basque whaling station, later adopted by the French. Evidence of at least one shipwreck nearby is a reminder that the improved nautical technology of the sixteenth century was no proof against the Newfoundland weather.

The rewards must have more than balanced the casualties, for the Basques remained, hunting the various species of whales that abounded off this bleak but beautiful coast. The sea around the Maritime Provinces is unique, with vast shoals that breed their own conditions and their own names. There was the Widow's Bank and Peter's Bank off the southern shores of Newfoundland, and the Sable Bank south of Sable island, which itself lies a hundred miles south and west of Nova Scotia. There was the Great Fishing Bank east of St John's and the telltale Whale Bank that lies slightly further west. Stories of immense shoals of fish on these new-found coasts encouraged England to claim the totality of North

America, but the vacuous words of monarchs and politicians did not stop the whalers. Whoever claimed to own the land and the coasts, whalers from different nations hurled their harpoons at the great black-bodied whales and carried the oil back to Europe.

It is unfortunate that few of these men were literate, or if they were, their writings have not survived or are not widely available, for their reminiscences would have opened windows on a virtually unknown historical room. What have survived are the writings of explorers, thorough seamen, but of a different breed from the professional fishermen and whalers. Where the explorers came, saw and returned home to document, the whaling men endured year after year. What the explorers saw as a once-in-a-lifetime novelty was routine working existence to the whalers, and while it was in the interests of the explorers to make a drama out of their voyages, fishermen and whalers hoped only for moderate weather and a profitable catch.

However, as the explorers probed the northern oceans, searching for a passage across the shoulders of the world to Asia, they left their impressions in a score of journals. As they sailed over the very same oceans as the early whalers, in the same sort of vessel and in the same period, their perceptions would be similar. In the absence of journals from the whaling men, those of the explorers will be substituted. For instance there was Martin Frobisher, a Yorkshireman who was almost wrecked off Greenland and who described an Arctic storm in summer:

> There fell so much snow, with such bitter air, that we could scarce see one another...nor open our eyes to handle the ropes...every man persuading himself, that the wynter there must needs to extreme, where they found so unseasonable a summer.[1]

The early whalers must have thought the same. Frobisher experienced much of what the whalers saw. He found icebergs off the coast of Greenland, which he named West England and claimed in the name of Queen Elizabeth. He had drums beat and trumpets blare when a true Arctic fog enveloped him. He was there when some of his vessels moored to an iceberg, as the whalers were to do. He got lost in a blizzard and sailed into the 'Mistaken Straits' that was later to become the Hudson Straits. All these things were to become familiar to the whalers. Adverse currents assailed his ships, low clouds obscured the sun, fog shrouded the vessels, crewmen were tempted to desert, the crew of *Buss Emmanuel* spoke of mutiny, and Frobisher prayed for Divine aid. 'Lord now help, or never!' The words could have come from the lips of a thousand whaling men over hundreds of years of tragedy and turmoil in the north.

Frobisher's entire endeavour failed. He did not find the Northwest Passage to Asia and he did not find gold, but he had made precedents. He had helped crack open the northern door and had peered at the wonders inside. He had met, albeit briefly, the 'countrey people' on Lok's Island near Frobisher Bay and, most importantly, he had chronicled his exploits. His voyages, like those of other northern explorers, had helped to unravel the mysteries of the Arctic. He had also opened up more waters to the whale hunters.

John Davis, a Devon man, sailed *Sunshine* in Frobisher's wake. Again there was no interest in whaling, but on his initial voyage *Sunshine* came across a school of porpoises. Tiny by whaling standards, even these creatures proved too difficult for the explorersto catch. Davis recorded that they lost 'fish, irons, pastime and all' as the porpoise swam off with their hooks. If nothing else, the failed attempt proves the level of skill that a whale fisherman required. Three times Davis probed into what he would see as the howling wastes of the north, hoping for a Northwest Passage, but finding instead ice, storms and frustration. Alarmed by a terrible roaring noise, the explorers found that it originated from two icebergs rubbing against each other, a portent of what was to come.

Rounding Cape Farewell, the ice-collecting tail of Greenland, Davis cruised north on the warm water current that was to carry many later whaling fleets. When he reached the entrance to a great gulf whose echoing vastness stretched west and ever west, he saw a tidal overflow 'loathsomly crying like the rage of the waters under the London Bridge'.[2] It was a homely enough description for the entrance to one of the world's greatest bays, later to be named after Henry Hudson. Two days of struggling against 'water whirling and roaring as it were the meeting of tides'[3] saw him win clear, but he did not discover the Northwest Passage. At 72 degrees, 46 minutes north, Davis reached a glacial wall, along which he cruised for thirteen days while the crew chipped at the ice that formed on spars and rigging. Then, unable to penetrate this barrier, Davis returned south.

Although he considered it a failure, the voyage had some positive results. Davis had reached and named Cumberland Sound and had found a school of whales. An accomplished Elizabethan, Davis also invented the backstaff and quadrant, which thrust forwards the science of navigation. Despite these concrete scientific achievements, it was his route along the West Coast of Greenland that would be more in the mouths of whaling men. The Davis Strait was to become one of the world's great whaling highways.

After Davis, the explorers felt their way into the labyrinth of the north, with William Baffin bringing a 45-ton vessel up the strait that Davis had probed. He crossed from Upernavik on the western coast of Greenland, passing over what would be Melville Bay, to Sir Thomas Smith's Sound. Then Baffin sailed south, naming Jones Sound and Lancaster Sound. He left his own name in the bay that he circumnavigated and eventually in street names the length of Britain's whaling coast. Dundee has its own Baffin Street, named after that Baffin Bay where generations of Dundee whalers spent their working summers. Barely recorded and nearly forgotten, the Scots were also among the early explorers, with John Cunningham sailing *The Lion* past Cumberland Sound and along the coast of Labrador in 1606. A few years later Scottish colonists landed in Nova Scotia, harbingers of the much greater invasion to come.

While these explorers introduced the high Arctic to whalers, later whaling captains would repay the debt by aiding and encouraging the explorers, to whom they gave the sardonic epithet of 'Discovery Men'. In time the whalers became the true experts in the ice, learning their skills in the bitter experience of a thousand voyages. Nonetheless, before the whaling men followed in the keel wake of the explorers, they first had to exploit waters closer to home.

While the Basques pioneered the whaling waters of Newfoundland, the Dutch sailed north and east. The Dutch were the maritime masters of the seventeenth century and they hunted the great whales that clustered in the seas around Spitzbergen. This high island is one of eight that together make up the Svalbard archipelago, stretching from 74 to 81 degrees North in the chill seas above Norway. Perhaps the seas are not so chill as those in the Davis Strait, for an offshoot of the Gulf Stream slithers offshore, creating a warm-water passage in these frozen latitudes. The milder climate of Svalbald is aided by cyclonic activity, so Spitzbergen has an average March temperature that varies from −8 to −16 degrees Celsius, and an average of +5 degrees in July, although the range can vary from −30 to +17.

Despite the Gulf Stream, the sea is dangerous with icebergs from calved ice that splits from the glaciers as they make contact with the sea, plus drift ice from the northeast and water ice that forms in the fjords. Superb mariners who named Cape Horn and who were in the process of becoming the world's leading sea power, the Dutch took all the dangers of Spitzbergen in their stride as they hunted the whales. Conditions around Spitzbergen created a splendid training ground, not only for the Dutch, but all the nations that would later mount whaling expeditions to the Greenland Sea and Davis Strait.

Once ashore, the Dutch found the islands mainly mountainous, with fjords and valleys that contrasted with the levels of their homeland. The lowland plains were more familiar, and the thick mist surely reminiscent of a North Sea haar. The islands are icy in winter and often flooded in summer, and even on the small percentage of each island that can grow plants, vegetation is sparse, with neither trees nor bushes. Nonetheless, there are reindeer and polar bears, arctic fox and short tailed voles that may have been inadvertent emigrants carried there on the whaleships. More important for the whalers were the pods of whales that swam freely off shore, and the four species of seals that included the great walrus with its whiskered snout and downcurving tusks.

This island group may have been that Svabald that the Norsemen discovered, the 'country with the cold coasts' that lay a mere four days sailing from Iceland. Nevertheless, not until the Dutchmen William Barents and Jan Cornelius Rip rediscovered these frozen northern peaks while searching for the North East Passage did whaling begin. It is interesting to note that there was a Scottish mariner sailing with Barents. There had long been a Scottish–Dutch connection through trade and shared religion; there was no reason why Scots seamen should not serve on a Dutch whaling ship.

Discovery of the islands, however, did not guarantee a monopoly, for the English too were learning how to exploit their nautical surroundings. Until the sixteenth century English mariners had been more notable for their piracy than their whaling skills, but they hired a handful of Basques to teach them the way of the hunter and then shipped north and east. Terming Spitzbergen East Greenland, they sailed their stout ships to the lee of its jagged peaks, where fat black whales floated in unsuspecting schools and blizzards of snow greeted the boys from the south.

With only the vaguest idea of geography, the mariners believed that Spitzbergen was connected to Greenland. As Denmark already claimed Greenland as a colony, the Danes attempted to have vessels from every other nation pay them for the privilege of slaughtering whales. Lacking the military muscle to enforce their laws, the Danes were out of luck, but their insistence was only one source of friction. The English Muscovy Company hunted here, hurling their harpoons into the docile black mammals that until now had dominated these northern waters. The Muscovy Company had originally sought trade with Muscovy, as Russia was then known, but instead found profit in blubber and whalebone. While the Danes hoped for money and the Dutch for dominance, the Muscovy Company from London followed their national predilection for aggression as they quarrelled with their fellow countrymen from Hull.

Whaling techniques were perfected off Spitzbergen, with seventeenth century whaling boats about 200 tons in weight, about two thirds the size of those used in the eighteenth and nineteenth century. They carried crews of 50, around the same as Dundee vessels of the nineteenth century. They sent small boats, known as pinnaces or shallops, out to hunt the whales, which were harpooned before being lanced to death, the identical technique that was used throughout the eighteenth and most of the nineteenth century. However, off Spitzbergen, the dead whale was towed to a shore station to be processed, rather than being towed to the mother ship to be flensed.

As it was the Dutch who had discovered this whaling paradise, the Dutch believed that they deserved to take the lion's share of the spoils. While other nations had shore stations to process the dead whales, in 1622 the Dutch founded an entire whaling town in the area and named it Smeerenburg, which meant Blubbertown. The name was appropriate, for the stench from vats of boiling blubber blanketed the ramshackle buildings and clung to the 15,000 people who lived and worked there. Most were seamen, but they were supported by coopers and blacksmiths, carpenters and bakers, all living under the misted mountains and supported by the hunters of the great black whales. Central to the town were the iron vats where whale blubber was boiled into oil to illuminate the filthy streets of Europe's expanding cities. When William Bruce, the Scottish scientist and polar explorer, visited the site at the end of the nineteenth century, he saw the remnants of wooden houses and wooden crosses protruding from the ground. The names were Dutch, both male and female, and coffins and pieces of human bone lay inadequately buried in the thin soil.[4] As in the Basque settlements in Newfoundland, this was a place of sadness as well as of profit, but Smeerenburg also reveals that women played their part in the early whaling trade.

If Dutch women were involved with early whaling, so were Scots men. Folklore speaks of mediaeval whalers in Scotland, men who lived in the Hebrides and sailed their long-luirist, a vessel that boasted oars and sails, to the deep seas around Rockall. These men hunted whales, towing the meat and blubber in rafts to Heisgeir to be boiled into oil. On more solid historical ground, King James VI was keen to see Scotland taking a full part in the maritime enterprise of the period, and in 1617 he issued a thirty-five year patent to Sir George Hay and Thomas Murray of the Scottish East India and Greenland Company. This company was based in Leith, Scotland's premier port. Greenland, of course, included Spitzbergen, and Scottish ships were successful enough to fill at least one ship with whale oil, but clashed with the English Muscovy Company. Not for the last time, a company with an English monopoly feared Scottish competition, and pulled both rank and the plug on the Scottish company.

In 1625 the Scots tried again when Charles first allowed Nathaniel Edward to fish for whales off Greenland.[5] He wanted the oil for his Leith soapworks, but rather than use Scottish crews, he sent Englishmen from Yarmouth. Again there was conflict with the English Muscovy Company and the Scottish enterprise folded. It was not until 1670 that the Scots tried again, this time with a nineteen-year monopoly granted by Charles II, but again there was little success. Following its own motto of 'Persevere', in 1682 Leith formed the 'Leith Whaling Company', sending out one vessel that year and two the next. As was common in the period, one of the Scottish ships had a crew of Dutch professionals, but the enterprise still failed and Scotland's whaling seemed destined to the same obscurity as her colonies of Darien, Nova Scotia and New Jersey.

Perhaps the Scots whalers were not searching in the right places. By the middle of the seventeenth century there were hundreds of whaling vessels from half the maritime nations of Europe scouring the seas around Spitzbergen. Whales became scarcer, first being exterminated from the nearer shores, then, as hunting continued in an ever-widening radius, from the surrounding seas. Whaling ships had to sail further and further from their bases to fill their holds with blubber and bone, but still the Dutch were the old masters of the art and their terms for whaling procedures stuck and were used by all in the lingua-franca of the Atlantic.

In 1707 Scotland and England, a United Kingdom since 1603, merged their parliaments and proudly proclaimed themselves the United Kingdom of Great Britain. If the other nations of Europe noticed at all, they would possibly believe that greater England had swallowed smaller Scotland; many from the southern nation still believe that is what happened. However, those people with forethought and any historical insight might have realised that the union of the oldest continuing nation in Europe with its larger neighbour and rival would create a unique alloy

of fire, determination and commercial acumen. After a shakedown period where dynastic differences were disposed of and both nations sized
each other up, the British set to work to become the most significant
nautical power in the world.

In 1733 the government embarked on a programme to remove Dutch
whaling supremacy. Despite the early discoveries by English seamen, it
was the Dutch who first exploited the whales of the Davis Strait, as it
was the Dutch who had ploughed the seas off Spitzbergen and fished
the herring shoals off Shetland. In the 1730s, over a hundred Dutch
ships harpooned and hauled the bowhead from its home, while the vast
majority of British ships followed old trade routes to Europe, and new
trade routes to the plantations of the Americas. Not that the Dutch
were totally alone in the Straits, for in 1728 a Scot by the name of Ian
Anders caught a whale in Disco Bay[6] on the West Coast of Greenland.
Scots, then, were again among the pioneers of the area, for it was not
until 1719 that hunting in the Davis Strait properly began.

However one whaler does not make an industry, nor does one ship
challenge a national hegemony. Dutch whaling ships brought in blubber that was changed to oil and whalebone that was flexible enough to
be used in the fashion industry. Dutch whaling ships brought in revenue
for the Netherlands, and, by implication, denied Britain these advantages, so that money that should have come to Britain rattled instead
into Dutch coffers. The British government planned to emulate Dutch
success in the Arctic.

At the beginning of the eighteenth century Britain did not own a
vast overseas Empire. Its trading ships were at least matched by those of
the Netherlands, France and Spain. Nor was Britannia unchallenged on
the waves; it took a series of hard-fought wars with the Netherlands and
France before the Royal Navy was properly recognised as a valuable
asset that required nurturing with recruits. Unfortunately, the Navy was
difficult to man on two counts: firstly, it was an unpopular service due to
the hard discipline, low pay and poor food; secondly, despite the number
of merchant ships that sailed from British ports, there was always a dearth
of trained seamen. Naturally, seamen preferred to sail in a merchant
vessel, where conditions may have been deplorable, but they at least had
the option of leaving at the end of every voyage. Men trained in the
Arctic whaling trade would be ideal for the navy, being used to harsh
conditions. The products of whaling were also increasingly necessary,
with whale oil a perfect lubricant for the machinery used in creating
woollen textiles.

In 1733 the government offered a bounty of £1 for every ton weight of a ship of at least 200 tons that sailed to the whaling grounds. There were few takers, but a doubling of the bounty in 1750 had more effect. In 1749 Britain had a mere two whaling ships; in 1756 there were 83. Naturally there were a number of conditions before the bounty was paid, not least that five supernumerary hands were taken on each voyage. These extra hands were known as Green Men or Fresh Men, and in theory were untrained seamen or landsmen. As well as the requirement for Green Men there were other, equally stringent requirements. The Customs officers at the port of departure had to measure the whaling vessel and check her equipment. The masters and mates had to make an oath that they were bound for the whaling grounds, and had to keep a log that recorded their voyage. The owners had to make a similar oath, and on the return of the vessel, the catch was examined.

Despite these restrictions, there was a flurry of activity from a dozen ports in Scotland, mainly in the Clyde and Forth, and a score in England. Few whaling companies survived the first frantic years as the reality of whale fishing in the Arctic eroded their enthusiasm and their capital and whaling became concentrated on Hull, Whitby and London. By 1776 Whitby alone sent fifteen vessels north. Although the Scottish ports of Dundee, Dunbar and Aberdeen had smaller fleets, the connection was genuine and strong.

One year after the doubling of the bounty, the Edinburgh Whale Fishery Company was founded, with the object of making soap from the blubber. At this period merchant adventurers invested their capital in a ship for a single voyage to the Greenland Seas, which were then recognised as stretching between Spitzbergen and Greenland proper. Perhaps it was significant that the Edinburgh ship was named *Tryal*.[7] The Edinburgh Company was only moderately successful, catching between one and three whales in its annual voyage to the north, but other companies followed in its wake. In 1756 there was an attempt to found a 'Whaill Fishing Company', and the importance of the bounty was obvious in a letter that stated 'there can be but a trifle lost, were the ship unsuccessful, the bounty given by the government being so considerable'.[8]

The first concrete proof of whaling from Dundee comes from Customs records of 1754 that say the ship '*Dundee* of Dundee is properly manned and equipped for the Whale Fishery'.[9] The same vessel sailed north the following year, and must have had some success, for by 1757 Dundee had doubled its investment, with *Dundee* and *Grantully* leaving for the whale fishing.[10] There is a hint that there might have been whale ships operating at an earlier date, as in 1760 the Collector of Customs sent his superiors in Edinburgh 'an account of the number of men employed in the Greenland Whale Fisheries for 12 years past.'[11] Despite this bright start, at the end of the century the Scottish whaling industry was a poor small sister to that of England or the Netherlands.

While the Dutch remained a major presence on the whale-fishing grounds, it was colonial craft that were stifling the adolescent Scottish whaling trade. New England possessed a whaling industry before 1690 and by 1748 there were 60 whaling ships at Nantucket. The ports of New England had two major advantages over those of Britain; they were closer to the whales and, with vast stocks of timber to hand, their ships were cheaper to build. In 1775 around 79% of British whale oil was imported in colonial vessels. Colonial seamen from Boston, Nantucket and New Bedford brought whale oil into Britain and, ironically, it was on her return voyage from London that a colonial whale ship carried the tea that featured in the infamous Boston Tea Party. It was ironical because the Tea Party was the prelude to the American Revolution that ended one period of American whaling and delivered a second kick-start to the British whaling industry. When thirteen of the British North American colonies rebelled and merged to become the United States of America, they lost their tax privileges with Britain. American whaling vessels were no longer so welcome in London and British entrepreneurs looked to the north.

With fewer colonial vessels bringing whale oil to Britain, the price rose. Simultaneously the dynamism of the Industrial Revolution created a demand for oil to light the factories that worked twenty-four hours a day and to fill the lamps that made the city streets safer for the expanding middle classes. Whalebone was also required as fashionable women hoped to look slimly elegant; whalebone stays and corsets became an essential item in any up-market wardrobe. As shipowners again pondered over the possibility of investing in whaling, Americans agonised over their choices. Many chose the profits of loyalty rather than the rhetoric of rebellion, and colonial whalers crossed the Atlantic to Britain. The Royal Navy and home-based privateers had been busy so there were rebel prize ships in abundance, ripe for conversion to whaling vessels. The American Revolution decimated the New England trading fleet. When the Dutch joined the ranks of the opposition during the French Revolutionary War, the Royal Navy captured their whaling fleet conveniently to remove the rivals to Hull and London and Leith and Dundee. The way was now clear for Britain to become Europe's leading whaling nation.

While London remained the main whaling port for many years, the northern towns entered the business in a determined fashion. Labour was cheaper in the north, there was less alternative employment and the seamen were hardy. Northern ports such as Dundee, Hull and Montrose had been trading with the Baltic for centuries, so the seamen understood cold climate sailoring. They were also that much closer to the Arctic, which was important in the days when a sailing ship could be delayed for weeks by contrary winds and a penny-pinching owner fretted over even one day's extra pay for the crew.

Scottish whaling was concentrated on the East Coast, where Leith, Dundee, Aberdeen and Peterhead all had sizeable fleets at one time, but smaller places were also involved. Kirkcaldy and Montrose, Bo'ness and Cellardyke, Dunbar and Burntisland all sent ships to pursue the whale. Other towns and villages contributed skilled seamen: Arbroath, Fraserburgh, the fishing ports of Fife, Easthaven and, always, the men from the Northern Isles. Given that by the early nineteenth century most whaling ships called at Orkney or Shetland to fill up with men, it is perhaps safe to say that without these islanders the Scottish whaling industry would have been gravely weakened.

By 1821 there were 6000 men in the British whaling industry, with many thousands more in shipbuilding and ship repair, rope and sail making and the myriad ancillary trades that supported the men at sea. In 1824 the government ended the bounty system when whaling was at its height, and the sturdy ships were reaping an annual crop of whales from the Greenland Sea and the Davis Strait. Throughout the nineteenth century the hunting continued, through periods of prosperity and depression. 1830 was a terrible year, 1835 and 1836 nearly as bad with ships and men lost in the ice, but until 1858 whale oil was still the major source for lighting and lubrication. That year Pennsylvania produced petroleum and the whaling industry's decline was only a matter of time.

Peterhead and, particularly, Dundee persevered, placing steam engines in whaling ships so they could venture into places that wind-powered ships could not, and enabling them to make two trips across the Atlantic a year. The second voyage was for whales, the first for the seals that ultimately subsidised the entire industry.[12] Dundee whalers were particularly fortunate to belong to a city that was fast becoming the jute capital of the world, for whale oil was used to soften jute before it was processed. Despite this new demand more than doubling the price of whale oil, centuries of slaughter made the task of hunting the whale more difficult. After experimenting with sealing and a desperate attempt to hunt in the far south, Dundee whaling also ended. In 1920 the last British Arctic whaling company, the Tay Whale Fishing Company, ceased operations.[13]

In hindsight, whaling could be seen as unforgivable slaughter of a peaceful animal or as a brave, romantic episode where courageous men endured unbelievable hardships. To the men who took part it was probably neither; whaling brought them a wage that paid the rent, put food in the mouths of their wives and children and left some over to spend on drink. Most of these men were not inhuman monsters who hunted for bloodlust, but ordinary people doing what they saw as a necessary job of work. The whales they hunted, however, were equally innocent.

2

THE QUARRY

Whales were the quarry of the whale ships, the reason for generation after generation of men leaving the warmth of home and hearth and wife to sail upon the sea in increasingly hostile conditions. Yet whales were not feared, as tigers were feared, or despised as snakes were despised, or taken for granted, as herring or cattle were taken for granted. Mankind seems always to have had an ambiguous view of the great marine mammals that provided so much. On the one hand whales have been viewed as a valuable commodity to be ruthlessly exploited, on the other they are regarded with affection and something like awe. In the most famous of all whaling books, *Moby Dick*, the great white whale is something beyond the ordinary, a creature verging on the supernatural. Whales must be unique in that they are the only prey that was worshipped by half the seafaring peoples of the world. Virtually every maritime nation has tales of whales, and virtually all the tales are of wonderment and respect.

According to the *Navigatio Sancti Brendani Abbatis*, the Irish seafarer and explorer St Brendan once landed his curragh on an island that was 'stony and without grass'. As he and his companions boiled a pot full of food, the 'island' moved away, so that Brendan declared that it was 'the biggest fish in the ocean'.[1] Although it is unlikely that Brendan the Navigator ever landed on a whale, the story is indicative of awe.

The near idolisation of the whale was not confined to any one continent or any one sea. Across the Atlantic, the Inuit, close companions of many Scottish whalers, have their own legends. They believed that the sea mother was warm-blooded. When she was a young human girl, a stormy petrel seduced her and took her into his domain. The father of the girl came to her rescue in a boat, but the petrel whistled up a storm, prompting the father to throw the girl into the sea. Naturally the girl tried to clamber back into the boat, so her father chopped off her fingers, which became seals, fish and whales. It is interesting that the Inuit echoed the belief of the old British seamen that whistling could call up a gale. Once the Inuit hunters had successfully killed a whale, they appeased the animal's ghost with religious rituals.

Other North American peoples were equally respectful of the whales. Before they began whale hunting, the native people of Nootka Sound, Vancouver Island, fasted for a week, slashed themselves with seashells and abstained from making love with their wives. They firmly believed that an unchaste man would never catch a whale. Malagasy people from Madagascar, who hunted whales in the late eighteenth century also performed religious ceremonies when they killed a whale, while those at the northern tip of the same island would ask a mother whale to look away while they killed her cub. Their style of whale hunting, however, was unmerciful, both to whales and men. After climbing on the back of the whale, they thrust a wooden plug into the animal's blowhole. Japanese whalers were using poison by the thirteenth century, while four hundred years later they rowed out to the whales in a flotilla of boats and speared them to death.

If whales were washed ashore in parts of South East Asia, they were afforded a funeral and their bones were placed in a temple. Further north the Koryat tribe of Siberia believed that whales sought revenge if one of their tribe was killed, but looked kindly on people that helped them. Every people that had contact with whales appear to have been moved by the presence of the animals. British whalers were no different; they were among the most superstitious of seamen. Perhaps this reaction is not surprising given the size and bulk of the whales and the fascination they seem to exert on the casual spectator. However it is unlikely that many British whalers were aware of a spiritual bond with the mammals they hunted, despite the respect that they certainly had.

Although whalers sailed to the whale-fishery grounds to catch their prey, whales were not fish and they did not live on the ground. There are seventy-eight species of whale, each as red-blooded and mammalian as man. They have a far larger brain than their human cousins and, contrary to our contemporary career-conscious craze, centre their life on their family. Current scientific opinion agrees that while mankind moved from water to land, whale-kind was once a four-footed animal that chose to move from land to water. Perhaps both species crawled across the same beach, existing in the same space, although hardly in the same era. The earliest whale fossils are around 52 million years old, so predate man by quite some time.

When they moved to the water, the limbs of the whales altered. The forelimbs broadened to enable the animal to thrust itself through the water, while the rear limbs disappeared completely. To complement their paddle-like flippers, whales developed a broad tail, with flukes that drive it through the sea at some speed. These flukes are a characteristic sign of whales, and are often seen as the animal dives. As many whale hunters found out, they were also a useful defence against hunting whaleboats.

It is likely that at one time there was fur on the whale, for vestigial traces remain in the form of bristles around the snout, but in all other ways the whale adapted to its marine environment. While land-based mammals have a complex bone structure that takes the weight of the flesh, organs and muscle, seawater supports the bulk of whales, which instead of bone have a fibrous tissue, covered with a layer of blubber. The blubber acts as an insulator, holding the body heat of the whales even in the bitter cold of the Arctic, but also acting as a buoyancy aid and an energy store. Unfortunately, once humankind realised that blubber could be boiled down to oil, the whale became a floating commodity.

Whales also adapted to their environment by enlarging the scope of their lungs. While a single human exhalation can expel about 15 percent of the used air from their lungs, whales can clear 90 per cent, with the resulting spout through its blowhole, properly its nostrils, a seven metre high sign of its presence. This spout was known to the whalers as a 'fall', and may be one source of the lookout's cry of 'A fall! A fall!' The spout was made up mainly of water vapour blown from the lungs of the whale, but mingled with a minute amount of water from the surroundings of the blowhole itself. Augmenting their immense lung capacity, whales have also developed large amounts of myoglobin, a globular protein that is present in vertebrate muscle. Oxygen attaches itself to myoglobin and is released when the whale most requires it. Because of the large lung capability and this presence of extra myoglobin, whales are able to remain underwater for periods up to fifty minutes.

In common with most mammals, male whales seduce the females, but unlike most animals the pair make love in an upright position. There is tenderness about their actions, with the great flippers stroking each other's body in a manner strikingly reminiscent of human lovers. As the act reaches its natural fulfilment the whales embrace each other and leap from the sea, creatures once of the land, now of the water, but always dependant on the oxygen in the air. Between ten to twelve months after the act of copulation a calf is born, always underwater, always with the ability to swim and perhaps with the father also present. Whales retain this family spirit by swimming in great herds.

For the first eight months or so after birth, the calf remains close to its mother, living for much of the time on her rich milk. If the calf dies, the mother will lift its body onto her back and carry it for days. There are many modern human mothers who could learn from such devotion.

While there were whalers that spent fifty hunting seasons in the Arctic and retired with a fund of knowledge about the area, whales spent their entire lives in the sea. A baleen whale that was fortunate not to meet a whale hunter could survive the three score years and ten allowed to humans, and add another ten years on top. In the heyday of Arctic whaling, few were so lucky. The blue whale, giant of the ocean, can live for a hundred and twenty years. Two generations of blue whale were enough to see the beginning of Britain's whaling industry in 1750 and the collapse of the last British whaling company.

Perhaps because they have evolved in an environment that lacks light, whales are dependent more on sound and hearing. Underwater visibility is at best limited and at worst non-existent. Even five fathoms down, white light is only 10 percent that of the surface. Another fifteen fathoms and there is only one percent of white light, so an alternative means of navigation other than sight is required. It is believed that whales, like porpoises, can produce sounds inside their head and propel them forward at great speed. When the echo returns, an analysis of the sound informs the whale of its surroundings. This system of navigation would be especially useful when the whales were navigating in the dark underwater of the Arctic ice, particularly when they were being pursued by a hunting pack of Scottish whaleboats.

Whale song through water is not only five times faster than sound carried by air, it also carries for great distances. It is a haunting sound, ethereal, adding to the loneliness of the Arctic. When the early seamen heard the sound throb through the hulls of their ships, they were struck with superstitious awe; some believed that spirits haunted them. Perhaps whale song was the origin of the Sirens of Odysseus, which called so perilously to his crew. There is no single song; each one is different, which may indicate a language as complex as anything humanity has evolved, but is more likely to hold a detailed picture of the whale's environment. The evidence of behavioural patterns, whale song and a brain larger than that owned by man indicates animals of some intelligence; their actions while being hunted tends to confirm this belief. Moby Dick may be fiction, but whaling history is filled with tales of whales that turned on their attackers, or eluded them with a mixture of cunning and strategy.

There are two distinct groups of whales, those with teeth that are known as *Odontoceti,* while those without are *Mysticeti.* There are sixty-six known varieties of the Odontoceti, which is the smaller species, generally under five metres long and including the dolphins that were so loved in the Mediterranean. They are hunters, preying on squid and crustaceans, although the orca or killer whale also hunts seabirds and seals, especially the young and vulnerable, with a brutality that matches anything in nature. Whale hunters of the Southern Oceans searched for the cachalot or sperm whale, which can reach 12 metres in length.

Scottish Arctic whalers were more interested in the Mysticeti or baleen whale. There are ten known species of baleen whale, grouped into three families: rorqual, right whales and grey whales, all of which have baleen in place of teeth. Although the whalers knew baleen as whalebone, it is not bone but a horny substance that descends like a flexible curtain from the upper jaw of the whale. There are between 160 and 360 pieces of baleen in the mouth of a whale and it is used in eating. The civilised west knew it as a flexible material with a hundred uses, most notably in the female fashion industry.

Baleen whales have been termed 'gentle giants' because of their lack of teeth, but in truth they are extremely skilled predators. They eat plankton, which is also known as krill, sea butterflies or Arctic shrimp. These creatures are so small that some are even microscopic. Plankton floats on the surface of the sea in huge quantities, feeding on the algae that in turn is nourished by sunlight. When the sun causes fields of algae to bloom, changing the colour of the ocean to green or red or orange by the sheer impact of uncountable millions of organisms, plankton will arrive to feed, and where there is plankton there may well be whales. The Arctic summer has virtually no night, so constant sunlight produces vast amounts of plankton-attracting algae. Experience taught the whale hunters to look for the discolouration of the ocean that was caused by blooming algae.

Plankton is so widespread in the oceans that it produces a large percentage of the Earth's oxygen; it rests only one step above algae in the food chain. The whales acted as the third link until mankind returned to the sea from where he had emerged aeons before, adding a fourth and final link to the chain, and perhaps damaging the fragile ecology of the planet.

Although effective, there is nothing particularly ingenious about the whale's method of feeding. They locate a plankton swarm and swim through with their massive mouths agape. When a large quantity of plankton is captured, the whale closes its mouth and squeezes the plankton between its tongue and the bristled, frayed edges of the plates of baleen. The water is then spat out and the plankton swallowed. There is another method of harvesting the plankton crop. If the swarm is scattered, the whale can submerge to some depth then swim to the surface in a spiral, at the same time blowing air bubbles that press the plankton inwards. When the prey is concentrated, the whale will rise upward; jaws open, and swallow them.

Baleen whales are probably among the largest creatures ever to exist, with the blue whale the true giant at up to 30 metres long. However, Scottish Arctic whalers could only watch and fume as these magnificent animals swam by, for with a speed of 14 knots the blue whale was faster than the sail-powered ships, and even if it was killed, it would sink. The whalers of the eighteenth and nineteenth centuries just did not have the technology to cope.

While the early Basques hunted the Right Whale, the *Balaena Glacialis*, the Scottish whalers were more interested in the Bowhead Whale, *Balaena Mysticetus*, which they termed the Greenland right whale. This animal is similar to the Right Whale but is larger, with an upcurving head that gave it its name and that can hold as many as 700 pieces of baleen. This baleen could weigh as much as one and a half tons, with some pieces up to four metres in length. A successful whaling voyage could account for ten or more of these animals, some of twenty metres in length and seventy tons in weight. Each kill meant profit for the whale-ship owner, and eased the financial burden on the cold and toiling whale hunters, the men who actually rowed the small boat. Each kill helped feed the whaler's children, pay his rent and clothe his wife. Each kill brought revenue into the country's coffers.

There was a half metre thick layer of blubber beneath the dark skin of a bowhead whale, which both attracted the attention of the whaler and proved the nemesis of the whale. If the whale moved slowly, the whalers would catch it; if it swam quickly, the blubber prevented its body heat from escaping so it died of heat exhaustion. It seemed that there was no escape for the whale, but there were many that ran and dived and lived to consume more plankton on another day. The odds might appear to be stacked in favour of the hunter, but the whale was streamlined for underwater swimming and could survive in the ice far longer than could any man.

When they were caught, whales were killed for the baleen and the blubber. In an age before plastic, baleen, once heated, was an ideal flexible replacement. As already noted, it had a hundred uses for Victorian consumers. Whalebone was used as stays and stiffeners in corsets, bodices and bonnets, hoops for the wide skirts so beloved by nineteenth century women, and spokes for the umbrellas that were becoming fashionable with imperial expansion into India. Whalebone was also made into brush bristles and watch springs, upholstery for middle-class sofas and drum skins that beat the army into battle from the Red River to Rohilikand. It was used in the manufacture of harps and chairs, beds and, at one time, weaver's reeds.[2] Tennis players bounced their shots from baleen strings and mothers chastised their children with whalebone whips; the civilisation of Victorian Britain could not get enough baleen.

Possibly even more important than the baleen was the blubber. Once brought back from the Arctic, whale blubber had to be boiled down to make oil. All the major whaling ports had boiling houses where the work was performed, but the unfortunate people who lived close by were not impressed by the smell. In an age of unpleasant aromas, the stench of boiling blubber was enough to make even a Victorian gag. Dundee's boiling house was close to the harbour, while Kirkcaldy had its Whale Oil Boiling House at Pathhead Sands. When there were proposals to build a boiling house at Burntisland the locals objected because of the stench.

Newhaven too had its boiling house at the Fisherman's Park, while the Shore of Leith also savoured the sickening stink of blubber boiling. Those people who braved the walk up the ingenuously named Boiling House Close spoke of Wood's Scent, for the whale ship owners were the brothers Wood. One brother sported a narwhal tusk walking stick, which, with his portrait, can be seen in Trinity House in Leith. Wood appears prosperous and serene, totally unconcerned at the reaction of his fellow citizens to the stench his works created.

Whale oil was commonly known as 'train-oil' from the Dutch word 'traan', a drop or tear. It consists mainly of glycerides of saturated and unsaturated fatty acids. From the seventeenth to the mid-nineteenth century, whale oil was used to light the more prosperous streets of the expanding cities. John Dyson said that by fuelling street lamps, whale oil 'made a bigger contribution to safety in the streets of London than the policeman'.[3] The *Aberdeen Journal* of 24 November 1830 carries an advertisement that is perhaps typical. It stated that William Chambers, Treasurer of Police, wanted six tons of best boiled whale oil 'for the public lamps of this city'. The oil had to be from whales that had been caught that season, guaranteed as best quality.

Aberdeen was not alone. Other cities and towns advertised for whale oil, while manufacturers used it for a variety of money-spinning ideas. Not all of them were detrimental to the people. The Scottish Convention of Royal Burghs claimed that 'the cheapness of train oil for burning is of great consequence to the poor...it is...of consequence in...soap boiling, currying and dressing of leather &ct'.[4] Until the seventeenth century, soap was hardly used in Europe, when sayings such as 'the clartier the cosier' hinted that a dirt-encrusted body was warmer than one scoured clean. Even in the eighteenth century, English women were notorious in Europe for their lack of hygiene, and washing with soap was an operation that was not performed until ordered by a medical practitioner. Only when whaling escalated in the later eighteenth century did the use of soap become widespread. Cleanliness might be next to Godliness in the Victorian pantheon, but its achievement was dependent on the usually grimy and unkempt whaling men.

The discovery of petroleum first challenged then usurped the position of whale oil as a provider of light. Whale oil, however, did not go quietly; it was used in manufacturing, first when 'batching' wool and later to soften jute in the great mills of Dundee. Whale oil was also used to waterproof or preserve cloth, and in the manufacture of linoleum, for which Kirkcaldy became famous, and to lubricate machinery. It filled domestic lamps and was used in making candles; and it encouraged wage-slavery by allowing factories to work non-stop, night and day. However, whale oil came at a terrible price. Thousands of whaling men never came back from the high latitude waters, and thousands of others were permanently crippled. The whales were even worse affected. Although one whale could provide up to twenty-five tons of oil, at the height of the whaling boom there was an insatiable demand and the great animals were killed in their thousands.

It has been estimated that between 1675 and 1721 the Dutch alone caught 32,907 whales. From 1750 the British joined them in the mass slaughter in the North, but before they could catch the whales, the hunters needed a ship.

3

THE BLUBBER BOATS

'Have mercy lord, your sea is so big—my barque so small'
Prayer of the Breton fishermen

Old time seamen were often intensely proud of the vessels in which they worked, claiming that, rather than being mere transport, they had a life and personality of their own. Perhaps it was for this reason that men from one branch of the seafaring trade often denigrated those from another. Rivalry between seamen who sailed on different routes and different types of vessel was common, and led to many impertinent comparisons. For instance, colliers from the northeast of England were known as 'Geordie Bears' and rumoured to be both uncouth and illiterate, while those that worked the fast packet vessels that sailed between Liverpool and New York were 'Packet Rats'.

When whaling vessels worked in the open ocean, they could be built like any other vessel.[1] As the whaling grounds became confined to more northern waters and some of the most hostile conditions in the maritime world, whaling vessels had to be sturdy; they were built for endurance rather than speed or grace. The change to specialised vessels began in the late eighteenth century. At the beginning of the nineteenth century, when the whalers were already fishing around Greenland and the Davis Strait, William Scoresby, the Whitby master, thought that whaling ships should be between three and four hundred tons 'of the best and strongest material.' He advised that they were 'flush decked' with 'hold beams laying low…to resist pressure of ice' with 'a flat floored burdensome hold for good stowage and carrying a large cargo.'[2] By and large, the Scottish whalers followed this advice, or had worked it out for themselves. Purpose-built whaling vessels were double planked throughout, with treble planking at bow and stern and were further 'fortified' with oak planks between two and two-and-a-half inches thick at the bow to help bludgeon through the ice. This extra planking extended right around the hull, but lessened to one inch at the stern. For further strength, extra planks of wood, known as 'ice plates', were fastened to the bows around the water

24

line.[3] There was also internal strengthening, with massive transverse oaken beams termed 'ice beams', 12 inches square, at the bows and stern.

Even at the end of the nineteenth century most whaling ships were built to the same design. Vessels built to such exacting standards did not come cheap, so whaling was an expensive investment. Compared to the elegance of the clipper, the topsail schooner or the majestic four-masted barque, a whaling ship of the early and mid-nineteenth century was short, stubby and simple. Seamen from other ships termed them blubber-boilers[4] and viewed them with something like contempt.

Interestingly, this supposed ugliness of whaling vessels continued until the second half of the twentieth century, with the factory ships of the Antarctic so ugly that one whaling man said of them, 'you couldn't change any line or spar of her anywhere without improving her appearance.'[5] The twentieth century factory ship had similarities to the earlier whaling ships other than to her lack of beauty; neither took a part in the actual hunting of the whale. The whaling ships that sailed from Hull or Peterhead or Dundee were little more than transports; they carried the whaling men to the hunting grounds and transported the produce of the whales, together with the hunters, back home. They were the mother ship from where the whale hunters put out on the icy waters in their cockleshell boats.

A lot of thought went into the conditions that the whaling men would have to endure. Some vessels, at least, were provided with box beds for extra protection against the cold, while government regulations set minimum standards for food. When *Dorothy* of Dundee was being prepared for the whaling season of 1830, her owners bought a great deal of material. New stores included crockery and butter, ironmongery and hardware, with coal and candles for the long Arctic nights. There were raisins and groceries, canvas for repairing the sails, a new mast, cheese, biscuits and flour, spirits and beef, peas, meal and barley, 25 dozen eggs, black and white paint, blocks and brooms.[6] With a voyage that might be six months long if successful, or three times as long if the vessel became trapped in the ice, whale ships also carried stores that would last. The McManus Galleries in Dundee hold a tin of preserved meat from 1846, painted red and labelled 'Robert Kinnes, East Whale Lane, Dundee.' A firm named Morton's of Leith also supplied tinned meat for the whaling trade. All had to be paid for from the profits from the last voyage. The Montrose Whale Fishing Company seems to have bought good quality fresh food for their crews. In 1822 they advertised for eight tons of 'best ox beef' for their vessels.[7]

The small stores of *Friendship* included seventeen pounds of tea, which was a luxury item at the period so probably intended for the senior officers, and one hundredweight of soft sugar. There were also fifty pounds of hard sugar, with coffee, pepper, two-and-a-half stones of candles, two gallons of vinegar, three hundredweight of cheese, three casks of molasses and, to ensure cleanliness, one bar of soap. Hopefully it was a large bar. There were also half a dozen bottles of sherry, a dozen bottles of port and a gallon each of brandy, gin and whisky.

The University of Dundee holds microfilm records of the Tay Whale Fishing Company, where lists of ships' stores remained virtually unaltered from year to year. Every voyage the ships loaded beef and pork, which originally was imported from Ireland, and despite their desire to encourage the whale fishery, the government still applied duty on the salt used to cure the meat.[8] Additional to the salted meat were biscuit and flower, peas and barley, molasses, coffee, raisins, sugar, vinegar, rice and rum. From 1847 oatmeal is added, but perhaps surprisingly, the supposed anti-scorbutic lime-juice was not carried until 1848 when *Advice* and *Prince Charlotte* loaded 15 gallons apiece.[9]

The bounty payments were crucial in regenerating British whaling, and equally important in creating many of the existing records of the industry. In order to receive the extra finance, the owners and the master of the whaling vessel had to obey strict regulations. One regulation said that whaling ships had to be accurately measured, for the bounty was paid according to the tonnage of the ship. Another stipulated that whaling ships should carry one whaling boat, that is the small boat that actually hunted the whale, for every fifty tons of the ship's weight. Experience had taught that the most successful whaling ships carried at least five whaleboats, so most whalers were at least 250 tons in weight. Despite Scoresby's advice, in the early years of British whaling there were few whaling ships of over 300 tons, partly because it was difficult to catch sufficient whales to fill a ship of that size. However, there were vessels of 350 tons and even larger, particularly in the later period.

Because of the possibility of fraudulent bounty claims, the customs officers were particular about the length and weight of each whaling vessel. When in 1773 'Messrs Waddell & Reid measured *Dundee* of Dundee with the greatest care and attention', rather than the 351.6 tons that Mr Tory, landsurveyor of Leith had calculated, she was 364.5 tons.[10] The difference was carefully noted in a letter that was sent down to the Edinburgh customhouse.[11]

One of the most successful of the early nineteenth-century Dundee vessels was *Estridge,* which had been built at Shorehouse in Sussex in 1777. *Estridge* was first mentioned in the Dundee records in 1800,[12] but was re-registered in Dundee in 1815. She was a 316-ton two-decked vessel with three masts. There does not appear to have been anything out of the ordinary about *Estridge*: at 98 feet long she was neither short nor long, like most whalers of her period she was carvel-built and square-sterned, with a standing bowsprit and no figurehead.[13]

There was some ambiguity about having figureheads on whaling ships. While many seamen believed that a figurehead represented the luck of the boat, and that the figure of a female could calm a storm, others believed that figureheads were only ice catchers. For instance there was *Truelove*, an American privateer that was captured by the British in 1780 and used as a whaling ship. The figurehead of *Truelove* was removed because ice gathered on it and created a dangerous weight at the bow of the ship. Nonetheless, in 1875 Alexander Stephen and Sons of Dundee built a whaler bearing the famous name of *Arctic*. At 828 tons gross weight she was large, at 200 feet 6 inches she was long and her 98 horsepower engines were powerful for her time. Stephen's gave her the figurehead of an Inuit holding a lance.

Estridge sailed from Dundee for at least twenty-five years, mastered first by Robert Webster, who was also part owner,[14] then later by George Deuchars, before she was lost in November 1825. Many whaling masters seemed to have at least one share in their ships; perhaps the managing owners believed that an interest in the ship would encourage the master to search more diligently for whales. It is also interesting that the Register of Shipping gave the height between decks. *Estridge* had five feet eight inches (about one metre 25 centimetres), which was adequate for an average-sized man of the time. In common with most whaling ships, she was owned by a company, in her case the Tay Whale Fishing Company.

The 304-ton *Friendship* was another well-known Dundee whaling ship that was captured in war when Captain Charles Adams in HMS *Chiffone* made her a prize in 1803.[15] As with most whaling ships, she was two-decked and three-masted, again without a figurehead, and was 102 feet 6 inches long. She was registered in Dundee in 1821 and her remarkably spacious six foot two inches between decks must have been popular with her crew. Unlike many ships, which are little more than names, quite a lot of *Friendship*'s history is known. In 1827 her master was James Chapman and The Friendship Whale Fishing Company owned her. There is a James Chapman named as a harpooner in *Monarch* of

Montrose in 1815, and if this is the same man, he had risen through the whaling ranks.[16] Two of the trustees of the Friendship company were the Dundee merchants David Ochterlony and Robert Stirling, while a third was a bookseller named George Miller, who seemed to have shares in a surprising number of ships. In December 1828 these three sold their shares to another Dundee merchant named Thomas Nicoll, who sold four sixty-fourths of the ownership to Thomas Davidson, shipmaster in Dundee, on 10 February 1829. Presumably this was the same Thomas Davidson who was also master of *Dorothy.*

It was common for individuals to own a few shares in a number of ships, for by that method the risk was spread. Investing, or adventuring, in ship ownership was a hazardous practice, as shipwreck was terribly common in the eighteenth and nineteenth centuries. Every major storm brought its quota of wrecked ships and shattered seamen along the coast of Britain, and the pages of Ship Registers are interspersed with sad little notes informing the Customs Officials that a specified ship is missing, presumed lost. Often the ship had gone down with all hands.

In March 1832, David Davidson became master of *Friendship,* but David Sturrock later replaced him. At some time Thomas Nicoll must have bought back his shares, for when he died in 1838, all 64 sixty fourths of the ship were transferred from his possession to his wife and children. In an age when women were supposedly protected from involvement in the harsh realities of business, it is interesting to read that Mrs Charlotte Robertson or Nicoll, his 'relict', was mentioned ahead of James Brydon Nicoll, presumably his son. The other beneficiaries are all female, being Mrs Margaret Nicoll or Ross, the wife of Daniel Ross who lived at Hawkhill Place in Dundee, Mary Nicoll and Eliza Ann Nicoll, both spinsters, and Charlotte Nicoll. All these women were Thomas Nicoll's children.[17] In April 1841 all 64 sixty fourths passed to Mrs Margaret Davidson, widow of Thomas Davidson, shipmaster, Alexander Davidson, shipmaster in Crail, and Peter Dron, shipmaster in Dundee, as trustees and executors of Thomas Davidson.[18] Later that year ownership was transferred to Elizabeth Shield, Allan Greig MacIntosh and William John Gray, residing in Newcastle.[19]

If the ownership of the ships was confused, it is unlikely that the crew was really concerned, as long as they were adequately protected from the elements and were suitably fed and watered. Compared to most merchant ships of the time, these vessels were heavily manned. In October 1777, the 365-ton *Dundee* of Dundee, with Thomas Robson as master, returned from the Arctic with 84 butts of blubber, 25 hundredweight of whale fins and her crew of 48 men.[20] Seven years earlier she had only 46.[21]

Another early ship was *Advice*, built at the noted whaling centre of Whitby in 1785, and registered in Dundee in 1816. Her statistics are very similar to those of *Estridge*, being two-decked, three-masted and one inch short of ninety-eight feet in length. Ship-rigged with a standing bowsprit, again she was square-sterned, carvel-built and lacked a figurehead. With Lanceman Webster as her long-serving master, *Advice* was owned by the Tay Whale Fishing Company.[22] The three trustees of the company whose names were given in the Register are David Brown, John Sine and John Hume. *Advice* was a successful and a long-lived ship, surviving decades of service as a whaling vessel in the north before being lost in the Davis Strait in June 1859.

Although Dundee was a shipbuilding centre, it seems that most of her early whaling vessels were built elsewhere. *Dorothy* was another well-known vessel, and larger than most at over 368 tons. She was built at Jarrow in Durham in 1812 and was working from Dundee by 1821. Again, she was two-decked and three-masted; slightly over 99 feet long, over 29 feet in breadth, ship-rigged with a standing bowsprit and no figurehead. Her builders were not quite so kind to the crew, with headroom between decks of just five foot eight inches. With James Deuchars as master, in 1826 the Dorothy Whale Fishing Company owned the ship, with the subscribing owners registered as William Wyllie, a teacher, James Laing, a shipowner, and James Thain, a Dundee merchant. Two years later her shares were transferred to Thomas Nicoll of 'Hawkhill Place near Dundee'[23] who also owned *Friendship*.

Three Brothers was another Dundee whaler which was built in Jarrow. At 339 tons she was around the same weight, and with two decks and three masts the same build, while her length of 98 feet was also average. Save for the six foot eight inches between decks she seemed typical of the vessels in the Dundee fleet during the early part of the century. Her registered owners were John Blair Millar, a Dundee merchant, John Calman, a shipbuilder, and John Gabriel Russel, an insurance broker, all of whom were trustees of the Dundee Union Whale Fishing Company. She sailed from Dundee throughout the 1820s, until she was lost in the terrible year of 1830, when nineteen of the British whaling fleet failed to return.[24]

Fairy must have been less comfortable to sail in. She was a Yorkshire-built three-master, 95 feet 6 inches long, carvel-built, square-sterned and without a figurehead, but with less than four feet eleven inches between decks, the taller members of her crew must have assumed a permanent stoop whenever they ventured down below. The Dundee New Whale Fishing Company owned her, with the Dundee merchant James Soot, a wood merchant named James Keillor, and John Calman, ship builder, as subscribing owners. In 1838 ownership was transferred to the Fairy Whale Fishing Company, with another clutch of owners including George Nicol and David Neith, Dundee merchants.[25]

All these early vessels were sail-powered, whether barque or ship rigged, and Dundee had played a notable, but not a spectacular part in the whaling industry. In 1858 all that changed when Gourlays of Dundee installed a steam engine into a whale ship, thus creating what was known as an auxiliary-powered ship. With the eminently suitable name of *Tay*, this vessel had many of the characteristics of the sail-only vessels. Like them, she was two-decked and three-masted, carvel-built with a square stern, but there were some significant differences. *Tay* had two quarter galleries, a female figurehead and, at 141 feet, she was nearly half as long again as *Estridge*. At 455 tons she was also considerably heavier. However, her engine room accounted for a great amount of space, as it was 25 feet long, and her coalbunkers took up even more space. *Tay* was the forerunner; the next half-century of Scottish whaling was to be dominated by wooden-hulled auxiliary vessels from Dundee.

Again, *Tay* was owned by a group of people, among them William Clark and James Kennedy Martin registered as shipowners, with the wine merchants George Floyd Alison and William Strong. *Tay* lasted until 1874, when the register said she was 'totally lost on the sixteenth of June while crossing Melville Bay on the way to the Davis Straits whale fishing'.[26]

Steam power, of course, was not new. In the late eighteenth century Symington's *Charlotte Dundas* had proved that steam-powered vessels were commercially viable, and in 1812 Henry Bell took his *Comet* from the Clyde into the open seas off the West Coast of Scotland. From that point steam ships had multiplied, so that by the late 1850s they competed with sail-powered vessels on many of the world's trade routes. The long-haul routes continued to be dominated by sailing craft, but as engines increased in reliability it seemed only a matter of time before steam challenged their position. Naturally, opinion was split about these new vessels. Seamen who had learned their trade perched on a yard-arm during the screaming squalls of the North Sea, or long-hauling to the Americas, called steam ships 'steam kettles', but the Victorian worship of Progress was nearly as strong as their devotion to the Lord. Steam continued its inexorable voyage across the oceans of the world.

Narwhal was another of the early steam whalers. Built by Alexander Stephens and Sons, which became the leading steam whaler builder in Europe, she was registered as a steam screw vessel. Even longer than *Tay*, 27 of *Narwhal's* 151 feet were taken up with an engine room. In 1877 Gourlay Brothers of Dundee built her new inverted cylinder, direct acting engine that gave her a full seventy-five horsepower. Although that may sound underpowered by today's standards, these engines gave Dundee whalers the ability to voyage to the whale-fishing grounds despite contrary winds, and to press through ice that would have been a formidable barrier to sail-powered craft. *Narwhal* was owned by the Dundee Seal and Whale Fishing Company, who were registered as James Soot, merchant, Robert McGavin, merchant, Alexander Stephen and Thomas Smith, merchants, all of Dundee, and the Arbroath merchant William Gibson. *Narwhal* was under the management of David Bruce of East Dock Street in Dundee.[27] *Narwhal* enjoyed an Arctic career that lasted until September 1884, when she was damaged by ice and abandoned off Cape Searle in the Davis Straits.[28]

David Bruce was one of the leading whaling ship managers of Dundee, also having the responsibility for, among others, *Camperdown*, a 154-foot long, 424-ton screw steamer built in 1860. David Duncan, an Arbroath manufacturer, owned the majority of her shares, while Alexander Stephen owned 25, James Yeaman, a Dundee merchant, owned 7, Peter Christie, a Fife farmer, owned 3 and William Bruce, shipmaster of Dundee, the remaining 2.[29] David Bruce also became part owner of whaling vessels, and his name is prominent in Dundee whaling circles in the last quarter of the nineteenth century. Like so many whaling ships, *Camperdown* sank in the Davis Strait.

Henry Gourley, who had so successfully re-invented Dundee's position in the whaling world, was also interested in using iron as a medium for whaling vessels. In 1867 he lectured the British Association on the advantages and drawbacks of iron whaling ships. Dundee, nevertheless, continued to build in wood.

Despite Dundee's long involvement with the whaling trade, it is her later whaling ships that are best remembered. While *Estridge*, *Dorothy* and *Fairy* are nearly forgotten, *Balaena*, *Polynia* and *Terra Nova* are still remembered. Perhaps that is because these vessels are later in time, or perhaps they held that special aura that makes some vessels a legend in their own lifetime. *Cutty Sark* was no better a vessel than *Thermopylae* or *Aerial*, but is better remembered; the Forth-built *Willie Muir* was renowned in Leith although she was only a ferry boat;

while *Sirius,* the first ship to cross the Atlantic under steam power alone, is hardly known.

These later whaling ships, however, had character and presence; in a way, they were part of a Dundee that had reached the apogee of its fame as Juteopolis and they carried the pride of the city on each voyage north. Built in 1861, *Polynia* was a two-engined barque-rigged vessel, 146 feet long and weighing 358 tons. Her owners included two Dundee merchants, William Penny, a Dundee shipmaster, and Peter Christie, a farmer of Scotscraig.[30] *Polynia* featured in one of the Dundee whaling songs, *The Old Polina*, where one line declares, 'No other ship could make the trip with Polina I declare'. That line shows a pride in the ship, while the song highlights *Polynia's* voyage across the Atlantic to the Newfoundland seal fisheries. After a thirty-year career, *Polynia* was in Lancaster Sound in July 1891 when the ice crushed her.

Even better known were *Balaena* and *Terra Nova*, both of which belonged to the last flourish of Dundee, and indeed British, Arctic whaling. When the Arctic catches declined, *Balaena* was one of the four Dundee vessels that sailed to the Antarctic in 1892 in a vain attempt to revive the whaling industry. However, after that adventure she continued to fish in the north, bringing home 750 seals, 250 walrus and 26 bears in 1898. *Terra Nova* was the last Dundee-built whaler, being launched in 1884 and owned by William Stephen. At 187 feet, she was long, but she had the ubiquitous three masts and two decks, while the figurehead of a demi-woman guided her through the seas.

Although *Terra Nova* was a whaler, she is better remembered for her part in the rescue of Captain Scott's *Discovery* in 1904. On that occasion her captain was Harry MacKay, a whaling master who had already taken her to the whaling and sealing grounds of Newfoundland. Scott used her in his 1910 expedition to the South Pole, and although he did not return, *Terra Nova* did, to continue to hunt off Newfoundland. Her career, long and distinguished, only ended in 1943 when a U-boat torpedoed her.[31] Dundee gave her that most distinguished badge of respect of naming a pub *Terra Nova* in her honour.

Although no Scottish whaling vessels have survived, they served as a model for *Discovery*, which was also an auxiliary-powered vessel. *Discovery* was built almost entirely of wood, at a time when the skills required for wooden shipbuilding were already declining. In her own way she serves as a requiem mass for the souls of the departed whaling ships and their crews. As an illustration of the level of skill that was needed, *Discovery* has 25 different types of wood. Her double-framed hull is 26 inches thick and is made up with three layers of wood. The outer hull is of pine and elm, with a core of Guyanan green heart and a lining of Riga fir, while her frames are of solid Scottish oak. Because no metal was allowed to disturb the delicate magnetism of her scientific instruments, neither a rivet nor an iron nail was driven into the hull of *Discovery*, so the wood had to be steamed into position. As it was her bow that would be first to make contact with the ice of the south, it was made with eleven-foot thick oak. The shipbuilders of Dundee were expert in their task, and made *Discovery* so strong that she survived two years trapped in the ice at McMurdo Sound, and has survived a varied career since then.

While *Discovery* was never intended to be a whaler, she is perhaps the best surviving example of Scottish whaleship building. However, her crew was never composed of professional whaling men, or, as they were often known, Greenlandmen.

4

THE GREENLANDMEN

'Sailors get money like horses and spend it like asses.'
Tobias Smollett

As in any vessel, there was a pyramidal system of rank in the Arctic whaling vessels, but one that was perhaps slightly less uneven than usual. At the apex of the pyramid was the master, who was responsible for the decisions that affected the voyage. He chose where to hunt and what course to set. The mate was next in command, followed by a second mate who in some cases was also a harpooner or line manager. Harpooners, line managers and boat steerers, or boat headers, were also classed as officers; these were the specialist whaling men, on whose skill the success or otherwise of the voyage depended. The requirements of the bounty stipulated that every whaling ship should also carry a surgeon, and there would be tradesmen such as a carpenter and sailmaker. Along with the cook and the ordinary seamen, often termed 'common mariners'; the total complement of a whaling vessel would be between forty-four and fifty, although that number increased in the later period when the vessels also hunted for seals from Newfoundland.

Surgeons were a rarity on merchant vessels, and many of the surgeons on whaling vessels were medical students or recent graduates whose journals provide invaluable evidence of the life of whaling men at sea. W. Gillies Ross, in his *Arctic Whalers*, suggests that Scottish medical students used the Arctic voyages as a means of providing funds for their university courses. Certainly many were young, but there is no doubt that their presence would have saved limbs and lives at sea. From 1822, the surgeon's qualifications had to be checked by an official of the Customs and Excise.[1] Despite the obvious hardships of the Arctic, there seems to have been competition for the post. When *Neptune* of Dundee advertised for a surgeon in 1880, there were 38 applicants, from as far apart as Ross-shire and Dorset.[2]

The masters of the whaling ships seem to have been accepted as respectable members of society. The most famous of them all, William

Scoresby of Whitby, wrote that he moved from Church Street 'a low part of the town and not genteel to the New Buildings and fashionable neighbourhood.'[3] The Dundee whaling masters seemed to establish small colonies close to the harbour. In 1809 William Deuchars, master of *Mary Ann*, William Valentine, master of *Horn* and James Webster, master of *Rodney*, all lived in the Seagate, while Adam Christopher, master of *Estridge*, lived in the Fishmarket. Although the shipowners did not live quite so cheek-by-jowl, in a small town such as Dundee they were all within reasonable distance of one another. Walter Newall of the Dundee Whalefishing Company lived in Castle Street, David Jobson senior, who owned *Rodney* and *Jane*, lived in the Murraygate, while David Ramsay, owner of *Estridge*, spent his home life in the Cowgate.

Dundee's Seagate seemed to be an important hub of the whaling world at the beginning of the nineteenth century, for by 1818 Lanceman Webster, master of *Tay*, George Thoms, master of *Calypso*, and Robert Coupar, the new master of *Estridge*, also resided there. By 1829 the offices of the Union Whale Fishing Company were located in the Seagate, near to Thomas Davidson, master of *Dorothy*. Five years later the Tay Whale Fishing Company and the Dundee Whale Fishing Company were in the same street.

Other masters of the whaling fleet were from the Murraygate, Crichton Street and King Street, all quality addresses in the city.[4] Overall, it seems that the Dundee whaling masters, like William Scoresby of Whitby, could live in the better parts of the town. Unfortunately the men who made up their crews are not so easy to trace. Until the bounty system ended in 1824, the regulations stipulated that the names of each member of the whaling ship crew should be recorded, but they did not give addresses. As the entries in census records and the *Dundee Book* gave only a general view of a man's occupation, the crews of the whaling ships were lumped under the general term of seaman. Every coastal town in Scotland had many seamen, of whom only a small proportion worked in whaling vessels.

Nonetheless, it is possible to locate at least the towns in which many of the early whaling men lived. During the wars of the eighteenth and early nineteenth centuries, the Royal Navy press-ganged many seamen into warships. For instance in 1755 the master of *Oswald* of Bo'ness complained that the Royal Navy had pressed 19 of his crew.[5] Whaling officers such as harpooners and boatsteerers could obtain certificates, known as protections, which exempted them from the press, while even 'common mariners' who were signed on a whaling vessel could be protected from voyage to voyage. Customs Records have the names of these men in Protection Lists, which in some record the town from where the seaman came.

In 1810 the protection list for *Advice* of Dundee lists four Dundee men among its specialists: the harpooner Robert Keith, boatsteerers Lanceman Webster and Thomas Fyffe and the line manager George Smith. It is more than probable that Lanceman Webster was the later shipmaster of the same distinctive name. There were also four men from Broughty Ferry mentioned: Thomas Webster the harpooner, John Kidd the boatsteerer, and Lawrence Lyall and Robert Webster the line managers. At this time Broughty Ferry was a small fishing village; not for a century would it become part of Dundee. The remaining specialists in *Advice* were the harpooners James Brown of St Monance and Alexander Donaldson of Anstruther, the boatsteerer William Wilson of St Monance, and the line managers Robert Ritchie, also from St Monance, and Robert Pattie of Newport.[6]

There is no doubt that, at least at this period, the fishing villages of Fife were heavily involved in whaling. There is a possibility that men sailed with people from their own communities. While *Advice* seemed to recruit from St Monance, *Friendship* had seven specialists from Dundee, three from St Monance, two from Cellardyke and one each from Pittenweem, St Andrews and Ely.[7] Among the Cellardyke men was a harpooner named William Smith.

There is a persistent legend that a Cellardyke whaling master named William Smith brought home the jawbone of the largest whale ever killed in the Arctic. The jawbone was placed at the back door of his house, where it remained for well over a century. The remains of the jawbone are now held by the Scottish Fisheries Museum at Anstruther. It is possible that the harpooner named William Smith was one and the same as the celebrated Captain William Smith and it would be nice to be able to support a piece of folklore with solid fact.

The same pattern is repeated in other Dundee ships of the period, with *Mary Ann* having harpooners from Dundee, St Monance and Crail, boatsteerers exclusively from Dundee and line managers from Dundee and Pittenweem.[8] That same year of 1810, *Horn* had harpooners from Dundee, St Monance and Pittenweem, boatsteerers from Dundee and Pittenweem and line managers from Dundee.[9] As a contrast, the specialists of *Estridge* were nearly all from the Dundee area, although some resided in the tiny villages of North and South Ferry, which were not then part of the city. There was only a solitary harpooner from

Pittenweem and a boatsteerer from South Shields among the Tayside men.[10]

In the 1811 whaling season, *Calypso* carried one of the Listons from Newhaven as a harpooner, with Andrew Greig from Woodhaven and two line managers from Newcastle.[11] In that same season the names of the 'mariners or common seamen' for *Friendship* included nine men from St Andrews, two from Kingsbarns, one from Leven and one from Balmerino, all in Fife.[12] In 1814 *Advice*, with Lanceman Webster as master, sailed with common mariners who were from Dundee, Broughty Ferry, St Andrews and West Wemyss, while *Tay*'s mariners came from Dundee, Pittenweem, St Monance, Colinsburgh, Anstruther, Earlsferry and Crail.[13] The early Dundee whaling fleet, then, seems to have relied heavily on the Fife ports for its personnel.

With the end of the French wars in 1815, there were no more lists of protected seamen, while the publication of bounty lists ended with the cancellation of the bounty system in 1824. Nonetheless, the names of some whaling seamen continued to be recorded. The University of Dundee holds the name, rank and wage bill of the crew of the whale ship *Dorothy* for the seasons of 1828 and 1829. The numbers are slightly different, with 41 crewmen mentioned in 1828 and 44 in 1829. There is also a list of oil money paid out in 1828; as the names of the crew do not exactly correspond to those paid wages, it is possible that the money was paid for the 1827 voyage. There are 49 men in the oil money list.[14] Some of the crew of *Dorothy* in 1828 had oil money slips that were paid in Pittenweem on the Fife coast.[15]

Dundee University also holds the crew list for *Dorothy* in 1834, which had the same geographical make-up as that of a generation before. An authority from some of the crew for oil money to be paid to Thomas Muir of Kirkcaldy indicates that seven of the crew were from that area. It is interesting that five of these men signed their names, with only two marked with a cross, so at least in this instance there was a high level of literacy. Two of the men were from Cellardyke, two from St Andrews and one each from Earlsferry and Pittenweem.[16] At a much later period at least one Dundee whaler came from Germany; in 1934 an Arbroath man spoke to a German official who had worked on a Dundee whaler before the 1914–1918 war.[17]

Whaling vessels used an apprenticeship system to qualify for the whaling bounty. In December 1783 the *Aberdeen Journal* carried an advertisement for 'several stout lads' to sail in the 'Greenland trade', adding that 'if they have served at sea, the better'.[18] Seven years later the same newspaper again advertised for 'two stout lads for the *Christian*, whale vessel'. This time the advert was age-specific, asking for boys between fourteen and eighteen, and adding, perhaps significantly, 'these from the country will be preferred.'[19] It may have been easier to train a Greenlandman from scratch, or perhaps the advertiser merely believed that country boys were more robust than those from the city, who may have already been weakened by years of work in mill or factory.

From at least the late eighteenth century, whaling ships recruited heavily in Orkney and Shetland. Possibly whaling ships had called at the northern isles before then, for the *Edinburgh Courant* of 22 March 1751 carried a story of 13 Shetlanders who arrived in Leith 'to be employed in the whale fishery'.[20] Given the nautical history of these islands, it seems natural that they should become involved in whale fishing. Indeed, whaling seems to have been as common in Shetland as it was along the Biscay coasts, if differently organised. There was an old Shetland saying that there were three Godsends, 'a stranger, a wreck and a caa of whales', and if the islanders did not possess the resources to hunt far out to sea, they took their opportunities when they were offered. Whales often appeared off the Shetland islands, and when a school was sighted, men put out to sea in a flotilla of small boats, drove them ashore and killed them in an ugly but efficient display of slaughter.

Although the islanders did the labour, the Crown claimed that whales were 'fish royal' and took their third, while the lairds took the same amount, leaving the remainder to be divided among the actual hunters. Many island lairds kept their tenants in near-mediaeval oppression, so a voyage to the Arctic was a relief and an opportunity to earn welcome money. However, there were occasions when the landlords refused permission for men to join the whaling ships.

At the end of the seventeenth century, Mathew Mackaile reported that 'the common people' of Orkney 'excell all people for navigation in small boats with 4 or 6 oars, and one or two sails'. It was men with exactly that skill that the whaling masters needed for whale hunting, so the whaling ships called at the northern isles, season after season. As one surgeon noted in his journal:

> We...are going to call at Lerwick...for the purpose of adding to our crew a number of Shetlanders, these men being said to be good and experienced sailors.[21]

Experience in boat handling was invaluable in the north. When Captain Markham joined *Arctic* for a whaling voyage, he commented that the stroke oar and line manager was 'a powerfully-built Shetland man, standing about six foot two inches, commonly called Big John.'[22]

Dr Barrow, in his book on Northeast England whalers, includes crew lists from whaling ships that sailed from Newcastle and Shields. The lists date from the middle of the eighteenth century and there are men from Lowland Scotland or Orkney on every vessel. For instance in the Whitby vessel *Henry and Mary* that sailed in 1756, the surgeon, George Ogilvy, came from Edinburgh; in *Sarah* that sailed from Shields in 1784, the cook and two seamen were from Leith and many of the seamen were Orcadians. As time passed, it seemed that more seamen were Scottish, and after the bounty payments ceased, the number of islanders increased even further; by the 1830s most of the crew of *Lady Jane* from Shields were from Prestonpans, Cockenzie and Orkney. The same vessel in 1848 had William Archibald from Pathhead near Kirkcaldy as mate, a surgeon from Glenmoriston, a second mate and a specktioneer from Prestonpans, a further eleven men from East Lothian and Fife, and picked up seventeen more seamen, a steward and two apprentices at Stromness.[23]

In 1866 the Hull whaler *Diana* sailed out of Shetland with a full crew of 51 men. When she returned, there were only two fit men on board after six months trapped in the ice of the Arctic. Twenty-six of her crew came from Shetland.

With every aspect of the whaling trade regulated by the bounty laws, the customs officers had to make due allowance for the influx of mariners from the isles. The ship master had to make an oath as to the numbers of men they had when they sailed from their home port, but the customs officials covered themselves by inserting the words 'and with more common men to be taken on board at Lerwick or Kirkwall' in the margin.[24]

Captain Markham, who sailed on *Arctic* in 1874, wrote that of the 55-strong crew 'a fourth part came from the Shetland Isles, one man is English, one a Norwegian and the remainder are Scotchmen, principally from the Highlands.'[25] Perhaps the make up of *Arctic*'s crew was unique, for there are few other references to Highlanders on board Arctic whalers. It is also possible that Markham's definition of a Highlander was elastic, and he simply meant a man from the northern half of Scotland. Nevertheless, some vessels certainly did not need to recruit men from the Isles. In 1808 the 'whole of the crew' of the Dundee whaler *Estridge* 'was completed at this port',[26] and it is unlikely that *Estridge* was unique.

One Shetland seaman, who was involved in the Antarctic whaling of the post-war period, believed that the mainlanders on the whaleships were bad seamen who knew about whales but needed islanders to man the boats and not panic in a gale as the whalemen did.[27] He might have been correct, up to a point. Photographic evidence, and those bounty records that record ages, indicated that many of the whalers were very young, but at the same time whaling was a trade that kept its appeal to a number of men. Crew lists in Dundee and Montrose often contain the same names, sometimes with the identical rank, occasionally with some promotion. For instance there was David Yual, who was a Greenman in *Mary Ann* in 1813, a common mariner in the same vessel in 1816 and a line manager in 1819. More spectacular was the already-quoted case of Lanceman Webster, who rose to master.

Men such as Webster certainly made their career in the Arctic; the Ingram Papers mention a Peter Ramsay of Kirkcaldy who died in *Erik* in 1874 after 56 whaling seasons as harpooner and specktioneer.[28] There was also the harpooner Edward Scott, who died in 1903 when he was 54 years old,[29] and James Webster who voyaged to the Arctic whaling every year from 1815 to his death in 1872.[30] Eighteen seamen are mentioned in all three of *Dorothy*'s crew lists, as are four line managers, six boatsteerers, and Robert Henderson the carpenter. Such continuity of crewmen suggests a stable and a happy ship with an efficient crew. Arthur Conan Doyle, who sailed as surgeon on the Peterhead whaler *Hope* in 1880, gave a possible reason for the seamen who returned year after year to the north. He commented that 'the life is so fascinating that I could imagine a man would find it more and more difficult to give up.'[31] Conan Doyle was a student at Edinburgh University when he signed on the *Hope*, but his seven months at sea seem to have been successful, as the Master asked him to return the following season. Conan Doyle refused; he thought that the work was brutal.

As with most occupations, the vast majority of men were working for the wages. British whalers were paid a flat rate supplemented by bonuses according to the amount of oil the ship obtained, and 'fast boat' money that depended on which boat got 'fast' to the whale. In 1829 a whaling seaman earned a basic 17s. 6d. (about 87p) a month, while a harpooner, a line manager or a boatsteerer earned £1. A cook earned the same, but the tradesmen picked up more. Robert Henderson, the carpenter of *Dorothy*, was paid 30s. (£1.50), John Donald the cooper 25s. (£1.25) and John Stevenson, the mate, earned £2. Naturally, neither the cook, carpenter nor cooper helped crew the small boats that caught the whale, so they would not share the oil or fast money bonus.

In the 1828 lists of *Dorothy*, the amounts paid for oil money vary from the £70 15s. 3d. (£70.76) paid to Captain Davidson and the £70

13s. 2d. (£70.66) to Alexander Donaldson, boatsteerer, to the 2s. (10p) paid to James Fernie and the 5s. (25p) owed by William Taylor. Excepting Captain Davidson, the average oil money paid was £22 4s. 9d. (£22.23). By the end of the century a harpooner earned 55s. (£2.15) a month, a boatsteerer earned 50s. (£2.50), a line manager 45s. (2.25), while an able-bodied seaman earned £2. An ordinary seaman, the labourer of the ship, earned between £1 and £1.50 a month,[32] although in all cases a good season's fishing could double the wages. As a comparison, the Master of a Tay Ferry earned about £2 a week, and a deckhand 24s. (£1.20).[33] These figures would indicate that a deckhand on a Tay Ferry could bring home more than double the pay of an ordinary seaman on a whaler, and without any of the danger. It is no wonder that the Greenlandmen were eager to hunt whales in order to supplement their income.

Given the low wages and the obvious dangers of working at high latitudes, what sort of men would crew the whaling ships? The opinions of the contemporaries of the Greenlandmen appear unfavourable. Christian Watt of Broadsea was both the daughter and the wife of whaling men, yet she still referred to them as a 'wild and rough lot',[34] while the Reverend John Mill, of Sandwick parish in Shetland, thought them 'curs'd ruffians'.[35]

However, outside her immediate family, Christian Watt would only meet the whaling men immediately before or after a voyage, when they would be on their worst behaviour. It is also possible that she was reporting from hearsay, repeating a popular idea rather than observing from personal experience. The writings of the Reverend Mill appear to be from a man with a rather jaundiced view of life, perhaps too narrow-minded to give an objective view of his subject matter.

In saying that, others who had personal experience of the whaling men could be equally scathing. Christopher Thomson was a landsman who sailed as a carpenter's mate on *Dunscombe* of Hull in 1820. He was a literate man who wrote of his initial perception of the whaling men, saying that the Greenland sailors were:

> Notorious for their daring and for their disrespect of speech; prefacing or ending every sentence with an oath, or some other indelicate expression.[36]

Swearing, however, might have been offensive to the more respectable members of society, but it was hardly a cardinal sin. Seamen were universally known for their foul language. It was a Scandinavian saying that swearing was absolutely necessary to make a good seaman,[37] while Sir Walter Runciman believed that when seamen were cursing, everything was all right, but when they started to pray the ship was in real danger. Runciman should have known; the son of Scottish parents, he had relatives who had fought in the Royal Navy during the war with Bonaparte, and he rose from a before-the-mast seaman to own a fleet of ships.

Although it would have been hard to find a Greenlandman who did not swear, not all would commit blasphemy, for that was a sin often believed to tempt shipwreck. The most famous of all unfortunate seamen, the Flying Dutchman, had been condemned to round the Cape of Good Hope forever, because he scoffed at the Lord. This strange interweaving of superstition and reverence appears to have been deep in the spiritual fabric of the Greenlandman.

Burn Murdoch, an Edinburgh Medical Student who accompanied the Dundee Antarctic expedition of 1892, thought the crew of *Balaena* 'looked rather grim'[38] when he first saw them in a Dundee shipping office. They were separated from the ship's master by a brass latticework, which he believed kept the officers safe from the crew on pay day. Presumably there had been occasions when recently paid crewmen had sought revenge on an unpleasant or unjust officer. 'Bully' masters and 'bucko' mates were common ogres in the nineteenth century.

Later in the voyage, Burn Murdoch thought the crew of *Balaena* 'a jolly motley crowd', that included 'Arctic whalers… South Spainers… men and boys from the East Coast fishing villages, and… men from the Shetlands.'[39] As this voyage was Burn Murdoch's first on a whaler, he could not be expected to be expert in the make-up of a typical crew, but the mixture might well have been typical. Burn Murdoch's book also reveals that some of the men were real characters. One such was Willie Watson, who had sailed on a nitre trader to the West Coast of South America, worked on an Arctic whaler and had also been a golf caddie at Carnoustie and a soldier in the Franco-Prussian War.[40] Such a combination of employment indicates that whaling may have been viewed as just another occupation.

Captain Charles B. Hawes, author of *Whaling*, said that after reading hundreds of logbooks and journals, he believed that the whaling vessels had a large proportion of madmen. Perhaps madness was a prerequisite to any seaman, but there were certainly adventurers and possibly misfits among the Greenlandmen. As well as Conan Doyle, the author of Sherlock Holmes, there was Ralph Wake, from Seaton House, who sailed as a harpooner on board *Friendship* of Dundee in 1815. He was a last-minute replacement for James Mackie who left the whaling service before he received his Protection for that voyage.[41] As Seaton House was the mansion house of Tarrie Estate, near Carlingsheugh, north of Arbroath, it is interesting to speculate why Ralph Wake signed articles on a whaling ship. James Tytler, the Scottish aeronautical pioneer, also sailed on a whaler.

There is a certain amount of evidence for anti-social behaviour from the Greenlandmen. Among the papers of the Dorothy Whale Fishing Company in Dundee University are a number of arrest warrants for members of the crew. One is for John Cunningham, an illiterate crewman, another for Alexander Bruce, the surgeon and possibly the best-educated man on board. It appears that he owed money to his aunt, Helen Bruce. The other arrest warrants were for Alex Ledgerwood, who owed £10 to Mrs Matilda Scott, and for John Shand, again for debt.[42]

The Greenlandmen seemed to have a reputation for wild behaviour. In 1860, when Captain Shewan signed some Peterhead whalers aboard his clipper *Cha-szu*, he warned the mates that whalers were 'little versed in the niceties of sea discipline and apt to consider that Jack was as good as his master.'[43] Shewan also wrote that their 'freedom and truculence of demeanour' made them 'by no means easy to manage.'[44] Nonetheless, he sought out Greenlandmen for *Cha-szu*, and as clipper ships could often hand-pick their crews, that fact reveals Shewan's estimation of the whalers' seamanship. Indeed, whaling men seem to have been prevalent throughout the maritime world. In April 1838, when 60 men from Shetland were made redundant by one of the periodic downturns of the whaling industry, they sailed to Sunderland and all found employment within a day.[45] While sailing northward in the Lighthouse yacht in 1814, Walter Scott mentions that 'some of our crew… had been on board Greenlanders',[46] while Captain Cook had two Greenlanders on his 1771 voyage. Being from the whaling port of Whitby himself, he would know their qualities.

Other explorers were even more dependent on Greenlandmen. William Scoresby, one of the most respected seamen of the early nineteenth century, started his career as a whaler. In his long and fascinating life he corresponded with William Banks of the Royal Society, spent an unhappy time in the Royal Navy, studied physics and chemistry at Edinburgh University and invented a device for taking deep sea temperatures. It was Scoresby who told Banks that he had found 2000 square leagues of the Greenland Sea between 74 and 80 degrees north clear of ice, which led to the first exploring expedition of John Ross. Scoresby had hoped he would be chosen to lead the expedition.

In 1818, the year that Ross and his 'Discovery Men' probed for the North-west Passage, the Secretary of the Customs in London issued a letter to the whaling men. They were now allowed to profit from any reward offered by parliament for discovering 'a northern passage between the Pacific and Atlantic Oceans, or for approaching within one degree of the Northern Pole.'[47] It seems that the government saw the Greenlandmen as useful auxiliaries in the race for the fabled passage.

Ross chartered *Isabella*, a Hull whaler, for the expedition, and many years later that same vessel rescued him from his second attempt at finding the North-west Passage. It was another whaling captain, Bernard O'Reilly, who said that a simultaneous expedition to sail over the North Pole was a 'closet lucubration'. Perhaps if Greenland captains had been consulted more, there would have been less loss of life in the official expeditions. William Parry, who had protected the Greenlandmen from French privateers in 1810, may have been impressed by their seamanship, for he brought a Greenland master, Mr Allison, on at least one of his expeditions. Parry was also one of the most successful Arctic explorers of his age. When the Discovery Men got lost, whalers were sent to find them. Sir John Franklin was one of the foremost explorers of his day, but when he disappeared in an abortive attempt to discover the North-west Passage, two whaling ships of the Aberdeen Arctic Company were among those who searched for him.

Not all the experiences with Greenlandmen were so positive. On his second expedition, John Ross used the Greenock whaler *John* as a storeship. The men complained that, without hunting for whales, they could not profit from their long stay in the Arctic. Even before they left Scottish waters, they mutinied and tried to persuade the crew of Ross's own ship, *Victory*, to join them and 'stand up for seamen's rights'. Scrambling ashore, the Greenlandmen went on a drunken orgy that resulted in many pawning their clothes to buy drink. Perhaps it is not surprising that, when on the next season's whaling voyage, they mutinied again, killed the master, drove the mate and a boat's crew away and wrecked the ship. Very few of the crew returned.

The ill-fortune of *John* is a reminder of what could happen at sea, but not all whaling men were as truculent. Admiral Seymour thought the whalers' crew of *Mazinthien* 'as fine a set of honest hardy seamen as one could find'.[48] Captain Markham, who had joined *Arctic* expecting to find the whalers 'filthy and disgusting', appeared pleasantly surprised, stating that 'at any rate for this voyage, the *Arctic*'s crew are an exception to the general rule.'[49] By inserting the word 'exception' Markham indicated that other whaling crews were not so good, a belief that Captain Adams endorsed when he stated 'that he had never put to sea before with such a good and sober crowd'.[50]

The wild reputation remained with whaling men even into the twentieth century. Writing in 1937, Basil Lubbock commented that 'in port... [Greenlandmen]... gave way to the wildest carousels'[51] and added, it is 'difficult to realise... how hard and wild, not to say violent, the Greenland seaman was.'[52] Nigel Gatherer, who wrote folk songs in the 1950s and 1960s, composed 'The Dundee Whaler', which contains the lines:

> You'll get into Lerwick to fill up the stores
> And ye'll spend a' your money on whisky and whores.[53]

Speaking about the song, Gatherer commented that Dundee whalers 'would often go on shore for terrible drinking sprees.'[54]

Late twentieth-century historians have also commented on the behaviour of whalers, with W. Gillies Ross arguing that they were 'given to boisterous and often licentious behaviour when authority was relaxed.'[55] Derek Flinn argues that 'when the whalers lay in Bressay Sound, Lerwick became one of the most notorious and riotous ports in Britain.'[56] James Irvine, a Shetland author, commented that, until the 1850s, the Town Council swore in Special Constables 'to cope with the riotous behaviour of the whalers.'[57]

Not all historians agreed. Gordon Jackson argued that 'Montrose whalemen were members of a tight knit community, with a sense of responsibility and camaraderie.'[58] The trouble in Montrose seems not to have been due to the behaviour of the crews, but caused by the lack of them. In 1812, with foreign wars eating up seamen, David Kinnear, manager of the Montrose Whale Fishing Company, asked to transfer 'certain of the protected men belonging to the *Eliza Swan* to the *Monarch*', because the company was 'at a loss for experienced fishermen to serve both vessels'.[59]

At the end of the nineteenth century at least, the whalers of Dundee were popular in their homeport. Burn Murdoch said that 'all Dundonians, from the small boys to the big shareholders, take a proud interest in them.'[60] Perhaps the best method of ascertaining the working behaviour of Greenlandmen is to ask the Captain. In 1850 the Mercantile Marine Act instructed all ocean-going vessels to keep logs that contained a column where the character of each member of the crew could be recorded.

In the case of *Chieftain* of Kirkcaldy, every crew member had VG—the highest recommendation—entered after his name. In that case at least, there could be no higher acclaim.

Whaling men then, came from the whaling ports, the small fishing villages of the coasts and from the northern isles. The shipmasters appear to have been accepted into the respectable areas of society, and many were intelligent and gifted men. It seems that there is some ambiguity about people's perceptions of the seamen who sailed before the mast. While some, such as the Reverent Mill, had a low opinion of them, they were accepted as capable seamen, despite the occasional glitch. Experience of working with the Greenlandmen seems generally to have raised the opinions of observers.

Although it is probable that most men sailed to the whaling for the wages, they may have returned, season after season, for a very different reason. There was the desire for a challenge, the comradeship and quite possibly the desire to escape. As Captain Hawes believed, some may have been literally mad, certainly many were eccentric, and perhaps some were searching for what academics would term the 'Other', an experience beyond the ordinary. Seamen never quite belonged in a largely land-orientated society, and many of the Greenlandmen would not be suited to the monotonous drudgery of industrialised society. Men who would be misfits in Dundee or Edinburgh or London found acceptance among their peers in the Greenland Sea or Baffin Bay. The psychiatrist Dr R. B. Robertson, in his book *Of Whales and Men*, labelled the Antarctic whalemen he worked with as 'psychopaths', meaning 'men with suffering minds',[61] men who were doomed to alienate themselves from civilisation in some way. Robertson's theory included men such as Shackleton and Columbus, or the countless pioneers who colonised Canada, Australia, Argentina or the United States. Nonetheless, however correct Robertson may be, in the eighteenth and nineteenth centuries, the Greenlandmen were viewed merely as seamen with a routine, if dangerous job. It was a job deemed necessary at the time, but one that most people would not willingly perform themselves. Therefore it was a job that had to be done by people slightly out of the ordinary.

5

SKETCHES OF SOME WHALING MEN

'S beag 'tha fios aig fear a bhaile,
Cia'mar 'tha fear na mara beo'
The landlubber knows not
how the mariner exists'—Gaelic proverb

While it is possible to trace the careers of whaling masters with relative ease, the lives of ordinary before-the-mast seamen are more obscure. A few, such as Lanceman Webster, can be followed as they rose from Boatsteerer of *Advice* in 1810[1] to mate of the same vessel next season,[2] and on to become Master in 1814.[3] There was also Robert Pattie, who was promoted from seaman to harpooner of *Advice* in February 1815.[4]

Most seamen, however, are more anonymous, mere names in bounty lists, blurred images on faded photographs, shadows that emerge in single mentions from the pages of logbook or journal; they are merely a part of an amorphous mass. Nameless and unidentified, they are included in such entries as: 'called all hands to tow the ship'[5] or 'the carpenter repairing the boat. The people on board doing Sundray jobs.'[6] Every log and journal carried the same kind of entry. The Greenlandmen were unheeded when they were working: 'Pepol Engaged varriously under the botswain',[7] and they were nameless when they reached the whale fishing grounds: 'called All hands to take the boars from below'.[8] They were even nameless in death: 'two men missing from the mates watch, must have been washed overboard'.[9]

Yet these were not mere automatons, but living, breathing people with hopes, dreams and aspirations, men with families and children, each one different even if they were viewed as one of the 'people' or the 'hands'. Unfortunately, the lives of ordinary people are only recorded when they perform some extraordinary deed, which either makes them famous or infamous. Even then, that deed has to come to the notice of somebody who has the ability and the desire to investigate and record.

Many of the Greenlandmen have left fleeting, partial memorials to their lives, but in most cases the historian has to rely on folklore for a base and on detective work to fill in a few of the gaps. Most Greenlandmen probably led comparatively stolid lives, sailing to the Arctic season after season and spending the winters either at home with their wives or sailoring on a different route. Some, however, led lives less ordinary, or were reported as having done so.

In 1875 *The Scotsman* published the obituary of a seaman from Fife named David Wilson. Born in 1792 at Brownhills, near St Andrews, he spent his boyhood on a Fife farm and ran away to sea on the Kirkcaldy smack *Maggie Lauder*. With some seagoing experience, Wilson signed on the Dundee whaler *Advice* and voyaged to the Arctic. As he was returning home, the Royal Navy vessel *Pinkie* approached with the intention of press-ganging some of the crew. The whaler fled, with Wilson at the wheel, but the faster *Pinkie* caught them. Wilson was pressed, but deserted at Jersey to rejoin the merchant service, only for a French privateer to capture him in the Bay of Biscay. Eventually Wellington's army rescued him, and Wilson was able to return to life as a whaler. Years later he settled in James Street, Cellardyke, as a fisherman, married, and raised eight children.[10]

Much of this story may be true, for adventures at sea were commonplace at the turn of the eighteenth and nineteenth century. There was a David Wilson, 'common mariner' aboard the Dundee whaler *Horn* in 1809,[11] and again in *Advice* in 1810.[12] Whether this was the same seaman is arguable, for David Wilson is not an uncommon Scottish name, but in 1810 *Advice* was mentioned as having given 'opposition' to His Majesty's Gun Brig *Pickle* commanded by Lieutenant Crawford, when the navy boarded the 'said ship'.[13] David Wilson is named as having a 'protection', but his name disappears from the lists for a few years, before reappearing in 1814 in the whaler *Mary Ann*.[14] Perhaps this is a coincidence, but an interesting one.

A suspiciously similar story is attached to Robert Pratt of Cellardyke. Folklore states that he was returning on a whaler when the press-gang grabbed him off Inchkeith, but he managed to jump out of the Royal Naval brig and onto a Forth ferry that deposited him safely in Fife. He joined a trader, only to be pressed again in London. He served in the navy for a number of years before a French privateer captured his vessel. Imprisoned in France, he escaped and made his way to England, then back to Scotland, where he rejoined the whaling fleet. Pratt made thirty-seven Arctic voyages before settling as a sailmaker in Cellardyke.

Again there is a fragment of documentary evidence, which may back up at least part of this story. In the 1808 season the Protection List for *Mary Ann* of Dundee included a Robert Pratt,[15] who was not present on any further lists until 1814, when the Dundee whaler *Three Brothers* had a Robert Pratts of 'Cellerdykes' on board.[16]

Cellardyke had its own whaling company at one time, and was the home to many Greenlandmen who served on the Dundee vessels, so it is hardly surprising that two of its seamen should be remembered. The Kirk Session records of Cellardyke do not always give Cellardyke whalers the best characters. In 1829 George Boyter was accused of not being a member of any church, and replied that he was often absent at the whaling. Robert Brown, another whaler, was both illiterate and 'very ignorant', but it was his predilection for pre-marital sex that caused the Session to prevent him from joining his whaling ship. Other Cellardyke men were either more righteous or more careful not to be caught. Three Dykers, William Davidson, John Muir and William Muir were on board the Dundee whaler *Thomas* in 1836. None of them returned when she was wrecked.

James McIntosh of Broughty Ferry was another ordinary whaler, who was better known by his nickname of 'Toshie'. He was a career whaler, with many Arctic trips to his credit, when he sailed north in *Chieftain* in 1884. Unlike most of the Dundee fleet, *Chieftain* was a three-masted schooner without an auxiliary engine. Built in Lossiemouth, she was square-sterned and carvel-built with a male figurehead, and was commanded by Thomas Gellatly.[17] On 26 May, *Chieftain* was off Greenland and had four whaleboats hunting for bottlenose whales, known as 'botleys' to the Dundee whalers. One boat caught a whale and towed it to *Chieftain* to be flensed, then returned to the hunting pack. It was a successful day, for the other three boats were fast to another whale, but as the boats came together, a fog descended.

Of the four boats, one was commanded by Captain Gellatly, a second by a harpooner named Bain, another by the second mate and the fourth by the spectioneer. As the fog remained thick, Captain Gellatly sent the second mate to search for *Chieftain*. It was normal practice in these circumstances for the ship to sound a gun or ring a bell, but perhaps the fog distorted the sounds. The second mate did not find *Chieftain*, but was rescued by a Norwegian schooner. When it became obvious that *Chieftain* would not find them, Captain Gellatly reorganised the boat's crews, ordering McIntosh to join Bain's boat, which had the most inexperienced men, and ordered everyone to make for Iceland, some two hundred miles away.

The boats had mixed fortunes. The spectioneer managed to reach land. Captain Gellatly steered safely to Brimness, where a Norwegian smack found him. Bain and McIntosh were not so fortunate. For at least fourteen days they steered their boat toward Iceland, but with an inexperienced crew they did not reach the land. When a storm blew up, McIntosh took the long steering oar, sitting for days in the stern and watching helplessly as the others died of hunger and exposure. McIntosh threw the bodies overboard. When he was found, he had to be cut free from the boat, and was so badly frostbitten that a Danish surgeon had to amputate both legs at the knee.

McIntosh never went back to sea, returning to his wife and son. He became a level-crossing attendant at Broughty Ferry and fathered another seven children, but was dissatisfied with the heavy teak legs that he had. The Reverend David MacRae found him a hand tricycle, on which McIntosh pedalled to London. The *Pall Mall Gazette* interviewed him, so preserving his story, and began a successful appeal for lighter cork legs.

A much earlier whaler was Robert Edgar of Montrose, whose descendants keep his memory very much alive. Robert Edgar was born in November 1795, possibly in the Parish of Craig, and was a harpooner on a whaling ship, retiring to become an itinerant preacher. Edgar brought many artefacts back from the whaling, including scrimshaw work, a mahogany-trimmed telescope and, most surprisingly, a Japanese pearl-handled sword. These souvenirs give a strong indication that Edgar was involved in South Sea whaling, so perhaps he sailed in one of the London-based whalers, or even an American vessel. He certainly returned to Montrose, where he lived with his wife, Ann Lowe.

Robert Edgar died on 19 March 1857, at Shore Wynd, Montrose, and was buried in Inchbraoch Cemetery, Rossie Island. His wife survived him by some twenty-seven years. According to James Gibson, the family historian, she was born in Laurencekirk and had no formal education. Lowe must have been very strong-willed as well as a devout woman, for she taught herself to read so that she could follow the church sermons. After the death of her man, Lowe brought up her family by mending nets and finding bait.[18] This last was a tedious, hard job that entailed early rising and long hours on beaches that were swept by North Sea winds, or standing knee-deep in the sea plucking mussels off slippery rocks. If a whaler's life was hard, that of his wife was equally so, and one wonders how many more women had to support their families in such a manner after their husbands failed to return from the Arctic.

That is a sobering piece of history that is never conveyed by the romantic image of a white-sailed whaling ship.

Alexander Alison is another mariner who is only known through the strenuous efforts of his descendants. His parents were Alexander Alison, a Dalkeith merchant, and Helen Dods, and they married in Dalkeith, possibly in 1794 or 1795. In that period in Scotland, the wife kept her own name throughout her life; it was only with the Anglification of Scottish culture that the absorbing of the wife's identity with her husband's name became widespread. As was obvious with Ann Lowe, Scotswomen retained their strength of character as well as their own name. From Dalkeith, Alison and Dods moved to London, where Alexander senior became a 'wharfe clerk' at Cottons Wharfe, near Bermondsey Street. Young Alexander Alison was born in August 1796 and baptised in St Olave's Church.

When Alexander senior died in 1803, young Alexander moved back to Dalkeith to become a tailor with his uncle, but at some time he ran away to sea. Documentary evidence for the next period is missing, but family lore, which is often surprisingly accurate, insists that he was shipwrecked, pressed into the Navy and escaped by running into one door of a pub and out the other, to hide in a field of corn. It was in 1812 that Alexander Alison worked as a whaler, when he signed a three-year apprenticeship on board *Lady Jane,* a Thames-built vessel owned by William Linskill of Tynemouth and Quentin Blackburn of Newcastle. On his first voyage he encountered a storm that lasted for weeks and reduced the master, William Holmes, to tears. He also made a promise not to swear, a promise he kept despite provocation by the other members of the crew.

When Alison left the sea, he became a tailor with the Highland Light Infantry in 1815. Seven years later, and by now married, he bought himself out of the army but was bankrupted when he refused to vote for one of his clients who was also a politician. Not a man to give up, Alison moved to London and started again. Interestingly, his grandson, Archibald Alison, worked for Levers Whaling Station in Stornoway between the First and Second World War. Passages from Alexander Alison's journal have been quoted in the text of this book.

Cornelius Frogett was not an ordinary mariner, but a shipmaster who for years commanded the Dundee brigantine *Rodney.* He was in command of *Rodney* from at least March 1790[19] and sailed, always to the Greenland whale fishery, until 1805, through the dark years of the French Revolutionary and Napoleonic Wars. In common with the other whaling

51

masters, Frogget commanded an armed ship and a crew of protected men, leaving Dundee in March and returning in July or August.

He does not seem to have performed any spectacular deeds, and his catches were no more than was expected. In 1800, for instance, he brought back 2 tons of whale fins, and 79.5 tons of blubber, from which 52 tons and 10 gallons of oil were extracted.[20] However, what the records do not show is that Frogget worked through some terrible personal tragedies. He was married to Jean Thompson, and on 1794 they had a son, David, who died when he was two. At the same time Jean was nursing their daughter, Jean, who died at seven months old the following year.

Intensely personal facts such as these help bring the Greenlandmen into perspective. Not only were they working in an extremely tough and dangerous business, made more difficult by war, they also had to cope with a family life that was complicated by long absences from home. If the whaling industry needed men with more than ordinary physical and moral toughness, it also needed whaling wives who were able to endure the unendurable without the support of their men.

Anno quinto

Georgii II. Regis.

An Act for encouraging the *Greenland* Fishery.

WHEREAS the Trade to Green- *Preamble.* land, the Greenland Seas, and Davis's Streights, in the fishing for Whales, Seals, and other Creatures caught there, is a very beneficial Trade to this Kingdom, not only in the employing great Numbers of Seamen and Ships, and consuming great Quantities of Provisions, but also in bringing into this Nation great Quantities of Fins, Oyl, or Blubber of Whales and Oyl Skins, and other Produce of Seals and other Creatures; and whereas the permitting the Importation of such Fins, Oyl, or Blubber, or other Produce whatsoever of Whales, Seals, and other Creatures caught by His said Majesty's Subjects in the said Seas, Streights, or in any other Parts of the Seas adjoyning thereunto, without paying any Duty for the same for a competent Time, may greatly contribute to the Encouragement and Support of the said Trade; may it therefore please Your Majesty that it may be enacted, and be it enacted by the King's most Excellent Majesty, by and with the Advice and Consent of the Lords Spiritual and Temporal, and Commons, in this present Parliament assembled, and by the Authority of the same, That it shall and may be

5 F 2   lawful

4

The Beginnings: Act of George II to encourage the Greenland Whale Fishery

The Prey: a Fin Whale. This specimen was killed off Scotland, but gives a good idea of the sheer size of the whale (Angus Council Cultural Services)

The Vessels: Eliza Swan, *one of the most successful Montrose vessels. In this picture, men can be seen whaling and seal hunting on the ice (Angus Council Cultural Services)*

The Vessels: Lord Gambier *of Kirkcaldy. When the vessel was lost in 1862, the local Inuit cared for the crew. This badly faded photograph is one of very few to show a purely sail-powered whaling vessel (Fife Council Libraries)*

The Vessels: Peterhead whaler Hope, *on which Arthur Conan Doyle worked as a surgeon. She is shown in Aberdeen Harbour, probably soon after her launch in 1873 (Aberdeen Heritage)*

The Vessels: the whaler Eclipse *in Arctic ice (Aberdeen Heritage)*

The Vessels: Peterhead whaling brig Alert, *commanded by Captain Alexander Davidson in the 1880s. She is shown here in North Harbour, Peterhead (Aberdeen Heritage)*

The Vessels: Terra Nova, *the last Dundee-built whaler, whose distinguished career included rescuing* Discovery *in 1904 (Scottish Fisheries Museum, Anstruther)*

The Vessels: Diana *in Godhaven harbour. 'Godhaven, a Danish settlement on the south west coast of Disco Island, was a place well known to the whalers.' (Scottish Fisheries Museum, Anstruther)*

The Vessels: an example of later British whalers, Southern Harper, *an Antarctic whale catcher of the post-war era; note the crow's nest high on the foremast (Angus Council Cultural Services)*

The Port: Montrose, 1822 (Angus Council Cultural Services)

The Port: Fit o the Toon at Arbroath, home of many whaling men

The Shipmasters: Alexander Davidson, who skippered the Peterhead brig Alert
(Scottish Fisheries Museum, Anstruther)

6

WHALERS AT WAR

'War, that mad game the world so loves to play.'
Jonathan Swift

During the wars of the eighteenth and early nineteenth centuries, British seamen had four formidable enemies. The first was disease, which was an ever-present scourge in any long-haul vessel. The second was the weather, for wind and waves exacted a shocking toll of the old sailing vessels. The third was the official foe, normally French privateers but often reinforced by French national naval forces, or ships from sundry other nations. American vessels were a particular nuisance during the 1812 to 1814 hostilities, and Danish privateers haunted northern seas when that country was on the opposing side. Despite this formidable list, possibly the enemy most feared by merchant seamen, including the Greenlandmen, were the press-gangs of the Royal Navy.

The official name for the press-gangs was the Impressment Service, although the name came from 'prest', a payment made to enable a seaman to reach an agreed rendezvous. There does not seem to have been any official form of impressment in Scotland before 1603, although James IV ordered that fishing boats were to be built and the burghs were to 'mak all the stark idill men within thair boundis to pass with the said schippis for thair wagis'.[1] After the Union of Crowns, Scottish seamen were vulnerable to impressment in the English navy, and as the century advanced, more Scots served the united Crown.

The eighteenth century was a period of intense naval competition, when dynastic wars divided Europe and the Royal Navy was in periodic, and often desperate, need of men. Coastal Scotland was as liable to be targeted as was England. There were various Acts that ordered towns to provide a quota of men for the navy, but there were never enough recruits, so forcible impressment was common. Usually this took place at sea, when homeward-bound vessels were stopped and stripped of men, leaving the master, mates and just enough of the crew to steer to port. In theory, the navy provided what they called men-in-lieu, members of the warship's crew who deputised for the pressed seamen. In practice the master of the stripped ship was left to struggle as best he could with an inadequate crew.

Service on board a man-of-war was not popular. Discipline was harsh, food was worse and there was an open-ended length of service. Unlike in merchant vessels, seamen could not leave at the end of a voyage if they disliked the conditions. What was worse, the pay had not risen since the seventeenth century. The possibility of prize money was dangled like a nautical carrot, but few seamen were lucky enough to serve under commanders such as Cochrane of the 'golden' *Pallas.*

When the bounty system for the whaling trade was first instituted, one of its primary purposes was to create a reservoir of trained seamen for the Royal Navy to use in the event of war. There was no secret about that fact; when the Royal Burghs of Scotland met to petition parliament to retain the bounty, they stated that the whaling trade:

> Has been for a long time considered of the greatest advantage to Britain in general, not only by furnishing a number of able and hardy seamen, as well for the service of the merchants as for manning his Majesty's fleets.[2]

The Convention of Royal Burghs was a meeting of the most important trading towns and cities in Scotland. Most of these towns were situated on the coast and represented a large proportion of the available merchant capital and financial enterprise of the nation. When it was time to renew the bounty, the Convention reminded the government that the whaling industry was:

> A nursery for seamen hardy beyond most others, who are at all times ready to be employed in the service of their country, by manning his Majesty's navy in the event of any sudden rupture among the powers of Europe.[3]

Yet when this sudden rupture occurred, as it did with remarkable frequency throughout the eighteenth century, the Convention was equally enthusiastic to prevent the Greenland seamen from joining His Majesty's ships. In July 1755, when the Seven Years War was in its infancy and the Admiralty was casting a predatory eye on the hardy seamen of the Greenland fleet, the Convention wagged a negative finger. Reminding the Admiralty that there was a 'general protection' issued for 'all fishermen… in the Firths of Forth, Clyde & Murray', the Convention, presided over by Lord George Drummond of Edinburgh, asked for a similar protection 'to the harpineers, linemen and boat stirers imployed in the whale fishery'.[4]

Lord George Murray was soon able to present a letter to the Convention from John Cleveland, secretary to the Lords of the Admiralty. Their Lordships had agreed not to press any seamen who had served on the Greenlandmen 'belonging to this part of the United Kingdom in the stations of harpooner, boatstearers, and line coillers'. The skilled whaling men on board Scottish ships were therefore safe, for Cleveland also said that if any were pressed unwittingly, they would be released 'upon proof of their having so served'.[5]

At that period, it seemed that the ordinary Greenlandmen, the so-called 'common mariners', were as liable to be pressed as were any other merchant seamen. English whalers were at least as vulnerable as Scots, and in 1790, when HMS *Champion* threatened to press men from a Whitby whaler, the Greenlandmen threatened resistance with harpoons.[6] That was not the only occasion on which the Royal Navy had to fight for their recruits. At one riot in South Shields, two men were killed and thirty-two pressed,[7] and when men from the Hull whaler *Sarah and Elizabeth* resisted, 'one man was killed belonging to the Greenlandman and 3 badly wounded.'[8] Referring to these incidents, Dr Barrow writes that in 1779, during the American War of Independence, there was a severe shortage of manpower in the Royal Navy and the naval officers were under instructions to press anybody regardless of protections.

Fear of the press gang could cause problems for owners as well as crews. When *Advice* was bought from London in 1804, her Bill of Sale arrived late, so the ship was not at first registered in Dundee. The owners had made up a list of the officers that would be protected, but until the Bill of Sale arrived, were unable to confirm Protections. In this instance, the crew had the choice between signing on unprotected or engaging with another vessel.[9]

Despite their obvious desire to avoid the press-gangs whenever possible, Dundee whaling men could resist with violence. In July 1810 *Advice*, under William Adamson, was off Thurso on her way back from the whaling grounds when HM Gun Boat *Pickle* sent a boarding party. A Customs report mentions that *Advice* gave 'considerable opposition', and advised that the bounty payment should be withheld.[10] It is possible that this was the incident in which David Wilson from Cellardyke was reported as being pressed by HMS *Pinkie,* and if so he may have been unlucky. An earlier letter from the Customs Collector of Dundee said that when whaling vessels return from the Arctic 'it very frequently happens that part of the crew leaves them off Cape Wrath or other places... for fear of being impressed.'[11] Perhaps *Pickle* was aware of this procedure and ambushed the returning vessels. If the voyage was complete, the protections may no longer have been effective.

Orkney folklore contains a wealth of legend about whalers and the press-gang, much of it tending to agree with the known facts. There is one tale, related by W. R. Mackintosh at the end of the nineteenth century, which tells of a whaling ship returning from the Davis Straits that was ambushed by a Royal Naval vessel off Orkney. After first trying to flee, the whaler then gave resistance, with the result that eighteen men were pressed, including one James Sabiston of Rendall in Orkney. The tradition is so close to the documented account of *Advice* and *Pickle* that it may well be true and argues for a closer investigation of folklore sources.

By an Act of King George III, protection against Impressment included 'six harpooners, six linemanagers and six boatsteerers and eighteen seamen as common mariners belonging to each such ship or vessel of the burthen of four hundred tons and so in proportion for any less tonnage'.[12] It was up to the Customs Officers to calculate the number of officers and men that were so protected. At least in the case of the Dundee Customhouse they appear to have been flexible, allowing *Estridge*, of 312 tons, to carry six 'of each description' and *Rodney*, of 176 tons, five of each. If the letter of the law had been strictly adhered to, the respective numbers should have been five and three.[13] The Dundee Customs officers had to seek permission from their superiors in Edinburgh, who were either humane men, or were alive to the commercial realities of the situation.

Protections were granted to named individuals after a bond, or monetary assurance was promised. Invariably there was a market for forged protections, with prices ranging from 8s. 6d. in Sunderland to an inflated £3 in London. Protections could not legally be transferred and somebody in authority, such as a Customs official, had to endorse them. Each whaling vessel was allowed a certain number of protections, depending on her size. It frequently happened that a man to whom a protection was issued was unable to make the voyage, in which case the ship's master wrote a 'petition' to the Custom Collector, who passed it on to his superiors. In March 1810 Alexander Young, master of *Eliza Swan* of Montrose, petitioned that Robert Lawson should be granted a Protection 'in room of George Brown as harpooner, the latter being in Ireland'.[14] This petition was granted, but the Collector asked if 'George

Brown or his sureties ought not to be called upon to answer for his default',[15] in other words, pay the amount of money he had bonded.

Even the whaling experts were not always protected when they sailed. The number of protections issued was strictly regulated, so when the protection for George Brown could not be recovered, Robert Lawson had to sail unprotected.[16] On another occasion, a Montrose whaler named David Mill was a protected line manager, but caught 'rheumatic affection', that curse of seamen. Although he surrendered his protection, his replacement, George Menmuir, was also 'to proceed in his place unprotected'.[17]

It is possible that some seamen accepted a protection for a whaling vessel as an insurance policy while they looked for a more pleasant berth. In 1808 John Fenton of Dundee was a line manager, but chose instead to sail to Jamaica, having first handed back his protection.[18] It was also possible for promotion to rob a whaling vessel of an experienced man. Such a case occurred in March 1814 when Richard Stark was protected as a boatsteerer on board *London* of Montrose, but instead accepted 'command of a small coasting vessel'. He contacted the Customs officers, and requested permission to 'be released from his engagement with the *London*'.[19] In 1810 James Brown, a St Monance man who was a harpooner on *Advice* in 1809, was promoted to be mate of *Raith* of Leith.[20]

Such instances of promotion confirm the seamanship of the whalers, and tend to reinforce the government's wisdom in creating the bounty system as a nursery for seamen.

If the Customs officers believed that the protections were vital, the men who had given their bond might be expected to treat them like gold dust, but sometimes they were careless. In 1811 a harpooner named Alexander Fenton had been granted a protection to sail on *Estridge* of Dundee, but 'having by Accident lost his Protection', was 'impressed into His Majesty's Service at Newcastle'. The owner of *Estridge*, Mr David Jobson, engaged Thomas Barclay instead, and requested that he be protected in the place of the unfortunate Fenton. On other occasions, the seamen just failed to appear, leaving the ship short-handed and the Customs officers scratching their heads. Such a case happened in November 1814 when Thomas Guthrie, who was listed as a line manager in *Three Brothers*, and Andrew Cargill, a boatsteerer in *Estridge*, both of Dundee, did not report. The Collector of Customs at Dundee asked the managing owners of the ships to 'produce a certificate that Guthrie and Cargill were serving in His Majesty's Navy'. When no such certificate appeared, the Collector requested permission to pursue their bonds.[21]

There were many reasons why a Greenlandman would not join his ship. He could have been captured by the French, as in the case of Alexander Sword, line manager of *Rodney,* or he could have deserted, as in the case of Robert Keith, boatsteerer in the same vessel.[22] Despite the undoubted hardihood of the whalers, some genuinely became sick. In 1814 Alexander McDougall was a line manager on the list of *Mary Ann* of Dundee, but owing to his 'bad state of health' he did not apply for a protection. Mr Patrick Nimmo, a Dundee surgeon, supplied proof of McDougall's condition and the ship owner applied to the Customs to put George Taylor in his place.[23] At other times, as in the case of James Steel of the Montrose ship *Monarch*, the protected seaman just 'failed to appear'.[24]

Protections were only valid as long as the person named was a member of the whaler's company. When Alexander McBay, once a boatsteerer on the Montrose vessel *Monarch*, was pressed in London in 1813, he claimed that he was protected. In an exchange of letters, James Paton, Collector of Customs at Montrose, informed Captain Richbell, the Regulating Captain in London, that McBay was not protected for the 1814 season.[25] McBay was unfortunate, for his name had appeared on the protection lists since at least 1810; presumably he was working on the coastal trade between whaling seasons.[26]

Although the French wars finally ended with the carnage of Waterloo in 1815 and the American war sputtered to a halt slightly earlier, whalers still had protections until at least 1816. That year William Anderson, manager of the Union Whale Fishing Company, wrote to the Customs, saying that William Spankie and James Smart had been unable to join *London* because they were at sea.[27] As in all these instances, there must have been a story; perhaps Spankie and Smart worked on a coaster through the winter close season, and the ship was delayed by adverse weather. After this period of time there is no means of knowing.

Although the press-gangs worried the whalers, they were only a danger in port and in home waters. As soon as the whaling ships cleared harbour they were in danger from enemy privateers. A privateer was a privately owned vessel that had obtained a licence to attack the enemies of its country, or the enemies of whatever nation had issued the licence. A vessel from virtually any state could apply for a licence, known as a 'letter of marque', from any other state, so a Swedish vessel, say, could sail with a letter of marque from Denmark that gave it permission to attack British shipping. In a sense, privateers were a poor man's navy and were often used by states without a strong national fleet.

Privateers were often little better than pirates. They sailed more for plunder than patriotism, with the owner, master and crew gaining most of the value of the vessels that they captured. There was no optimum size for a privateer; a small rowing boat crammed with armed men could pose just as much a threat to an unarmed and undermanned coaster as could a man-of-war. Whaling ships, however, were not undermanned, nor did they hug the coast. A privateer would have to be sizeable to threaten a blubber-boat, and even a medium-sized vessel carrying a letter of marque could represent a sizeable financial outlay. A British letter of marque cost between £1500 and £3000, and to that must be added the cost of armament, provisions for the crew and the gear of the vessel herself.

Despite these drawbacks, every maritime state used privateers during the wars of the eighteenth and early nineteenth centuries. Those that posed the greatest threat to the Greenlandmen came from France, Denmark and the United States. In May 1777 alone, 21 privateers from the raw young Republic slid out of Boston. With the Royal Navy concentrating its efforts on the English Channel, northern waters were ill-defended. In October 1808, a Danish privateer cut out the Montrose sloop *James and Margaret* from a sheltered bay in Orkney and put the crew ashore on Hoy.[28] Eight years earlier a cutter-rigged privateer was haunting the coast between Montrose and Aberdeen, capturing the brigantine *Ranger* of Aberdeen and chasing others.[29] Either of these vessels would have been a threat to the Greenlandmen on their passage north from Dundee, Montrose or the Forth.

It seems to have been United States privateers that posed most danger to the whaling ships. The Reverend John Mill mentioned American privateers in his diary: 'we were alarmed with American privateers being on the coast, and had taken two Greenlanders',[30] while the *Aberdeen Journal* wrote of them in August 1777,[31] and again in 1780.[32] Despite its preoccupation with the south coast, the Royal Navy did spare vessels to protect the whalers; for instance in 1809 HMS *La Sybille* sailed north to escort the whaler convoy that sailed to Greenland waters.

The Greenlandmen, however, were not the quietest of seamen and made provisions for their own defence. In April 1781 a whaler captured a French privateer and brought her as prize into Bressay Sound,[33] and at least one whaling vessel was refitted as a privateer.[34]

Customs Records contain many references to whaling vessels being armed. In March 1793, with the French Revolutionary War just begun, the Montrose whalers *Eliza Swan* and *George Dempster* gave security for arms to be carried. Both vessels carried two swivels (an anti-personnel weapon), one harpoon gun, two blunderbusses and one 'musquet'. Together with twenty-five pounds of gunpowder and fourteen pounds of shot, the total hardly seems enough to scare off a determined French rowing boat, let alone a privateer packed with red-capped revolutionaries.[35] The arms were only carried on the condition that they were brought back home, and the master had to account for any ammunition expended. An accompanying letter calls harpoon guns 'implements of fishing', which perhaps suggests that the use of such devices had to be explained. In 1792 the Society of Arts had offered a reward for the best 'improved harpoon gun'. Montrose vessels certainly carried such weapons, but at that date they were not reliable and hand harpoons continued to be used for many decades. It was not until the mid 1860s that Swen Foyn's swivel-mounted harpoon gun finally replaced the hand-thrown harpoon.

At the early stages of the French wars, not every ship was armed. The Dundee whalers *Tay* and *Rodney* took out security for their voyage, under the condition that they sailed 'north about and not through the British Channel', with the additional note that 'these ships not being armed for their defence.'[36] It would appear that the security was less if the vessels kept clear of the Channel, which would be more dangerous on account of enemy vessels. The French were more active the following year, capturing *Dundee* of Dundee[37] and *Raith* of Leith. While the crew of *Raith* recaptured their vessel, the Royal Navy boarded and retook *Dundee*, but not before William Souter, her master, had been carried away into captivity.[38] Folklore claims that her mate remained hidden on board during the French occupation and re-emerged when the Navy arrived. *Dundee* was an elderly vessel, having first sailed to the whaling from Dundee in 1754.[39]

The recapture of *Raith* might be the incident referred to by the Reverend Mill, who said that French privateers captured a Greenland vessel and put sixteen men on board, leaving the mate, a Shetlander named Bonsk Lyons, and one man on board. Mill claims that Lyons waited until eight of the Frenchmen were drunk and imprisoned them below deck, used a whaling knife to drive the other eight into a whale boat and then brought the ship into Bressay Sound.[40]

Being taken prisoner to France was perhaps even worse than being press-ganged, for the French incarcerated British seamen in gloomy fortresses, often many miles inland. Some of the luckier men could return home after a comparatively short period of imprisonment, such as the case of Peter Stiven, master of the Arbroath brigantine *Hunter*. He was captured by the French warship *Sylph* while on a voyage to Norway in 1805, and returned to Arbroath in December 1808.[41]

By 1805, after twelve years of war broken only by the Peace of Amiens, it appeared common practice for Scottish whaling vessels to carry arms. *Estridge*, Robert Webster, master,[42] *Jane*, William Christopher, master, *Horn*, William Vallantine, master,[43] *Advice*, James Webster, master and *Rodney*, Cornelius Frogget, master[44] all carried defensive arms to the north. *Estridge*,[45] *Jane*,[46] *Horn* and *Advice*, at least, had also been armed when they worked on the foreign and coasting trade between whaling voyages.[47] By 1808 *Mary Ann*, William Duchars, master, was also armed.[48] Orders in Council stipulated that whaling vessels could carry armaments 'not exceeding one carriage or swivel gun for every ten tons burthen of the said ship' and 'one musket or blunderbuss, one pair of pistols and one sword or cutlass for every person borne on the books'. Each weapon was permitted twenty rounds of powder and ball.[49] The licenses to carry arms, like the protections, were to be renewed with every whaling voyage.

In theory, a 300-ton whaling ship could thus carry up to thirty cannon, which would make her a formidable enemy to a privateer, and quite a handful even for a small warship. The 187-ton *Rodney* was licensed for 'eight carriage guns and fifteen muskets' in February 1810.[50] *Rodney* had already been licensed to 'carry arms for defence when employed in another trade'.[51]

When the 1812 war with the United States broke out, the Royal Navy was already fully stretched holding back the privateers of most of maritime Europe, blockading the French and allied fleets and providing escorts for the vital convoys that kept Britain fed. With vessels that were often chronically undermanned and ill-trained, the Navy attempted to stem this new flow of enemies, but the sea was wide and the Americans merged superb seamanship with powerful ships. In July 1813 a warship wearing the Union flag approached *Eliza Swan* of Montrose, hailed her and sent a boat. When the boat arrived, the lieutenant in charge claimed he was from HM frigate *Alexandria* (could be *Alexandra*), and asked Captain John Young to come on board with his logbook and papers. Captain Young complied, to be informed that he was now a prisoner of Commodore John Rodgers of USS *President*.

There were other prisoners on board from the seven merchantmen *President* had captured, and Commodore Rodgers placed them all on board *Eliza Swan*,[52] after agreeing to a bond of £5000 for ransom. Montrose Museum holds the ransom note. *President* looted *Eliza Swan* of a boat, some fishing line, provisions, harpoons and a sail, as well as the whaling licence.[53]

Overall, warfare was unkind to the Scottish whalers, but even so, Dundee at least increased her fleet. In 1793 the city sent four vessels to the whaling grounds, but by 1815, after twenty-two years of nearly non-stop war, it sent eight. Unfortunately there do not seem to be any figures for the number of whales captured during the war years, but in 1792 Dundee vessels brought home ten black whales and forty-one seals, with 83 hundredweight of whalebone and 75 tons of oil. In 1816 Dundee whalers captured 73 whales, with 950 hundredweight of whalebone and 968 tons of oil. Difficult conditions or not, the Dundee whaling industry came through the war years remarkably well.

7

'FAREWELL DEAR SCOTIA'

'Many waters cannot quench love; neither can the floods drown it.'
Song of Solomon 8:7

Possibly the two most emotional times for any whaling man, as for his wife and family, were the day of departure and the day he returned to port. When the whaling ship was about to sail north, both parties knew that the voyage would last for at least four months, and possibly for very much longer. There was always the very real chance of death or disablement in the north, either with the entire ship being lost or through one of the hundreds of accidents that could befall seafaring men. At the time of parting, all the petty misunderstandings that beset any marriage must have been regretted or forgotten, leaving the enduring love burning clear. Families gathered in what the *Aberdeen Journal* called 'a great concourse'[1] as the ships departed.

March or April was the traditional departure time, while the winter snow was still a fresh memory or a chill presence underfoot and the grey North Sea lashed malevolently against the harbour walls. By an Act of George III, whaling vessels could only claim the bounty if they left harbour on or before 10 April, unless there was some 'unavoidable impediment or necessity' in which case they were allowed until 25 April.[2] Vessels that sailed later than 10 April had to state the reason, in writing, to the Collector of Customs at their port.[3] In one recorded instance, *Monarch*, *London* and *Eliza Swan* did not leave Montrose until 12 April 1813; the Collector accepted their explanation that there had been contrary winds.[4] Sometimes the harbour was clear of whaling ships much earlier; in 1809, all the Dundee vessels left between 20 February and 21 March, save for *Mary Ann* that left on 4 May and was thus disqualified from the bounty.[5] Bad weather was probably the main reason for ships being delayed from sailing on the prescribed date. In 1810 the Collectors of Customs at Dundee reported that *Friendship* failed to sail on time as 'the weather was constantly averse for Ships sailing from this River going to the Eastward or Northward during the period mentioned'.[6]

In the eighteenth and early nineteenth centuries the whale ships headed for the Greenland Sea or Davis Strait, but later, with the advent of auxiliary engines, some left Scotland around February and crossed to Newfoundland first. They spent time with the sealers of Newfoundland and returned to Dundee or Aberdeen, before heading out again for the whaling grounds. Either way, the departure from their homeport was filled with emotion.

It seems to have been a tradition among whaling men that they stupefied themselves with drink the night before departure. In Fraserburgh and Peterhead this carouse was known as a 'foy', which simply meant a farewell feast or departure. Foys were not peculiar to whaling men, but were held for various reasons, such as when somebody moved overseas or obtained another job. As they were also held when a working season ended, they appear to have marked any sort of change from one episode of life to another. The police seem to have been tolerant of these occasions, allowing the Peterhead men, at least, space to indulge.[7]

The effects of these celebrations could last until after the ship pulled away. Admiral Seymour sailed with the Dundee whaler *Mazinthien* in 1867 and thought the crew were still not 'over sober' when they sailed.[8] Other men would be suffering from sore heads, while the 'Greenmen' (first-time sailors) would also be seasick when the ship hit the open sea.

In Dundee, and in some other ports, on the last Sunday before sailing the fleet was decorated with ribbons, people of the port came on board and the minister preached a sermon. On the day of sailing the whaler's girl would hand him a garland as a good luck charm and a love token. The garland was of ribbon, with one knot for every whale the ship would catch, but it was bad luck to count the knots. If they were married, whalers had to buy their own ribbons from a wise woman, a speywife, who blessed them. As the vessels left Dundee, the crowds hurled pennies and oranges onto their decks, to bring luck in the days ahead.

The intense emotional scenes that marked the departure of the whaling fleet were remarked upon in journals and newspaper reports. The *Dundee Directory* of 1875 commented:

> An equally animated spectacle is presented to the frequenters of the Marine Parade when the whale ships are departing for their hazardous cruize in high latitudes. The departure of these vessels for the sealing and the whaling is always witnessed by large crowds, and incidents of mingled excitement and amusement frequently arise.[9]

A paper read in Broughty Ferry in 1885 also tells of children, sweethearts and wives beside a departing ship, with cheers, crying women and waving handkerchiefs.[10]

W. Burn Murdoch, who sailed as assistant surgeon and unofficial artist on *Balaena* on the Dundee Antarctic Expedition of 1892, wrote at some length about the scenes as the ships departed. He mentions 'wives and children... picking their way about the decks', and, when *Balaena* eventually left the dock, 'the last of the crew bade good bye to their wives and children... leaving many a... face wet with tears.'[11] Captain Markham, who sailed as a passenger in *Arctic* in 1874, also wrote of the emotional scenes at departure, quoting a seaman who said that on parting his wife 'would have cried a pint of tears'.[12]

It seems that a surprising number of Greenlandmen were married. Burn Murdoch mentions that 'almost all the crew, old and young, are married',[13] and when a seaman fell from the rigging of *Spencer* of Montrose in 1825, the *Montrose Review* commented that the man was recently married.[14] The evidence suggests that the whaling men cared for their wives, with many of the journals written by the ship's surgeon mentioning the attitude of Greenlandmen toward their women. A common entry reads: 'this night being Saturday it is customary for sailors at sea to drink to the health of Wives and Sweethearts.'[15] The letter of a survivor from the wreck of *Hebe* starts 'Beloved Wife' and ends 'Thine to death', which suggests more than mere companionship.[16]

It was not unknown for a Greenlandman's oil money to be paid to his wife, as in this note: 'please pay the bearer Janet Cunningham oil money due to me from the ship *Dorothy*, signed by me (X) john Cunningham's mark.'[17] Even the landsman Christopher Thomson, normally a critic of the whaling men, mentioned that they remembered their 'wives and sweethearts'.[18] In the letters written by the elder Scoresby, whaling captain of Whitby, to his 'loving wife and children', as much space is devoted to family matters as to whaling.

Contemporary whaling ballads sung by the seamen also reveal something of their feelings:

> We leave behind us on the shore
> All them we love most dear
> We leave our sweethearts and our wives
> All weeping round the pier.[19]

Even the scrimshaw work of whalers could be revealing; there exists the tooth of a sperm whale that has been decorated with the image of a man parting from his wife and children.[20] The Greenlandmen did not seem to forget their wives even in times of stress. When *Empress of India* sank in the ice and her crew was being rescued, men from the rescuers joined the crew in looting the doomed ship. While many ran to the rum lockers, 'one man got a wooden (box) he had promised his (wife) to bring her back a box to wash her dishes in.'[21]

Nonetheless, the relationships of whaling men could also be volatile. Captain Markham wrote that some of the men of *Arctic* were happy to escape from 'the thraldom of a jealous and ill tempered wife',[22] and the surgeon Alexander Trotter, who sailed on the Fraserburgh whaler *Enterprise*, was scathing of Greenlandmen from Shetland. He wrote that when they returned from the whaling 'they live on their money setting their wives and daughters to cultivate their little bit of land.'[23] Walter Scott, who visited the Shetland Islands in 1812, also mentions that the Shetland women were 'rather slavishly employed... I saw more than one carrying home the heavy sea-chests of... husbands, brothers or lovers discharged from on board the Greenlander.'[24]

While they were at sea the Greenlandmen had fond memories of their women, but once ashore in a port not their own, they behaved in exactly the same manner as generations of seafaring men had before. The whaling song about Newfoundland that contained the line 'a health to all the girls out here and to our wives so fair'[25] may not prove that Greenlandmen cheated on their wives, but it points to the possibility. Statements from elderly Inuit such as 'I... remember the Scottish whalers. My... father was one of them',[26] reveal that some Greenlandmen at least could have families on the western side of the Atlantic. Perhaps these were the unmarried men, but such behaviour tends to corroborate the statement of William Scoresby junior, who wrote that 'no class of men... enjoy and appreciate so much the society of the softer sex, as sailors.'[27]

It is a great pity that the wives and women of whalers wrote even less than did their men, but what there is appears to confirm the strength of their relationships. In Whitby there were various traditions that revealed something of the attitude of whalers' wives, including throwing shoes to wish their men luck and wearing their shifts inside out to ensure fair weather and a successful voyage. Of course, these superstitions may be self-seeking, for a successful voyage would bring money into the family home and the life of a widow would be even harder than that of a married woman. At least one whaling wife composed a poem to her departing husband:

> May guardian angels prove your steps attend
> And guide you safe unto your journey's end
> In every stage of life may you most happy be
> And when far distant oftimes think of me.[28]

When the apparent sophistication of the lines was queried, Dr Robb of Dundee University commented 'I think I am prepared to believe it could have been written by a working-class Victorian woman with literary leanings... I don't think it is too good for such a (presumed) writer.'[29]

In his book *Of Whales and Men*, the psychiatrist R. B. Robertson pointed out that the community of a whaler was damaged because of the lack of women. Although Robertson was writing about the Antarctic whalers of the mid-twentieth century rather than the Arctic whalers of the eighteenth and nineteenth, no single sex community can ever be entirely natural. Perhaps that is why Neptune brought his wife when he visited on May the First, and perhaps why the master's wife was so popular when she ventured to sea.

Of the twelve British women known to have accompanied their men to the whaling grounds in the century preceding 1920, only one, Margaret Penny, left a journal. Her husband, William Penny, was one of the most innovative whaling masters. An Aberdeen man, born in 1809, he sailed on his first voyage at twelve years old and was mate of the *Traveller* by 1833. Six years later, as master of the *Neptune*, he heard of a whaling ground the Inuit called Tenudiakbeek, but could not then explore. Aberdeen whaling was in decline, and next year Penny commanded the town's only remaining whaler, *Bon Accord*. Aided by an Inuit named Eenuoolooapik, he probed into Tenudiakbeek and with the casual arrogance typical of Victorian explorers renamed it Hogarth's Sound. Now it is known as Cumberland Sound.

Penny helped search for the missing explorer Franklin in 1849 and 1850, and the following year overwintered in Cumberland Sound. By 1853 he was a prime mover in the Aberdeen Arctic Company, again overwintering in Cumberland Sound as he commanded *Lady Franklin*. Although he caught 28 whales, either the Aberdeen ships, or the Americans who were also overwintering, brought cholera that devastated the Inuit. It was Penny who suggested using steam-powered ships in the Arctic, but Dundee that exploited the idea, Penny who introduced overwintering, but Dundee seamen who followed the idea through. He was an ideas man, and his wife lived his dreams.

Unfortunately, Mrs Penny did not write of her personal feelings, but surely only a devoted wife would leave the domestic comforts of Victorian Aberdeen to spend a year in the downright discomfort and danger of an Arctic whaling ship. Unless she was afraid that Captain Penny would find a temporary wife among the Inuit. Whatever her feelings for him, Captain Penny had a high regard for his wife, for on one occasion Margaret Penny 'was left in charge of the ship'.[30] Other whaling wives had a less prominent role, as in the case of Captain Murray in 1889, who brought his wife because the voyage promised to be longer than normal.[31] It is entirely possible that other whaling masters brought their wives without recording the fact; a detailed examination of surviving whaling logs may well find anomalies, such as unpaid assistant surgeons.

There is no doubt that, on the admittedly meagre evidence, the women left behind were strong-willed individuals. One of the few who wrote at some length was Christian Watt, the daughter and wife of whaling men. Her comments on her fiancée indicate an affectionate man who did not get things all his own way. 'James Sim left for the whaling at Greenland. He had pleaded to be married right away, but I wanted time to think.'[32] By the time Sim returned, Watt had decided to accept his proposal. The impersonal 'James Sim' had been promoted to 'My sweetheart' who 'returned from the whaling' to be 'married in the middle of the floor'.[33] As was the custom among Scottish fishing families, the wife was in charge at home, with Watt claiming that she ran the house and her man gave her every penny he earned.

The bond of marriage may have been close, but the puritan morals of Victorian Scotland built some unassailable barriers between men and women. When Watt admitted that she was 'a certain way again', her mother told her to speak quietly as her father 'did not know of such things.'[34] Watt thought it strange that a man who had fathered eight children did not appear to understand the process of pregnancy.

The attitude of the children of the whalers is even more difficult to ascertain. There is no doubt that the sons of whaling masters followed their fathers to sea at an early age. John Smith, son of Captain John Smith of the Leith whaler *Baffin*, was only eight when he sailed with his father in 1832. John Smith junior remained at sea when his father retired and eventually became master of the crack clippers *Min* and *Lahloo*. Young William Scoresby was ten when he first joined his father, and John Murray was also a child when he followed his father to sea. Each youngster stowed away on his father's ship, which might indicate affectionate feelings toward their respective fathers. Both boys also became whaling masters.

Stowaways were not uncommon, as young boys swarmed on board before the vessel departed, and hid in one of the many places of concealment. In 1894 *Diana* had three stowaways, *Polar Star* had two; in 1889 *Chieftain* unloaded four stowaways when she called at Stromness; in 1901 *Eclipse* dropped off six at Peterhead, but *Esquimaux* must have been a favourite ship, for in 1900 she had twenty stowaways on board.[35]

The constant repetition of names in the whaling ships argues that generation followed generation into the forecastle as well as into the captain's cabin. The younger children that were left to wave on the quayside were no doubt only biding their time. Those at Whitby recited a rhyme that was intended to bring their fathers safely home:

> Suther Wind Suther
> An Blow mah Father heam t'mah Mother.

Watt's writings reveal her memories of her father, a fisherman from Broadsea by Fraserburgh who became a whaler. 'He was a smart man who believed in learning', she wrote, adding, 'we had a happy childhood in a Christian home.'[36] Watt, however, had no illusions. She also wrote that whaling was 'a very dangerous job costing many young lives.'[37]

Before these young lives were put into danger, before the ships sailed from Dundee or Fraserburgh, Montrose or Peterhead, the owners and masters had a great deal of preparatory work to do. While the bounty system endured, the Customs officers were also busy, with their records riddled with references to the whalers preparing for the Arctic. Even as the ships sailed back from the previous season, the officers were busy ensuring that they had enough stationery for the next, as they made requests for items such as: 'one quire of Owners Whale Fishery Oaths' and 'Certificates of Ships Equipt for the Fisherys'.[38] Whaling may have been a physical, dangerous occupation, but there was much tedious paperwork supporting the ships.

To qualify for the bounty, whaling ships had to produce a number of documents, but before they were granted the certificates, the Customs officers had to measure them to ensure they were the correct ships, and that they were of the correct weight. There were strict regulations for 'admeasuring ships', with the breadth not to include the sheathing or doubling that was so essential to whaling vessels. The length was to be taken in a straight line along the keel, 'from the Back of the Main Stern Post to a perpendicular line from the forepart of the Main Stem under the Bowsprit.' If the measuring officer came across 'anything unusual...in the construction of the vessel' that was there to increase the tonnage, and therefore the bounty, he was to either cut it off or make allowance so that there was 'no fraudulent evasion of the law'.[39] If the situation was not straightforward, the Officer consulted his superiors. In one instance *Dundee* lost her figurehead when she 'ran foul of another Ship', so the officer enquired if this alteration had to be registered.[40]

Not only the ships, but also the whaling boats were measured and licensed. The Customs officer had to send the measurements and a description of each boat to Edinburgh, with a statement that he had 'no reason to suspect that said boat has been employed in illicit trade by the present master or owners or is intended to be so employed'.[41] Once certified, the whaling boats were stowed away safely for the voyage to the whaling grounds. There were surprising differences between the boats; Scottish boats tended to have a transom stern, while English were double prowed. Some boats were painted in the same colours as their parent vessels.

As important as the weight of the vessel, the legality of her longboats and the date of her sailing, was the composition of the crew. The Bounty Laws of King George III demanded that every whaling ship had to carry one apprentice for every fifty tons weight. The apprentices were to be between the ages of twelve and twenty. In 1823 this law was altered so that each ship had to take an apprentice for every one hundred tons weight.[42] In 1816 the Montrose vessels *Eliza Swan* and *Monarch* each carried six boys, presumably apprentices.[43]

Alexander Alison was in a desperate condition when he was apprenticed on board a whaler. He had a berth on board a vessel out of Yarmouth, but the owner had taken a dislike to him and ordered him to leave the ship in South Shields, where he had no friends and no money. For a few days Alison had survived in South Shields, suffering physical hardship and much mental torture. A sympathetic woman had taken him in and fed him, but still Alison thought of himself as an:

> ...Outcast among men. Went down to the key where the ships lay saw men and boys eating and drinking all seemed happy and comfortable but me. No home no food a stranger in a strange land. Went back to the place where I slept they offered me something to eat and said they would do what they could for me in getting another ship for me. In a few days they so far succeeded in getting a promise from the mate of a Greenlander and in about a fortnight after the owner whose name was Blacklin of North Shields and who owned the *Lady Jane*—Greenland ship of 402 tons.

> Promised to take me as an apprentice for 3 years—this was
> in January 1812—I was Bound in February—we began to
> rig out the Ship which was to sail in March for Davis Straits.

The requirements for whaling ships to carry a quota of 'Green' or 'Fresh' men, who were to be 'a Person not a seaman, or having ever been at Sea before',[44] was intended to build up a reservoir of trained seamen for the merchant service and particularly the Royal Navy, but there seem to have been occasions when the law was sidestepped. In a letter written in 1790, Mr Philips of the Edinburgh Customhouse informed the Dundee Collector that when a Greenman deserted his ship the previous season, the master replaced him with a seaman. The Commissioners refused to pay the bounty and resolved to treat any similar cases in the same manner.[45]

Greenmen could sometimes have a tough time on board, and were often the butt of rough humour. One of the most famous halyard chanties was *Reuben Ranzo*, otherwise known as *Goodbye Farewell*, which was about a tailor who became a sailor on board a whaler. One version is:

> He came in onboard a whaler,
> Spare a penny for Reuben Ranzo,
> Ranzo, boys, ranzo.

A halyard chanty was a working song that was sung as the men hoisted the sails. In decrying a man who was not able to perform all the work of an able seaman, *Reuben Ranzo* perhaps gives a seaman's view of the Greenman system.

The names of officers were scrutinised as carefully as those of the men. When the mate of *Advice* was named in one document as Robert Evans and in another as Thomas Evans, their Honours in Edinburgh asked the Dundee Collector for an explanation. The Collector told their Honours that the mate was named Robert Evans and 'that we are extremely sorry at the mistake'.[46]

By 1821 it seemed to be the practice in England to allow seamen to ship as Greenmen, provided they had never before sailed on a whaling ship. Their Honours in Edinburgh sent a circular letter to each Scottish customhouse advising that they did the same.[47] Ironically, it was possible for Greenmen to earn more than landsmen, who were ostensibly higher in rank. Such was the case in 1818 when sixteen-year-old David Greig shipped on board *London*. As well as a lump sum of £6, Greig was given clothes that were valued at £4 10s. On the same four-month voyage a landsman earned only £7 10s. A suspicious Customs officer wondered if

Greig was properly qualified to be termed a Greenman, but an enquiry by the Customs cleared the owners of any wrong-doing as 'he never was at sea before he entered the *London*, and does not seem, though rather young, unqualified.'[48] The normal wage for a Greenman was £1 for the voyage, plus one shilling for every ton of oil brought back.

While the oil and fast money could not be calculated until the completion of the voyage, it was the practice for the owners to board the vessel before departure and pay a month's wages in advance. 'The owners came on board and pay'd each man One months advance. 6 men not coming forward it was proposed to proceed to Lerwick for the remainder.'[49] This procedure was not confined to whaling ships, for in South-Spainers, the ships entered the 'Horse Latitudes' when the crew had worked off their advance payment, their 'dead horse', and celebrated the fact that they were now earning money again by tossing a symbolic representation of a dead horse overboard. It would be interesting to know what proportion of this advance money was paid to the wives and families. Although much would be rattled over the counter of dockside taverns, some small amount would be used to buy seaboots, foul and cold-weather gear.

After 1824 the bounty was no longer paid and whaling vessels were 'no longer subject to the said conditions and regulations'. There was some doubt whether it was legal for whaling ships to sail without a surgeon, and the Customs officials investigated. They ruled that an Act of King George IV that ordered that any British vessel carrying at least fifty people had to carry a surgeon 'does not extend to vessels clearing out for the said fisheries, having no passengers on board, but only the master and crew'.[50] Nonetheless, whaling ships continued to carry surgeons.

Stores were equally well regulated by the bounty laws, with a humane government allowing a certain amount of tobacco and coal to be shipped free of duty. While tobacco, like rum, was essential for morale, a supply of coal ensured that the crew would not freeze to death. Customs officers, parsimonious or mistrustful, ensured that the allowed amount was not exceeded. In 1799 the Commissioners of the Customs ruled that a ship with fifty men, bound for a voyage to the Greenland Fishery, was allowed four chalders, or six tons, of duty-free coal. Any coals above that weight had to pay duty.[51] This allowance seems to have caused some difficulty, with the Montrose whalers, at least, believing that nine tons of Scottish coal was equal to six tons of English.[52] Montrose vessels seem to have regularly carried more coal than was permitted, with the Montrose Collector reminding the Customs Board that if 'the period of the voyage… were to be protracted the said allowance would not prove too much.'[53]

The Dundee Collector also got himself in trouble for allowing the vessels in his area to ship more coal than they were allowed. In a letter written in 1808 he gave the quantities of coal shipped on the Dundee whalers as: *Jane*, 19.25 tons; *Mary Ann*, 18 tons; *Horn*, 18 tons; *Advice*, 19.25 tons; *Estridge*, 19.2 tons; and *Rodney*, 16 tons. As a defence, the Collector reported that David Jobson, Managing Owner for *Jane* and *Rodney*, and Walter Newall, Managing Owner for *Mary Ann* and *Horn*, had assured them that these quantities were 'nothing more than they thought necessary for such a voyage.' It is possible that the Customs officers believed that whaling ship owners shipped duty-free coal and sold it off to a third party at a profit.

The Collector assured his superiors that the coals were 'really and truly' used on the respective ships and that on one occasion some of the whale ships ran out of coal and 'were reduced to the necessity of burning their lumber previously used for stowing the casks.'[54] However bad the conditions must have been for the Greenlandmen on their under-heated ships, the Customs officers in Edinburgh were not sympathetic, and the whaling ship owners had to pay duty of £22 19s. 4d. farthing on the excess coals carried.[55] In 1808 the Collector of Customs listed the amounts of coal that *Eliza Swan* of Montrose used, between 5.5 chalders in 1805 and 14 chalders in 1806. The difference depended on the quantity the ship brought back the previous season, for *Eliza Swan* did not work between whaling seasons, so used none of the coal.[56]

From the customs records, it seems that Montrose vessels were flexible in their regard to the amount of stores carried. However in a letter to his superiors in 1810, the Montrose Collector stated that he believed the stores were 'bona fide intended for the subsistence of the crew of the said vessel only, being 45 in number.'[57] Some items were nearly as important as coal. There was rum, which was vital to the morale, and possibly the health, of very many British seamen; there was coffee, on which a drawback of duty was allowed,[58] and there was tobacco. In a letter of March 1833, the Collector at Dundee said that the whaleship owners were 'urgent to know how they are to be supplied… with the benefit of drawback', as each vessel carried about fifty men 'and of course their consumption is considerable'. In the same letter the Collector said that the owners wanted a quantity of duty-free tea for each vessel.[59]

Only when the vessels were correctly manned for the whaling season and the stores were on board, could the masters and owners apply for a certificate that would allow them to claim the whaling bounty.

A typical example is *Princess Charlotte*, a 375-ton sailing vessel that operated from Dundee between 1820 and 1856, when she was sunk. In 1823 her master, William Adamson handed the following documents to the Customs Officer:

A certificate that the ship is Properly Manned
A Master's Oath that the Ship is intended to proceed
An Oath of one of the Owners that the Ship is to proceed
A certificate that Security is given
A licence for the Ship to Proceed[60]

The security was a promise to pay a penalty if the bounty conditions were not met. In 1820 the penalty was treble the bounty.[61] But even when all the conditions had been satisfied and the certificates signed and confirmed, the master could not merely sail away before the assigned date and do as he wished. There were some very vital and demanding tasks that he had to perform. Every whaling ship had to keep a log that detailed when land was sighted, what land it was, the distance and direction from the ship, and the soundings taken at the time. The logbook also had to record the time and position where 'any whale or other creature living in the sea' had been killed.[62]

There were occasions when the licence did not arrive in time, leaving the ship's master and owner with a dilemma; should they sail without the licence, trusting that they would receive the bounty on their return, or delay sailing, possibly until after the official departure date? David Kinnear, who owned *Monarch* and *Eliza Swan,* chose the former course in 1814. He sailed on 9 April and simultaneously protested the non-arrival of the licences.[63] On the return of the ships, the Customs collectors backed David Kinnear's protest, saying that the ships only sailed 'to ensure an early fishery' and to avoid a 'perilous' exposure in the Bay of Montrose.[64]

Despite all the arduous work and the reams of paperwork expended, despite the foys and the ribbons that streamed from the rigging, not everyone was sentimental about the final departure of the whaling ships. Before he sailed on the Dundee whaler *Arctic*, Captain Markham, RN, stated that the 'scene on board an outward bound whaler on the eve of departure has been described to me as both filthy and disgusting.'[65] He may have been correct, for a ship full of drink-sodden seamen and their tearful wives would not have been the most edifying of sights.

Nonetheless, there were many more men like John Wanless, who, when *Thomas* hoisted sails and slid down the Tay, spoke of 'my throbbing heart on seeing my town sink in the horizon'.[66] It is easy to imagine him hanging over the taffrail, watching the slopes of the Law and the tall chimneys that already lined the Scouring Burn slide astern. The seagulls would be circling and screaming around the spiralling masts and some of the Greenmen would already be experiencing the first rush of seasickness. There would be handkerchiefs fluttering from the knot of women who watched the ship that carried their men sliding out of the Tay, and perhaps a burst of drunken singing from one or two of the experienced hands. The parting thought of Wanless, as *Thomas* butted her bowsprit into the North Sea waves, was for his homeland.

'Farewell dear Scotia' he wrote,[67] and prepared for the voyage ahead.

8

THE VOYAGE OUT

'It happened on a Tuesday three days out of Dundee
The gale took off her quarter boat and a couple of men you see
It battered at her bulwarks, her stanchions and her rails
And left the old Balaena *boys, a-frothing in the gale'*
The Ballad of *Balaena*

Not every ship sailed directly away from Dundee toward the whaling grounds. In some cases the vessels remained in the roadstead, between Dundee and Broughty Ferry, for a couple of days until the weather was favourable, or until the crew was sufficiently sober and fit to work. In 1815, for instance, *Three Brothers* left Dundee on the first of March, but did not leave the roadstead until the fifth.[1] On the first day of the voyage, the Master called the roll to see how many of the crew had preferred to continue the celebrations, or had succumbed to the pleas of their wives to remain at home. Available evidence suggests that most of the crews turned up. In 1834 John Wanless recorded that 'names were called from the roll and only one was found absent.'[2] Fifty years later, Mathew Campbell, the surgeon of *Nova Zembla* in 1884, reported that they were late in getting up steam as some of the crew were still saying good-bye to their families, but when the roll was finally called 'every one answered to their names'.[3] However, not all voyages started so auspiciously. On the barque *North Pole* of Leith in 1837, James Lyle noted that with '6 men not coming forward it was proposed to proceed for Lerwick for the remainder.'[4]

John Wanless recorded that 'the men were properly divided into three watches, mates, Captains and spectioneers'.[5] The better masters used the three-watch, or quarter-watch system, which meant that men off duty could get a decent rest. The two-watch, or half-watch system meant that men were on duty twelve hours out of every twenty-four. Although the most religious captains observed Sunday as a day of rest, it was more common for whaling ships to work a seven-day week. Christopher Thomson was not the only seaman who quoted the old sardonic rhyme:

Six days shalt thou work, and do all thou are able,
On the seventh day wash the deck and scrub the cable.[6]

During the first few days, while the ships steered north along the coast of Scotland, the dregs of alcohol were sweated out of the crew and the Greenmen began to learn the reality of seafaring. It was now that the stowaways began to emerge; when the mate of *Nova Zembla* put a number ashore he supplied them with a couple of biscuits and the advice that they could 'find their way back the best they could'.[7] The voyage to adventure of these young boys ended with a weary walk back to Dundee.

As soon as the ships were out of harbour the frustration of administrative details was exchanged for the dangers of sailoring. The North Sea is as dangerous a stretch of water as any in the world, and not all the whaling ships reached the whaling grounds. On 1 April 1813, five Aberdeen whalers, including *Oscar* and *St Andrews*, slipped out of Aberdeen Bay into a day of variable winds and with a strong tide running. The ships anchored to await better sailing conditions, but the wind shifted to the northeast, so it was blowing them onto a lee shore, and strengthened to gale force. *St Andrews* cut her anchor cable, set her stay and mizzen sails and, in a display of fine seamanship, clawed past Girdle Ness. Closer inshore, *Oscar* could not find the sea room and was driven ashore at Greyhope Bay in front of a helpless crowd. Two boatloads of men capsized while Captain Innes and a handful of men escaped to the forecastle for a while before they also were washed into the sea. Only one seaman and the mate survived. *Oscar* had been a fine ship, two-decked and three-masted, slightly over 101 feet long, carvel-built and with a male figurehead. She was as seaworthy as any other whaler, and her loss a sobering warning of the perils off Scotland.

Seventy years later Captain Souter's Dundee whaler *Mazinthien* ran aground at South Bay, Peterhead, on St Patrick's Day. Again, she had anchored to shelter from a storm, but dragged her anchors in some atrocious weather. All attempts at rescue by firing rockets failed, and it was one of the crew who eventually got ashore in an act of true heroism, and the line he carried saved the life of all 29 men on board.

These vessels were only two from a long list of whaling ships that had been wrecked off Scotland. As far back as December 1674 the Bayonne whaler *St Martin* had been forced onto the shore at Huna, Caithness, followed the next year by *St Pietas*, also from Bayonne, which was wrecked at Papa Stour on her voyage home. In 1823 the Hull ship *Fame* was burned while on her way to the whaling grounds. There was an unknown

Gothenburg whaler driven ashore in Broad Bay, Lewis in December 1786 and *Horn* of Dundee that took the ground at Kingsbarns in Fife in November 1862. The amount of losses was high but not unusual; virtually every edition of most nineteenth-century newspapers carried stories of shipwreck. At a time when ships were nearly as common as commercial motor vehicles are today, a shipwreck was as newsworthy as a fatal car crash, although the Victorians frequently liked to add poignant and gruesome detail that would be deemed tasteless in the enlightened twenty-firstcentury. In January 1843 alone, there were 240 ships wrecked. One three-day spell cost 500 seamen their lives.

By the closing decades of the eighteenth century it was customary for whaling ships to call at either Shetland or Orkney to buy provisions and take on seamen. It seemed to be traditional for vessels bound for the Greenland Sea to call at Stromness in Orkney, while those for the Davis Strait headed for Lerwick in Shetland.

Most whaling journals have entries such as: 'We… are going to call at Lerwick… for the purpose of adding to our crew a number of Shetlanders, these men being said to be good and experienced sailors.'[8] Sir Walter Scott, who visited Shetland in August 1814, described Lerwick Bay as a 'most beautiful place, screened on all sides from the wind'.[9] However, when he got ashore he thought Lerwick was 'a poor looking place'. Scott said that the whaling ships took around 1000 Shetland seamen a year,[10] which reveals the importance of the islanders to the whaling industry. As far back as 1781 a group of Shetland lairds proposed supplying their tenants for the whaling fleet.[11] The arrangement was intended to ensure that the lairds retained power over their men while simultaneously removing the power of agents. The arrangement was to be between the shipowners and the lairds, while the Shetland seamen, already paid less than the mainland seamen, would end up receiving even lower wages.[12] It seems that the lairds were paid 45 shillings a month for each man they supplied, while encouraging the Royal Navy to impress those tenants who signed on a whaler without permission.[13]

Nevertheless, agents remained important in Shetland and Orkney. In Lerwick, many agents were merchants, obtaining berths on the visiting whalers for any man who wanted to put to sea. In the 1860s the fishing boat owners Joseph Leask and George Reid Tait were most prominent. Later Tait's successor, John Leisk, and Alexander Sandison were equally successful, although the most powerful was William Spence Smith.

The men of Orkney seem to have been as eagerly sought. One of the most prominent nineteenth-century agents was Mrs Christine Robertson, who doubled as a Stromness merchant. The *Statistical Account of Scotland, 1791–1793* said that there was a scarcity of male servants in Orkney as they were either in Greenland, on Hudson Bay ships or in the navy. South Ronaldsay was singled out as having young men going to the Greenland fishing, where they proved 'excellent sailors'.[14]

The northern isles may have provided excellent sailors, but it was not only Walter Scott who was unimpressed. John Wanless thought that the men of Stroma were 'shaggy haired... with a heavy scent of peats', although 'the peat reek was not made in so great abundance now'.[15] Stroma had been notorious for its smugglers in the past, and peat fuelled the fires that powered the illicit whisky stills.

When the ships rode at anchor in Bressay Bay or off Stromness, the islanders took to their small boats. They surrounded the whaling ships, bartering fresh fish, chickens and superb knitting for whatever the ships had to spare, which was often old shoes and clothing. To the islanders, this was the 'Greenland time' while the whalers were 'Southern Boys', 'Greenlanders' or 'Greenlandmen'.

Already some seamen had decided that whaling was not for them and took the opportunity to slip ashore. In 1787 the *Aberdeen Journal* carried an account of five men who deserted at Stromness, but who were recaptured and placed in the Tolbooth of Kirkwall.[16] William Barron wrote of a seaman who deserted at Shetland because he had a dream that he would not return home from the Arctic.[17] Other seamen sought different diversions. When Alexander Smith, chief engineer of the Dundee whaler *Camperdown*, called at Lerwick, he 'availed myself on Sunday, along with John and the Doctor, of the opportunity to go to the church.'[18] Nonetheless, most whaling men followed the age-old tradition of mariners ashore and headed for the nearest watering hole.

Derek Flinn argues that 'when the whalers lay in Bressay Sound, Lerwick became one of the most notorious and riotous ports in Britain',[19] and there certainly seems a charming harmony in the surviving records of visiting whalers. In April 1787, the Reverend Mill mentions that the Royal Navy was in Bressay Sound 'to keep the rough people' from 30 whaling vessels 'in (l?)aw (e?) and order, least when drunk and mad with gin they should set the town of Lerwick on fire.'[20] Christopher Thomson's observations of the behaviour of the crew of *Dunscombe* while in Lerwick also appear to fit the pattern: 'Companies of sailors, the greater part of them reeling drunk, were parading about.'[21] He believed that: 'nine-tenths of the Greenlanders, if they can command plenty of grog, and a fresh sweetheart, it is the sum of their enjoyment.'[22]

Knowing that there were months of hardship ahead, the Greenlandmen would make the most of the whisky dens and shebeens of the islands. Seamen would dance away their last hours of freedom and drink themselves insensible. Some would hope to spend a few frantic minutes with one of the less moral of the island girls, whose dark eyes would compare the Southern Boys with the men who were native to the islands and, as so often, choose what seemed the more exotic. Romance would be brief and sporadic, the high wail of the bagpipe a farewell to the land and the reek of peat smoke a sweet perfume as the raucous mariners spent the last of their first month's earnings in dissipation and carnality. Some of the Greenmen, warned by kindly companions, would invest in a bottle of Shetland whisky against the traumas ahead. To some of the islanders, this descent of hundreds of wild young men was a financial bonus, to others it was a threat, and there were inevitable confrontations between rival ships and different cultures.

In March 1817 the behaviour of the whalers was so bad that the Sheriff Substitute issued a circular requesting that the whalers 'conduct themselves with sobriety' and asking the shipmasters to 'prevent them committing any disturbance or breach of the public peace.' The whalers were ordered to be back on board their ships by nine o'clock each night unless they were on duty. Men that were ashore at night were to have a ship's boat, in case they disturbed the town or stole the local boats. Any breach of this curfew was to be related to the Lords of the Treasury, 'which would be attended with serious consequences to you.'[23] Presumably the serious consequences meant that the bounty payments would be withheld.

With the ship fully manned and provisioned and the last stragglers hounded from the whisky dens, the whaling ships hoisted anchor and sailed for the whaling grounds. Barron recorded that when the ships were ready to leave Stromness, the local bellman toured the town to round up her crew.[24] Their departure time depended on the two lords of mariners, the wind above and the tide below. An adverse wind could set them back for a day or a month, so the ships waited in frustrated idleness in the harbour.

As the hunting years passed the whalers had to seek further afield and into more dangerous seas, probing deeper into the ice for the diminishing number of whales. They hoped to be at the whale-fishing grounds just as the ice melted. If they were too early they could only wait at the frozen barrier. If they were late, they would be wasting whale-fishing time. Those who hunted in the Greenland Sea headed north for the vast area between Spitzbergen and Greenland, while those who dared the Davis Straits or Baffin Bay sailed along the 58th parallel to avoid Cape Farewell. Perhaps some of the Greenmen murmured at the ominous sound of the name Farewell, and doubtless the experienced hands would warn them about that cape at the southern tip of Greenland, with its reputation for fogs and icebergs. Nonetheless, Farewell was the gateway into the fishing waters of the Davis Strait and a whole selection of new tensions. Most ships would head for the West Water or the Baffin Bay fishery that had been discovered in 1818. It was an area rich in whales but even more dangerous for the ships.

However, before the whaling ships could begin to earn their wages, they had to reach the whaling grounds, and the North Atlantic is a notoriously cruel ocean. Alexander Alison in *Lady Jane* left Orkney with the help of a pilot, but once the pilot left:

> It began to blow and increased all night. We were under close reefed Topsails and foresail—every hour the wind increased till it became a perfect hurricane and continued without the least interruption for 6 weeks during which time we were sometimes under bare poles and sometimes under storm staysails. For 4 weeks we were lashed to the decks and bulwarks on the quarter deck—our regular pumps which are called chain pumps became choked and consequently of no use and the only pump we had left was a hand pump, at which 4 hands was lashed for 2 hours together alternatively night and day.

As every wave washed over *Lady Jane*, she continued toward the whaling grounds. Every Sunday the Master had prayers in his cabin, with the surgeon also reading a sermon, for many whalers took their religion seriously. It was after divine service that the Master:

> Came on deck and turning his eye to the larboard quarter which was then the weather side he observed a sea at some distance. Perceiving his situation he called for the Botswain to bring his axe and clear the mast to [see?] if he could [save?] the ship. He inquired also how much water there was in the Ship, the mate sounded the pumps and there was four feet water.

The situation was bad. The ship was taking in water and a large sea was racing toward them. As Runciman would have said, it was at times like these that seamen stopped blaspheming and started to pray. Alison continues:

> Death stared us in the face—no way of escape. I thought of home—such as it was—the Mate went down to the hold and found the water increasing rapidly arising... the water was coming with great force—this caused every one to think and the stoutest heart on board sunk within them. The captain stood and cryed like a child. He was a husband and a father all on board were very much affected... I... seemed to be totally inconscious of my condition... suspense hang on every countenance... the Sea came and the Ship was in the trough of it, it literaly hung above us. But God who has all power caused the ship to rise to it and when upon its bosom—we were completely among the clouds—Oh how every countenance beamed with joy and thankfulness for this merciful deliverance. And we were as those that rose from the dead for we had passed the sentence of death upon ourselves, but the winds and the waves obey God and are subject to his control and can do harm to none but by his permission.
>
> I read my Bible oftner after this and thought myself Serious.

Despite their escape from the wave, *Lady Jane* was still not out of danger. She was still taking in water, and they could not repair the leak without unloading everything, which was obviously impossible during an Atlantic storm. Perhaps because Alison had given himself to the Lord, he was granted another example of divine aid:

> The ship having sailed like a Washing Tub—every Block and Tackle was shook out of its place. At one time the main Tackle broke loose and I was sent to secure it and whilst in the Act of doing so she shipped a Sea that reached as high as our Main top carrying every thing before it so that I was completely lost for some seconds in the sea. The rest of my shipmates... sung out to me to hold fast but I could hear nothing. Providentially I was inabled to keep my hold and the first thing they saw of me was my red night cap for which they were glad for we had a few days before lost a fine young man that was out on the Bowsprit fastening some loose gear belonging to the Spritsail yard the ship diped

bows under water and part of the forecastle at the same time and he sunk to rise no more for ever. He was a fine young man to be married when he returned.

Lady Jane continued her voyage, and the leak also continued, until:

> Our cook, who had a wooden leg, one day contrary to the Customs and Manners of Sailors the ship liying on her Beam Ends. After he had cleaned his Coppers and gathered up the dust—Instead of going to leeward with his dirt to throw it over Board with great difficulty scrambled up to the Weather side no easy task for them that had two legs to do let alone a man with but one—and threw his dust over board. The dust flying in his face paying him for his trouble but strange to say that was the means under God by which the leak was stoped. The Suction occasioned by the Water rushing into the hole—drove Sinders and some loose dust into it almost effectively stopped the leak, so that we made no more water only what we had shipped for when we got into smoother water and unstowed the hold we found the leak and the cause of its stoping.

Seven weeks after leaving Orkney, *Lady Jane* 'made the Ice and we drove and steered in that time about 2200 miles'. Her experiences with foul weather were certainly not unique. In 1797 *Eliza Swan* and *George Dempster*, both of Montrose, left Stromness in Orkney and 'were in company on the afternoon of the 4 March in lat 69.33 North'. They parted soon after and since then 'no accounts whatever have been had of the ship *George Dempster*, whence it is inferred that she must have foundered at sea, on her outward voyage'.[25] The blunt, nearly laconic statement hides a human tragedy; fifty men written off, leaving perhaps thirty widows, children made fatherless, sisters deprived of their brothers, parents of their sons. Contemporary seamen believed that she was carrying too much canvas for the weather conditions. Her master was David Christie, and his English widow proved again that the women of whalers were a resilient bunch. Rather than buckling before her loss, she opened a school that became something of a legend in Montrose.

When Peterhead built an iron whaler named *Inuit* in 1858, she had a successful sealing season. The following year *Empress of India* sailed out. Her designers and builders intended her to start a new dawn in whaling; a steel-built ship with a 12-foot thick bow, a crew of 110 men and eleven boats. Unfortunately she was lost, her steel plates rent apart by ice, and

Inuit sank the same year. The wooden-hulled Dundee whaler *Narwhal* helped rescue the crew, at the same time looting the ship. Relations were not all cordial, as the rival crews were 'showering the most obscene oaths upon each other.'[26]

Looting abandoned vessels was common practice among the whaling men. When *Thomas* came across a ship wrecked in the ice, Wanless wrote that '*Lee*'s boat was there with the crew plundering her.'[27] In 1819 *Monarch* of Montrose removed 20 casks of blubber from *Diamond* of Aberdeen. *Diamond* is one of the most famous of whalers due to the folk song that was bawled out in whaler's foys all around the coast. 'The *Diamond* is a ship, my lads, for the Davis Strait she's bound'. However there was nothing to sing about when *Diamond* was abandoned in the bitter ice of the north.

After the experience of *Empress of India*, it was clear that the future did not belong to steel whalers but to the steam-powered wooden vessels that Dundee was to become so expert in building. Yet not even all the cunning of the shipbuilders' art, the experience of whaling skippers and the technological improvements of steam power could prevent the sea from taking her due in death and injury. The tragedies continued.

In 1884 Mathew Campbell, surgeon of *Nova Zembla*, filled in his journal with the succinct report: 'two men missing from the mate's watch, must have been washed overboard'.[28] In February 1886 *Aurora* left Dundee and hit heavy weather on her Atlantic crossing. Huge seas threw the helmsman across the wheel, smashing his ribs, and another three men were injured, one badly. Seafaring could also cause death by less direct methods: 'William Cowsfoot apprentice Departed the ship at the surgeon reports from influenza of the lungs.'[29] The sea might well provide a living for those who sailed her, but she was a cruel mistress who demanded her toll in blood and suffering.

Alexander Smith, chief engineer of *Camperdown*, mentioned that his 'poor friend John' suffered from '[sea] sickness since we left Shetland,'[30] and presumably many of the Greenmen were so afflicted. Nonetheless, respectable men such as Smith seem to have had a low opinion of their fellow seamen. Smith thought that they cared 'not a tuppence for your Neighbour,'[31] while the artisan landsman Christopher Thomson thought the Greenlandmen were 'illiterate'[32] and, except for seamanship, were 'Lamentably sunk below man, and seemed to partake of the animal.'[33] R. P. Gillies, a passenger on the London whaler *Leviathan* in 1822, would have agreed. He mentioned that London whalers treated Shetlanders 'with... over bearing insolence and brutal cruelty.'[34] Robert

Wilson and Thomas Twatt, who sailed on the Newcastle whaler *Grenville Bay*, thought that their shipmates were 'quite careless about learning. There is scarcely a boat steerer... that knows the alphabet.'[35] Burn Murdoch also slighted the seamen on *Balaena*: 'the needs of this class of man are simple, merely food and covering.'[36]

The comments of surgeon Wanless of *Thomas* in 1834 suggest more sympathy with the seamen. After discovering inferior quality stores on board, Wanless complained that 'poor sailors are imposed upon by every person in whatever line of business they deal'.[37] Burn Murdoch commented that many of the men in *Balaena* had sailed in 'coffin ships' that were 'old, over-insured, undermanned.'[38] The *East of Fife Record* of 29 October 1869 mentions a speculator in an unnamed northeast port who bought wrecked ships, patched them up with pitch, canvas and oakum and sent them back to sea. When they sunk, often with loss of life, the owner claimed the insurance.[39]

There were fewer complaints about the Greenlandmen's attitude to work: Surgeon Trotter of *Enterprise* commented that he was 'getting some clothes washed today by two of the sailors... they seem to do their work pretty well.'[40] Captain Markham thought the crew of *Arctic* was 'a fine sturdy set of fellows, evidently intending work if they get the opportunity'.[41]

Other writers also comment on the men working. When they were not immediately required for work on deck, the seamen would often be employed in the tween decks. The common mariners could be spinning ropeyarn or picking oakum; some writers would bracket these tasks together in short phrases such as 'pepol Engaged varriously under the botswain.'[42] Simultaneously the specialists such as the cooper, sailmaker, carpenter and blacksmith would be working at their trades. The combination could create a scene that suggested something familiar to a homesick man: 'when our Blacksmith, Carpenter and sail-maker are all at work and the other men being at something or other, it puts me in mind of a Seaborne Parish'.[43]

Each sea-borne tradesman was an expert with a long apprenticeship behind him and an intimate knowledge of his craft. For instance the sailmaker would know by touch the difference between the Number One canvas, as stiff as millboard, and the fine quality Number Six. He would be able to handle his sailmaker's palm in any conditions, and could lay his hand on the sail pricker, sail stabber, seam rubber, pegging awl or stitch mallet. He would keep his needles in a 'grease horn', which was the horn of a sheep kept half full of lard, to ease the passage of needle through sail, for grease caused rot in canvas. The horn may well have been strung around his neck on a lanyard, and he would sit on a canvas cushion at his bench, with the sail on his knee and a fid stool, pierced for the different sizes of fid, at his side. He would have fids of bone and of ivory or bone, each a miniature marlinespike used for reaming out grommets, for splicing and for piercing canvas.

The other specialists were as knowledgeable about their trade, men without whom the ship could not operate, as irreplaceable in their own way as were the harpooners or the master. Each was a single piece in the unit that made up the crew of the ship. However, despite the necessity for team-working on board, there were often squabbles and personal disagreements. Alexander Trotter seems to have disliked the men from Shetland, commenting that they were 'continually complaining'.[44]

In an age when people genuinely believed that smoking kept away cholera and the smell of rotted seaweed was healthy, it is not surprising to hear that seamen thought that sea water was a cure for many ills. 'Sailors complain more of a wet jacket with rain than a good ducking with salt water. They say you are more liable to catch cold with water from above than below'.[45]

When they were not engaged in working the ship, whaling seamen spent their free time in a variety of occupations, few of which met the approval of the serious-minded Engineer Alexander Smith. He mentions men 'Spinning Yarns, Card Playing, dancing or Singing and such frolics... No praiseworthy effort will likely be produced from such frivolities.'[46] Smith hoped that the officers of the ship could set an example on behaviour to the crew. That may not always have been possible. Mr Martin, the mate of *Narwhal* in 1859, was so foul-mouthed 'that he even astounded and astonished the crew.'[47]

Christian Watt was less scathing about the off-duty occupations of the Greenlandmen: 'my father was a grand fiddler... at the whaling in the Arctic he would play in the hours off duty.'[48] Other seamen were equally musical: 'often I get a glimpse of the concert I heard in the tween decks which was generally well atended'.[49]

Thomson mentions the whalers carving on bones 'with a penknife, divers cyphers of the initials of their sweethearts, with borders of diamonds, squares and vandykes, or tooth ornaments'.[50] Carving the initials of their women must have reminded the whalers why they were working in such a hostile environment, while museums hold examples of scrimshaw work that testify to the whalers' skill. On occasion the seamen were more boisterous, either forcing the Greenmen to clamber over greased poles or when they were 'playing tricks with each other and for some nights past have been making fun by blacking their neighbours faces.'[51] There seems to have been a knife game played on board, when the 'watch at eight o'clock' were 'amusing themselves by throwing their knives upon the deck into a square divided 41 times'.[52]

Critical of the forecastle hands, Thomson was just as censorious of the officers, whose 'leisure hours were frittered away in low conversations, card-playing and a song.'[53] There was one card game that seemed unique to whaling men: 'a game peculiar to whalers called "Scratch the ten"—which shall obtain possession of the ten of trumps'.[54] Nonetheless, in 1892 Burn Murdoch commented that the crew of *Balaena* had the 'utmost reverence for books'.[55]

Captain Markham perhaps gives a reason for the whaling men's seeming waste of time, commenting that although there was a little excitement, life on a whaler was 'rather weary and monotonous when confined to an area of a few miles... to cruise about in'.[56] Sometimes the men would believe they saw a mountain range to the north, but the old hands knew these were only clouds and termed them 'Cape Flyaway'. More commonly sighted was the Aurora Borealis, which set the northern sky ablaze with colour.[57]

In a whaling ship, the relationship between officers and men could be complex. The brass barrier mentioned by Burn Murdoch was only metaphorical at sea, and sometimes it seemed very ethereal. Harpooners, line managers and boat steerers shared the hardships of the 'common mariners' while hunting whales, so must have developed bonds of comradeship, but these men were of a lower rank than the master and mate, who navigated the vessel. Captain Markham, however, remarked that it was the custom on *Arctic* to call the harpooners by their Christian names,[58] which suggests an amicable relationship between officers and men, at least on that vessel. An occasional laconic notice in a newspaper, such as the 'all Hands are enjoying good health' of Captain Deuchar,[59] reveals at least recognition of the crew. It was common at the time to refer to the crew as 'the people', as Captain Archibald of the Kirkcaldy ship *Chieftain* did in 1852: 'people employed variously'.[60]

When South Spainers marked the Crossing of the Equator with an elaborate ceremony, whalers had their own celebration to mark their arrival at the edge of the ice, the whale-hunting grounds, or on the first day of May, depending on the custom of the ship and the port. It was a tradition that lasted as long as sail, but faded away with the greater urgency brought by steam.[61] While it lasted, the ceremony must have been a nervous time for the Greenmen, who would realise that something was about to happen, but would be unaware exactly what. 'At 8 o'clock pm all was quiet except the rumour of shaving those who had never been at the Straits'.[62] There would be expectancy among the old hands, then a 'bell rung as sign of the approaching Neptune with his comrade'.[63]

By tradition, Neptune was the oldest seaman on board, and his court supported him, including Mrs Neptune. All would be dressed in outlandish costume, most with long beards of white hair or dripping green seaweed. Some of the Greenmen might attempt to hide, but all were dragged before the Sea God. The ceremony differed in detail but it was always humiliating, sometimes painful and always welcomed by the old Arctic hands. Usually Neptune or his assistants would cut the hair of the Greenman and would then shave him, literally or ceremonially, with Neptune wielding a massive, often notched and blunt, razor. In some vessels the Court baptised the Greenmen with a helping of tar, in others with an obnoxious mixture based on a tub of urine. Barron speaks of Neptune appearing when eight bells struck at midnight, when the 'lazy' were 'lathered with coal tar... powdered with crushed chalk and resin.'[64] It was now that the forewarned or cautious Greenmen produced the whisky they had purchased at Lerwick, and bribed Neptune to let them off gently.

After the baptising came the festivities, dancing and fiddling and drinking. Often one last bottle of whisky was produced, opened and poured into the sea, a libation to the waters, an ungrudged sacrifice for a successful voyage, a fervent prayer for a cargo of whales and a hope for a safe return to wife and sweetheart and dockyard tavern. When they were still in port the Greenlandmen had collected ribbons, some from their girlfriends, others bought from spey-wives or snatched from the bonnet of an unwary female, who, in a whaling port, may not have been a reluctant contributor. Now all the ribbons were fashioned into a garland that was hoisted to the masthead as a circle of luck from the entire crew. Encompassed by the ribbons and held secure by the best wishes of the men, the love of their women and the blessings of the spey-wives, was a model of the ship or an effigy of Neptune, a charm to watch over the ship until she returned home. The bond was sealed with more whisky or anything else alcoholic that came to hand, and so the ship pressed on, into the ice.

9

THE HUNT

'Oh Pilot! Tis a fearful night, there's danger on the deep'
Thomas Haynes Bayly, *The Pilot*

In the eighteenth century, most of the whaling ships hunted in the Greenland Seas, cruising anywhere between Spitzbergen and the east coast of Greenland. By the nineteenth century, more rounded Cape Farewell and probed into the Davis Strait. They hugged the west coast of Greenland, with the night-time temperatures below zero and the ocean spray freezing on decks and spars and rigging. Sudden gales would shriek through ratlines that glistened with frost, while slowly sliding to starboard the tall peaks of Greenland pierced the sky.

As they sailed north, the whalers prepared for the hunt. The whaling boats were recovered from below, with one ready for instant work, 'on bran'. Equipment was stored in the boat, from the flag that would be placed on a dead whale to the all-important lines that were coiled carefully for use. As the log of *Chieftain* of Kirkcaldy succinctly recorded: 'at 8 called all hands and commenced taking out the boats and coiling the lines.'[1] While checking the lines, the fishermen revealing the cunning skill they had perfected with the baited long-lines in the homelier water off Pittenweem or Cellardyke, Broadsea or the Cockenzie Reef. The specktioneer, who was the man who cared for the harpoons, checked them over, sharpening the soft iron with a file, shaping the barbs with a blacksmith's die and spanned them in to their shafts. The name specktioneer, or spectioneer, comes from the Dutch *spek*, for blubber, and *koning* for king; a specktioneer was a blubber king.

The master posted a man aloft; not only to search for whales, but also to look out for ice as the current here constantly thrust icebergs large and small toward the ships. The look-out would sit in a 'crow's nest', a very practical shelter, rather like a large cylindrical drum, with an entry-flap at the bottom, a plank for a seat, and a telescope, often known as a spy-glass, for efficiency. There was usually a speaking trumpet and signal flags to help the loo-out communicate with any boats that were out on the water. Often there was a strip of canvas placed around the nest for extra protection, and even a canvas hood. The earlier whalers had an even higher perch, known as a 'bird's nest', situated at the masthead, to provide a larger circle of vision. Sometimes the look-out may have been supplied with a rifle in case he sighted a narwhal close to the ship.[2] William Scoresby is one of the men who are credited with inventing the crow's nest.

Only Arctic whalers used a crow's nest; the ships from Nantucket or New Bedford that spent years scouring the waves of half the world had less need of shelter; their look-outs sat on the cross-trees or hung onto the rigging. While the southern fishing vessels sent the younger members of the crew up, the Arctic ships needed an experienced pair of eyes aloft, for the look-out was there to give warning of danger as well as to act as the eyes of the hunter. In quiet weather, large bergs were easy to see and to avoid. Smaller pieces, known as 'washing pieces' were harder to see, but there was real danger when a northerly storm drove the ice against the ships. Double-planked or not, a wooden ship was a fragile thing when faced with the terrible power of ice. Experience taught men to scan for water made dark by the presence of plankton, known as 'good whale water'. They watched for an 'ice blink', which was a light reflection of ice in the sky, for whales hunted their food close to either ice floes or shore ice.

Only when everything was cleaned and ready did the captain allow another celebration. There would be a toast to the success of the voyage, hopeful glances at the bright bitterness of the Strait, and the ship would continue to batter northward, with the whaling boats hanging ready on greased davits and the wind sighing mournfully through the rigging. The ships did not cruise alone; there was often a fleet of vessels in sight of each other, and it could be quite a social occasion. Every whaling ship master had grown up in a tough school, they would know each other, personally or by name and reputation, and at any time one could decide on a 'mollie', a drinking gathering of his peers. The name could come from the mollie or storm petrel that was so abundant. In the days before radio the whalers had their own unique system of codes, and summoned a mollie by hoisting a bucket to the mizzen topgallant head.[3]

A whaling ship could cruise for days or weeks without sign of a whale. If it made an entire voyage without a kill it returned 'clean', which dented the finances of the owner, who still had to pay for the stores on the ship as well as the crew's wages and for maintenance. Fitting out a whale ship was expensive; in 1877 it cost the Tay Whale Fishing Company of Dundee 'an expense for outfit and men's wages of nearly £2000 each ship.'[4] The company's two ships, *Victor* and *Intrepid,* managed to kill thirteen seals between them, making 39 gallons of oil at 2/6 per gallon, or slightly less than £5 for the season. Without oil and fast money, the crew were also impoverished, so would probably have to search for another job over the winter.

The return of the whaling fleet was newsworthy, and the local papers noted the success or otherwise of the ships. In 1869 the *East of Fife Record* reported that:

> It is to be feared that the whale fishing at Davis' Straits this year has proved almost a complete failure... as late as the eleventh September all the rest of the Dundee fleet were clean.[5]

Clean ships were more common in the early years of the industry and as the Arctic industry drew to a painful close. In the early nineteenth century whales were more plentiful and voyages could be short and profitable. As the ship cruised north, heading for the rendezvous at the Devil's Thumb, just north of Disco Island, the Greenlandmen would be ready for the call 'A fall! A fall!'[6] that signified that the fall of water from a whale's blowhole had been seen. The *Montrose Review* argues that the word came from the Dutch 'val', meaning 'haste'.[7]

Whatever the derivation, once the lookout shouted the words, the ship burst into frenzied activity as men rushed toward their boats. One watch would be already on deck, the others below. Each boat's crew was pre-selected and every man knew his position and job. While those fortunate enough to be on duty would be fully clothed, others would have been in bed, and would run from the fug of the forecastle to the freezing temperatures on deck clad in nothing but 'woolen underclothing, the rest [of their clothing] in a bundle under their arms'.[8] In some vessels these bundles were known as gaskets. Even when they lay in their berths, most of the whaling men had their Arctic clothing in a ready-to-hand bundle.

There would be little time to dress as the men hauled at the oars, racing across the sea with the bow perhaps kicking up silver spindrift, perhaps pushing aside brash ice as they sped toward the sighted whale. The crew of the first boat to make fast a harpoon into the whale gained extra 'fast' money, but there was often pain before the gain, as the Greenlandmen had first to reach the quarry. Sighting a whale from the crow's nest was one thing; finding the animal amidst the ice floes and chopped water of the Arctic was another. It was in situations such as this that experience counted. No matter how strong the back of an oarsman, or how skilful he was at rowing, unless he knew the tricks of the whaling trade he was a child in the Arctic.

Each whaling boat had a crew of seven; six oarsmen under the command of a boat-header. While it was the Master's job to bring his ship safely to the whale fishing grounds and back, it was the responsibility of the boat-header, or boat-steerer, to command the whaling boats that rowed out to perform the actual kill. Of the three officers in the boat, the boat-header's task was the most seamanlike, for he commanded the strokes of the oarsmen. Rather than a rudder, whaling boats used a steering-oar, a long oar placed on the steering-side, the starboard side, of the boat. The boat-header had to calculate where the whale should be, and he had to get his boat there as fast as possible.

Nonetheless, the boat-header was not left entirely alone; the master of the ship helped all he could. Often he stood in the crow's nest and directed operations with signals, but if it was misty, or if ice floes obscured his vision he must have peered in frantic frustration as his boats pulled away. There were occasions when the master could play a more positive role, and double the catch: 'the captain was at the masthead and sighted another fish a good distance from the ship.'[9]

The boatsteerer knew that the bowhead whale was slow but so nervous that it would dive if it sensed danger. Accordingly he approached from astern and if he were ultra-careful he would order the oarsmen to muffle their oars, that is, place pieces of cloth in the rowlocks so they made less noise. Once positioned, the harpooner, or harpoonist, took over. These next few minutes were the epitome of whaling, the romantic image retained in folklore. They were also amongst the most dangerous.

The harpooner always took a bow oar, which he discarded only when the whale was close. Then he would stand, balancing in the bow of a boat that might be rocking wildly in a heaving sea, and lift the harpoon from its rest or 'mik' that was always in the starboard bow. There are examples of harpoons in museums scattered throughout Scotland; the museums at Broughty Ferry and Anstruther have harpoons that have been contorted into weird shapes by the efforts of the whales to escape, and they have to be hefted for their full weight to be appreciated. A very skilled harpooner could use the sharp edge of the harpoon to slice through the tendons in the tail of the whale, so it could neither swim nor dive and must lie there helpless for the *coup-de-grace*. The vast majority of harpooners used more traditional methods and threw the harpoon over-hand, with either one arm or two.

The harpoon itself was a three-foot-long weapon of iron, with wicked, flat barbs and a reverse barb, or 'stop wither' to prevent it from working loose. In 1880 a hand harpoon cost around 35 shillings.[10] The iron itself weighed about four pounds, and there was a five or six foot long shank or handle of hickory or ash, which fitted into a socket in the iron. The shank was attached to the 120-fathom-long whaling line by a length of rope known as a 'foreganger', which could be up to nine yards long. E. Keble Chatterton wrote that the line was 220 fathoms long, of two-inch tarred hemp.[11] Throwing this cumbersome implement called for rare skill and judgement, as well as courage.

The harpoon was not designed to kill the whale but acted as a giant fishhook that held it, until it was exhausted. Although apparently sticking to traditional methods, the whaling industry could be surprisingly innovative. In 1831 a Leith whaling ship had a trial with harpoons laced with prussic acid, but the crew refused to cut open the poisoned whale.[12]

Professional seamen wrote whaling logbooks because it was their job, not to entertain; their entries are tersely businesslike. 'Joseph Swankie got fast at noon—fish dead';[13] or 'William Latto got fast to a fish.'[14] 'At 2 Mr Jones got fast with the gun and hand.'[15] Journals can be as laconic: 'nineteenth July Our cautious spectioneer, an old Greenlander named Jack Knight fired his gun and got fast, hoisted his flag.'[16] Although the whole purpose of the voyage was to kill whales, there was often drama at the apex of the hunt:

> One day after 3 days and nights cutting up 3 large fish and pulling them away, another fish was seen. Boats were lowered down, the fast boat came up to her, she was harpooned the boat I was in was the second or 2d harpooner, the Whale went to the bottom remained there some time, came up— as soon as she appeared the first boat threw a lance which mortaly wounded her, the fish blew blood and nearly sunk the Boat with the quantity... the Boat I was in got right on top of her back—she raised herself, shuddered upset the boat, went down to the Bottom and died—upwards 600 fathoms deep. The ice began to close in upon us. The ship could not get near us—the wind shifted—increased the intensity of the cold. For want of exertion my circulation flaged... laid down in the bottom of the Boat for dead—the Fish was wound up by windlass from the bottom, to the

surface, the ship was got at. When alongside I was pulled up (so they told me) by a rope, placed before a large fire some food [?] given me—restored, but sir the sensation of returning circulation baffels all description.'

As soon as the metal imbedded itself deep in the flesh of the whale, the oarsmen had to back water quickly, for the animal would lash its great tail. A direct hit with those flukes could shatter a whaling boat and leave the crew to flounder in the freezing sea. Even a glancing blow could capsize the boat, with the same effect. It was the job of the boat-header to ensure that neither of these eventualities occurred. However it was much more likely that a harpooned whale would dive deep or 'sound', submerging and heading away at some speed. The boat-header had to calculate where it would reappear.

It was not unknown for the more professional headers to invest in a watch; they knew how long the animal could stay under water, and would use their experience to work out its probable movements. If they were skilful or very lucky, they would have the boat waiting where the whale broke surface. Thirty minutes was a normal time for a whale to remain submerged, but some could survive up to two hours: a long wait for the Greenlandmen. As they waited, the boatmen would raise a flag to signal to the ship that they had harpooned their fish.

It sometimes happened that the whale dragged boat and crew in its wake in what American whale men termed a 'Nantucket sleigh-ride'. At times the speed of the whale could reach 10 miles an hour.[17] More commonly, the whale would swim more slowly after the first agonised surge, and now the linesman or line manager earned his money. The Line manager ensured that the three-quarters of a mile of line was stowed properly in its storage space; he made sure it played out properly, keeping the fish hooked. As Conan Doyle phrased it, 'there is the line whizzing swiftly under the seats and over the bows between your outstretched feet'.[18]

If the whale moved at speed, the line would rush free so quickly that the friction could set the bollard-head alight. Then pannikins of seawater were used to keep the flames away, but some boats were pulled bows-high through the water in a cloud of smoke. When the whale tired and slowed down, the line-manager would hook some of the line around the bollard-head, exactly in the fashion of a fisherman fighting a fish. Again, this operation needed skill and judgement, for if the line was too short, the whale could pull the boat under water, too long and the whale might escape. The linemanager also had to ensure that none of the crew was entangled in a loop of the rope, for that man could be flicked overboard, or could lose an arm or his head if the whale lunged forward and the rope suddenly tightened. A man could also be pulled overboard and lost, so 'that man goes to his death so rapidly that his comrades hardly know he has gone'.[19] It was more common for the line to break and the whale to be lost. In the season of 1873 *Xanthus* of Peterhead lost a reported 13 whales when the lines broke.[20]

Catching the whale was the highlight of the voyage. Conan Doyle wondered 'who would swop that moment for any other triumph that sport can give',[21] but for most of the Greenlandmen it was a time of commercial, rather than sporting, triumph. Nonetheless there was also some personal satisfaction; when 'one of our young harpooners' on *Nova Zembla* harpooned a whale, 'everyone on board is very glad he has been successful as he is a very pushing young man.'[22]

Other boats would join the fast boat, adding their harpoons, so the whale had to drag two or three boatloads of men, each a new drain on its strength. If, as often happened, the hunt took place among the ice, the whale could swim beneath an icefield, leaving the boat-header the choice of leaving the boat and following on foot or remaining at the edge and paying out the line. Even the mightiest whale had to surface sometime. The boat-header might order a man to clamber to the top of a berg to search for the animal. If they had chased the whale across the ice, the Greenlandmen would lance the surfaced animal and decide how to manhandle it back to the ship. One method was to remove the flukes, weigh the animal down and haul it hand over hand beneath the ice to the boat.

When the water was clearer, the chase was by boat, and would continue until the whale was too exhausted to run. Only when it stopped did the boats close for the kill, still keeping a respectful distance from the tail. Even experienced Greenlandmen were in danger here; in 1825 the mate of *Advice* was killed when harpooning a whale.

The fight could have been long and arduous; Scoresby mentions a whale that fought for forty hours, but once the boats closed in, the whale was doomed. The Greenlandmen used whale lances for the kill. These were spears about six feet long, on the end of a four-foot-long handle, and they were thrust into the heart or lungs.

If the whale started to blow blood through its blowhole, somebody would shout out: 'its chimney's alight!' and the hunters would know that they had their prey. Only when they were sure that the whale was dead did the Greenlandmen prepare the animal for the next stage.

While his men were out hunting, the master was not allowed to be idle. The law said that no bounty was to be paid unless he inserted in the logbook 'the time when and the latitude in which any whale or other creature living in the sea shall have been killed taken or caught by the crew.'[23] When *London* returned to Montrose in September 1815 the log was checked and 'though a whale was killed on the second June no observation appears to have been made nor reason assigned for the defect'.[24] On occasion the master could put forward excuses, normally based on the safety of the ship during bad weather. In 1807 James Ireland, master of *Rodney* was taken to task for omitting some of the necessary entries. The owners had already provided him with extra printed instructions reminding him of his obligations, but Ireland defended himself by claiming that the ship was among the ice and added that he was 'yet young in the Trade.' He also promised to do better next time.[25] The Customs officers were aware of the dodges; when the master of *Eliza Swan* claimed that he could not make an observation because of thick weather, the Officers pointed out that the log recorded 'the weather was fine and clear.'[26]

Later in the century the hunters used a harpoon gun. There had been various trials throughout the eighteenth century, with an experimental swivel gun used at Rotherhithe as early as 1731 and a more advanced version tried in the Greenland Docks some forty years later. Although many whaling vessels, including those sailing from Montrose, carried a version of the whaling gun by 1790, it was not until 1812 that George Wallis created a harpoon gun with a more reliable mechanism. In 1844 William Greener of Newcastle brought out a weapon that proved popular, and British whaling vessels carried variations of the Greener gun until the end of the century. Low and Duff of Dundee made their own harpoon gun, which was about five-feet-long with a three-foot-long barrel. As so often, Dundee was in the forefront of new technology, with Alexander Henry, of Martini-Henry fame, demonstrating his new breech-loading whaling gun in the Tidal Harbour in February 1874. Captain Walker of *Erik* and Captain Yule of *Esquimaux* performed the actual firing of the weapon.[27]

While the master was attending to administrative tasks and attempting to steer his ship clear of danger, the whale hunters had their own problems. If the chase had lasted for hours and conditions were poor, then the boats might have difficulty in finding their parent ship. In the intervals between taking soundings and sightings, the master would help all he could by sounding the ship's bell, firing a signal gun or positioning a good man in the crow's nest to search for the boats.

First the hunters streamlined the whale by fastening the fins beneath it. Then they made holes in the flukes and threaded through a cable, the other end of which was attached to the boat. After that began the long row, with the islanders of Shetland or Orkney proving their expertise with the oars. If the men had breath to spare they might sing; Lubbock said that 'Highland Laddie' was a popular rowing song. The truly fortunate hunters would have a stern breeze and could hoist the sail; if more than one boat were involved in the kill, they would tow together, so lessening the weight. If there was only a single boat, it might have to tow a dead weight of perhaps fifty tons through a choppy sea, or through brash ice toward a ship that they could not see. They would listen for the signal gun or the bell, and hope. Sometimes men did not return, or came back with frostbitten limbs. The experience of James McIntosh of *Chieftain* was not unique.

When they reached the ship, the still harder work began, as the whale had to be flensed. Thomson mentioned the work ethics of the whalers, noting, slightly caustically that they did not admit to tiredness: 'they must not even think of it, much more complain... for to name it would be rank mutiny against the blubber lords.'[28]

Once at the ship, the whalers waited for calm weather before they stripped the whale of everything useful. The spectioneer supervised as men fitted spurs on their feet so they would not slip, mounted the whale and began work. A long strip of meat beside the backbone was removed, the only piece of whale meat to be eaten, then the head was hacked off and hoisted aboard. After that the men used flensing knives, long poles fitted with great blades, to slice off the blubber. When removed, the blubber was handed to the Kings of the Blubber who stored it in casks.[29]

There was a science in this butchery. First the whalers removed the 'kant', or 'kent', which was a strip of blubber from around the neck, placed a harness known as a 'kent purchase' around the gap and, with this harness attached to a windlass, slowly turned the body, simultaneously slicing off lengths of blubber.[30] As they worked, clouds of fulmar petrels, known as 'mollies', besieged the men and fed on the carcass. The noise of a molly has been described as 'something between the cackle of the hen and the quack of the duck'.[31] For most of the whaling period the whalers used block and tackle to hoist the blubber on board, where it would be stuffed into casks for the voyage home. The casks were stacked in tiers in the hold, with the larger casks, of 300 or 400 gallons, at the bottom and the smaller at the top. By 1870 the Dundee vessels were fitted with 'large iron tanks for holding the blubber.'[32] These tanks had a manhole at the top and were more convenient than casks.

The baleen was cut from the mouth of the whale, hung like so many garments on a washing-line until it was dry and then stored away. However, anyone who aspired to cleanliness would have been driven to distraction by the mess that accompanied the flensing. The mate would lay down sawdust, at 5 shillings the keg,[33] to soak up the blood and fat, but the boots of tired men would trail the resultant filth through every corner of the ship. The smell of blubber and death would cling to the ship for the remainder of its voyage. Despite the toil and sweat and carnage, flensing was not unpopular. The Greenlandmen knew that their bonus was growing with every piece of whalebone and every barrel of blubber. This bloody, filthy, raucous business ensured that they could feed their families and pay the rent through the winter. Only when the carcass was stripped of everything useful, the remains, known as the kreng, were pushed away and the ship would resume its hunt.

As well as whales, the Greenlandmen hunted seals, walruses and polar bears, with sealing becoming more important as the number of whales declined. After the introduction of steam-powered whalers to Dundee in 1859, the ships made two trips. The first was to Newfoundland, where they picked up a parcel of Newfoundland sealers, sealed for a month or so and brought their cargo back. The second was a traditional whale hunt. There were many types of seal in the Arctic, with the Greenland seal, *phoca groenlandica*, the most common. The Greenland seal gathered in their thousands on the ice floes, with around 500,000 killed annually off Newfoundland alone by the end of the century. Other seals included the *phoca barbata*, or ringed seal, the *phoca hispida*, or floe-rat, and the *phoca foetida*, the bladder-nosed or hooded seal. By the end of the nineteenth century, seals were more important than the ever-declining whales. Lubbock claims that even when they had an engine, Scottish whalers usually hunted under sail, as the whale's acute hearing could detect an engine at some distance. It is possible that the early engines were noisy, but whaling skippers would also be reluctant to burn coal unnecessarily that might be needed for the voyage back, or if the ship became trapped in the ice.

The birds that flocked around the ship seemed irresistible to the officers. In 1884 Campbell wrote that he 'saw a great many birds... we shot about half a dozen.'[34] Surgeon Trotter also enjoyed shooting at birds: 'I think I have shot about a hundred.'[35] Just as willing to join in the Victorian lust of slaughter, the crew baited hooks with fat and tossed them in the air for the birds to catch.

Whalers also sought the narwhal. In the Middle Ages the long spiral tusk of the narwhal was viewed with almost superstitious awe. Some people believed that it came from the mythical unicorn, which was the name the whalers gave to the narwhal: unicorn or 'uni'. Narwhal tusks could be eight feet long, but the shorter lengths were often used as walking sticks, with the surface carefully cleaned and polished.

Many of the journals mention bear hunts: 'towards night a bear was observed... nearer still he came... pop, pop went five guns.'[36] 'This morning before breakfast I went away with the second mate, bear shooting, we shot three... we were away from the ship forty minutes only.'[37] Although the officers treated bear hunt as sport, the skins were sold, and sometimes the entire animal. In 1903 Frederic Lucas of the American Museum of Natural History requested that Professor D'Arcy Wentworth Thompson of St Andrews University obtain a 'fully grown polar bear' for him.[38] A further letter asking for 'walrus skins' in 1908 revealed that a bull walrus sold for 'about £30', while musk ox were '$100 a pair.'[39] Mr Kinnes, the agent, seems to have had a range of prices for the animals, with the skin of polar bears averaging around £20 each. There does not seem to have been a universal law of ownership, for in Peterhead the bearskins appear to have been the personal property of the ship's master.[40] On at least one occasion a bear skin was brought home in a bad condition. In 1817 an undressed bear skin in *London* of Montrose was 'not worth the duties' as it was 'in a perishable state', so the Collector of Customs requested 'directions for the sale thereof'.[41]

If profit and not pleasure was the motive for bear hunting, the time of year when the bears were shot was important. The coats of bears shot at the end of winter, when they were white, were more valuable than the yellowish fur of late summer. Some hunting, however, was purely for the pot: 'The chief and carpenter went ashore after hares and the chief shot two'.[42]

The whole purpose of the voyage was to hunt, and success was calculated by the slaughter of seals and whales. If a ship returned 'full' there was profit for the shareholder and pennies for the crew. If she were empty or 'clean' there would be gloom in Peterhead, Dundee or Leith. The experience, skill and fortune of the master was crucial in deciding when to risk his ship to make a profit, but even the best master knew that fate or luck often took a hand when the ships were hunting in the ice fields of the North. The crew often looked for a lucky master rather than one with years of experience.

The perils of whaling did not end with the weather, the cold and the lashing of the whale's tail. There was another, hidden hazard that could hit the whalers. In 1802 Alexander Young, master of *Eliza Swan* of Montrose, reported that eleven of his crew were endangered by what he termed 'Mephitic Air' from his cargo.[43] Coopers perfected their skill during a four-year apprenticeship, but even their best-made cask might leak after being stored in a storm-battered ship. Leaking whale oil created dangerous gas in a confined space. The more successful a ship had been, the more chance there was of sulphuretted hydrogen or sometimes phosphine gas in the hold, either of which could temporarily blind and would cause nausea among the crew. Whaling ships were renowned for their evil stench, and gas from the blubber was just one more aspect of their working lives with which the whale hunters had to cope.

10

DANGERS OF THE ICE

*'I did not like the whale fishing… there is no sight for the eye of the
inquisitive after the first glance and no variety to charm the mind…
desolation reigns around, nothing but snow or bare rocks and ice.'*
John Nichol

In the eighteenth century, the majority of whalers hunted in the Greenland Sea or on the Western Coast of Greenland. Few ventured far into
the Davis Strait or saw the need to cross Baffin Bay, for there were whales
closer to hand. As the years passed the supply of whales gradually diminished, as they had in the Bay of Biscay and at Spitzbergen, so the
Greenlandmen had to search for new whale-fishing grounds in waters
ever more dangerous. Whaling logbooks give scant notice to the sighting of icebergs: 'At 4 PM passed a berg. At 9 passed another berg.'[1] 'Lat
61 degrees 28 N ship plying to the north and among many bergs.'[2]

It was in 1817 that two British whaling ships, *Larkins* of Leith and
Elizabeth of Hull, pushed the whaling frontier even further when they
steered west across Baffin Bay. When they followed the 77th parallel
they found the 'West Water' that was to become the happy hunting
ground for a new generation of whalers. Their success was confirmed
the following year when Wigtown-born Captain Ross RN thrust even
deeper into the unknown. However, if the West Water was an Aladdin's
Lamp for the whalers, then the genie was often in a cantankerous mood.
The short 150 mile passage across Melville Bay claimed so many whaling ships that it became known as the 'Breaking-Up-Yard'.

Despite the avarice of humanity, as long as the whaling ships were
powered by sails, their movements were dictated by wind and current,
as much as commercial pressure. A warm water current caresses the West
Coast of Greenland, inviting the whaling ships northward, to Disco and
Duck Island and to the sardonically upthrusting stack of rock known as
the Devil's Thumb. Whaling men had an unusual skill in affixing unusual names to geographical features, such as the formation known as
Kettle Bottom-up, which was also known as Sugar Loaf Hill.[3] It was at

the Devil's Thumb that the whale ships gathered, and from here they struck out westward, across the Breaking-Up-Yard toward the promised whaling grounds.

The passage was treacherous, with shifting ice and hostile winds. As *Narwhal* entered Melville Bay in 1874, Thomas Macklin wrote that there was so much danger that all the ships 'get up all their provisions on deck so as to be ready to leave at a moment's notice, in case of an emergency, also, every man packs up his chest.'[4] The precautions were necessary. In 1819, ten ships were lost, in 1821 there were fourteen and the worst year was yet to come. There was always one consolation; Greenlandmen, in common with all other British seamen, would always help their comrades in distress. When a ship was wrecked, another vessel would take in the crew, despite the obvious hardships of overcrowding and short commons that ensued. In 1826, when Captain Duncan of the London whaler *Dundee* took the crew of the wrecked *Harlingen* on board, he commented that 'the people... were all readily and kindly received by... our whole crew.'[5] Assistance was not confined to passive friendliness. At a time when their own ship was in danger and everyone was suffering from severe cold and scarcity of provisions, when the master of *Grenville Bay* called for volunteers to help the crew of the wrecked *Advice*, twenty-one men stepped forward.[6]

The northern shore of Melville Bay is composed of islands of solid rock, with shallow, heavily iced water. In the winter ice covers the entire bay, so the whalers had to wait until the spring thaw before they attempted a passage west. Usually they would see a narrow gap appear, dark water beckoning them toward the whales. Sometimes they sailed too early and were trapped in the ice.

The Greenlandmen knew that tide and wind would eventually thrust the ice westward, and they knew that there was a south-flowing current from Smith Sound that would then disperse it. A southerly wind would open a passage, but if the wind shifted west or even southwest, ice, known as the middle ice, would close the passage and endanger the ships. The Greenlandmen also knew that the best fishing ground was Lancaster Sound, to the south of where they would cross Melville Bay. There was a stark choice to be made: gamble on the ice melting, or return home clean.

In 1830 much of the whaling fleet made such a gamble and sailed west along a narrow passage; nineteen of them were lost. This was a fabled year, when a thousand whaling men were camped on the ice in a great debacle known as the 'Baffin Fair'. The sea had been kind as the ships sailed north, with 50 whalers rendezvousing at the Devil's Thumb in early June. *Eliza Swan* of Montrose led 23 ships into a narrow opening, moving slowly in single file. Then the ice had closed. The ships were divided into smaller groups as the wind strengthened into a gale and the ice piled up, squeezing the ships. Ice lifted *Eliza Swan* bodily and thrust her against the ship next in line, leaving her damaged but afloat. *St Andrews* survived, although four of her planks were stove in, but four ships were sunk in quarter of an hour and others followed, helpless before the ice. July brought more gales that sunk more ships including *Baffin* that had once been skippered by Scoresby, as the whaling fleet suffered its worst ever disaster.

With their ships sunk or trapped, the Greenlandmen caroused on the ice. Basil Lubbock argued that whalers believed discipline ended once a ship was sunk, and the evidence seems to bear him out. They called a southerly wind an 'ale wind', as it destroyed ships and allowed the men to plunder the liquor stores on board. For three weeks the men were free of restraint; a few died, but most joined the remaining vessels when the ice loosened its grip. The master of *St Andrew* was not impressed with the behaviour of the Greenlandmen: 'it is miraculous that so few lives were lost. Many of the shipwrecked crews were insubordinate, and would not save provisions, particularly those who could lay hands on spirits.'[7] To add to the financial cost of sunken ships, twenty-one returned clean that season.

The Baffin Fair marked the beginning of a bad decade, with ships lost nearly every year, many sliding quickly under the ice, but others lingering with their hulls shattered and their crew scattered among the fleet. However sentimental the Greenlandmen were when they left their wives, they viewed stricken ships as mere objects of plunder. In 1834, when *Thomas* of Dundee came across a vessel wrecked in the ice, the first thought of the crew was for pillage. They were not alone. 'When we came to the wreck the *Lee's* boat was there with the crew plundering her; they got little, so clean had she been picked that not one article we could have taken.'[8]

1835 was another bad year, with the ice so thick at Disco that the fleet steered south to Cape Walsingham before chancing the Breaking-Up-Yard. Even on the western side of Melville Bay the ice was too dense for whaling and by the middle of October eleven ships were trapped. *Middleton* and *Dordon* were soon crushed, with the crew of *Middleton* nearly mutinying and *Dordon's* men raiding the liquor store. Following a barbaric custom that seemed unique to Greenlandmen, they set fire to the wreck so that tall orange flames reflected weirdly on the ice as the smoke of the funeral pyre rose black into the Arctic sky. Two more ships sunk, but others wrenched free, so by December only five were still trapped, facing a long Arctic winter.

The conditions on board were terrible. There was ice in all the cabins, while the coal, so parsimoniously rationed by the Customs Officers, was running short. Frostbite was joined by scurvy, men hunted polar bear and the Arctic fox while death stalked the decks of ships now vastly overcrowded with survivors. It was not surprising that there was scurvy on board; Dundee whaling ships carried little or no fresh fruit and the first mention of lime juice, which itself was not always effective, came in 1849.[9] It was the shipowners of Hull, who still had the largest whaling fleet, who petitioned the government for a rescue expedition, and James Clark Ross, the London-born Scottish explorer, who led it.

Although Ross took the Hull whaler *Cove* across the Atlantic, he was too late, for *William Torr* had sunk and the other surviving whaling ships had escaped. Inuit had tried to help the crew of *William Torr* but they had all died. *Viewforth* limped home to Kirkcaldy in February with six of her crew dead and the survivors speaking shockingly of starvation and scurvy. It was another devastating year for the whaling industry.

1836 seemed no better, with fifty-six ships sailing to the Davis Straits and six ships becoming trapped in the ice. The Dundee vessel *Thomas* was lost, while exposure, hunger and disease claimed the lives of yet more Greenlandmen. The casualty list reads like the aftermath of battle: sixteen men died on *Norfolk*, forty-two on *Advice*, forty-five on *Dee*, twenty on *Grenville Bay*. David Gibb, who was a crewman on *Dee* when she was trapped in ice, wrote of whalers missing their wives 'now the husband had no smiling partner to comfort him… to soothe him in his sorrows'.[10]

This time, however, there was something done. In December 1836 shipowners and masters from Dundee and Peterhead petitioned the House of Commons to help the crews that remained in the ice.[11] There was also a request that the hospital at Stromness should be ready to care for the sick. Although the Admiralty was not keen on sending a Royal Naval vessel into danger, in January 1837 the Treasury advertised a Bounty of £300 to the first five vessels that sailed 'carrying an Extra Quantity of Provisions.' These vessels had to make log entries that proved they reached the 'Edge of the Ice to the Southward of 55 Latitude' and Customs Officers had to check the extra provisions they carried.[12]

There were no decades quite as bad as the 1830s, but there was a steady trickle of casualties and ice remained a constant hazard for the whaling vessels. Nevertheless, the Greenlandmen developed methods of coping with their environment. To create a safe harbour in the ice, the men would use ice saws—long, clumsy tools that needed practice to master. In 1826, Captain David Duncan of *Dundee* wrote: 'all hands employed sawing the ice around the ship… the immense labour and fatigue attending this operation may easily be imagined.'[13] The second half of the statement reveals the master's appreciation of the effort involved.

When a ship was sailing into ice, the master gathered the crew on one side of the deck and had them run back and forward. Lubbock called this operation 'overing', although Dundee whalers seemed to simply call it 'rolling the ship'. In June 1884 *Nova Zembla* became stuck in the ice and the master called all hands 'to roll the ship which they did with a will, so much in fact that her boats almost touched the ice and at last got through into loose ice.'[14] The gyrations of the vessel often weakened the ice sufficiently for the ship to ease through. If the ice was too thick, the crew lifted a whaling boat under the bowsprit and let it fall, which was a crude but sometimes surprisingly effective method. The later auxiliary powered vessels could often just barge through, depending on their 70-horse-power engines and reinforced bows to shoulder aside the ice.

If there was clear water but no wind, or a narrow passage through the ice, the men could go into the boats and tow the ship. William Barron reported that the men boat's crews sang as they towed, with their voices echoing in the ice.[15] If the passage was too narrow for the boats, men would clamber onto the ice and pull her through by sheer muscle power. Virtually every whaling log contained entries like William Archibald's laconic 'all hands towing among loose ice',[16] or 'called all hands to warp through the ice.'[17] Captain Davidson was equally terse when *Dorothy* was stuck in the ice in June 1834: 'called all hands and warped the ship through.'[18] Sometimes a man would encourage their labour by playing the bagpipes.

On other occasions James Webster, master of *Advice* used the ice as a reason for not taking soundings. 'Upon fourth April last, Cape Elizabeth bore N by W dist. 5 Leagues… no opportunity of Soundings as they were beating to windward thro Bay Ice.' The same reason was used on 15 May when: 'At midnight Whale Fish Islands bore E by N dist 5 or 6 Leagues Dog Island SE 3 miles no soundings they being surrounded by loose ice and Ice Bergs'. And again four days later when 'Lively Isle NE by W 8 miles no soundings as they were employed killing a fish and a great deal of ice round them.'[19]

Icebergs were also useful as a supply for fresh water: 'we got nearly a tank of ice off a small berg in the afternoon, we being in great need of water.'[20] Ice might be very dangerous but it was also a preservative. In 1826 *Active* of Peterhead was abandoned in the ice with her cargo of seven fish. Next season she was recovered and brought home. This was not the only occasion when Greenlandmen found a previously abandoned whaling ship. Barron mentions finding a spar protruding from an ice floe and 'to all appearance a vessel was underneath' He added that that type of ice was known as 'Sound ice' that broke up only every seven years.[21] Some Greenlandmen could even enjoy the cold, as when Wanless noted that 'some of the men were snowballing each other.'[22]

Scottish newspapers published reports of whaling ships lost in the ice as soon as they could, but before radio or telephone, the relatives had to wait for confirmation from vessels returning from the same area. In October, the *East of Fife Record* confirmed a rumour that *Abram* of Kirkcaldy, commanded by Captain Souter, had been lost. The master of *Polar Star* of Peterhead reported that *Abram* had been frozen in while crossing Melville Bay, and when the ice broke up, large bergs had crushed her 'to pieces'. The *East of Fife Record* also said that the crew were reported 'all saved', and the ship and the oil money had been insured.[23] It was a bad year for Kirkcaldy, with another of her whalers, *Lord Gambier*, lost at the beginning of the season; a third vessel, *Chieftain*, would also be lost.

Decades of experience taught the whalers so much about ice that they created a vocabulary all of their own. Small icebergs about the size of a small house were known as 'growlers' because of the noise they made. Pieces that fell from large icebergs were known as 'bergy-bits', while a whaler that made fast to an iceberg for whatever reason was 'fastened on to the floe.' Barron reported that off Godhaven in Greenland 'we made fast to an iceberg near a large glacier, where we stayed some time in hopes of getting north.'[24] In calm weather ice could form beneath the sea; if the temperature dipped to 29 degrees Fahrenheit ice would form on the surface. This was 'bay ice' to the Greenlandman. Mixed with snow, this covering became a glutinous 'slush' that could impede the passage of a whaling boat. Unmixed, bay ice could form at eight or nine inches thick, through which a steam-powered whaling ship could slice a passage with some ease. When the ice is thin, the ship leaves a narrow wake. When the ice is thick and white, it becomes more brittle and easier to sail through.

When bay ice spreads out it forms into discs known as pancake ice, which can freeze together into floe or field ice, with a land floe being a floe attached to the land. If the sea rose and smashed floe ice the result was known as 'pack ice', and when the movement of the sea piled one piece of pack ice onto another, the Greenlandmen knew the result as 'hummocky ice'. At the edge of any pack was 'brash ice', which was basically the debris of the pack. There were also 'streams' of ice, which were long barriers of ice that formed at right angles to the direction of the wind. When wind or current pushed two or three of these streams together, they could create an impenetrable barrier of ice.[25]

If a whaling ship was caught between a stream of ice and the land, it had little chance of survival, so an experienced whaling master would be alert for the signs. He would also know that a newly formed ice field was easier to break through than a more established field, and that he could sail through a narrow channel between ice by alternatively pushing with the starboard and then the port bow.

Every nineteenth-century fisherman had a large store of weather lore and whale fishers were no exceptions. There were various tried and tested signs for foretelling the weather. A northerly swell warned of a coming storm, an echo returning from a large iceberg promised a helpful north wind, while mist from the fissures at Cape Searle was a sure sign that a fog was coming.[26]

Despite all the knowledge that the whaling men accumulated over the decades, even the later, steam-powered whaling vessels often steered into trouble. The Ingram Papers tell of *Columbia* being lost in the ice in 1869, and a boatsteerer, Alexander Walker, sued the Dundee Seal and Whale Fishing Company, who owned the vessel, for four months' wages and oil money. Walker was an experienced Greenlandman with a decade of whaling behind him, and he claimed that *Columbia* was 'lost through carelessness'.[27] It is probably significant that the master was on his first whaling voyage.

In 1872 SS *Polynia*, commanded by William Walker, was trapped between two ice floes, with a barrier in front of her. In company with *Erik*, *Polynia* attempted to find a passage, but gave up after eighteen days and headed south. The ships tried again at Cape Searle, but were again stopped by a barrier of ice. While *Polynia* probed into a channel between two floes a fog descended. Simultaneously the floes on either side pushed together, damaging *Polynia's* propeller guides and displacing her propeller.

Ice continued to build up, with eighteen feet on one side, seven on the other, and it pressed *Polynia* until she was at an angle of 45 degrees, with the pumps fighting constantly to control a leak. As the crew pre-pared to abandon ship, the ice suddenly eased and *Erik* was able to come close and tow *Polynia* to clear water.[28]

Not every ship was as fortunate as *Polynia*. A glance through the entries in the *Register of Dundee Ships* reveals a depressing list of whalers that were lost in the ice. *Resolute*, built Dundee 1880, is recorded as 'vessel crushed in ice and totally lost 27th March 1886 off Ireland Rocks, Fogo Island, Newfoundland'.[29] *Our Queen*, built Liverpool 1860, was the 'vessel wrecked and totally lost 18 July 1879 in the opening of Ad-miralty Inlet, Lancaster Sound, Davis Straits by being crushed between two fields of ice.'[30] *Princess Charlotte*, built at South Shields, was 'lost in Melville Bay, Davis Straits 14 June 1856.'[31] Lanceman Webster's *Ad-vice*, built at Whitby 1785, was 'lost Davis Straits 23 June 1859'.[32] *Dundee* is reported 'abandoned in Melville Bay, Davis Straits, 15 August 1863'.[33] *Narwhal* was 'damaged by ice [and] abandoned off Cape Searle, Davis Straits on second October 1884, and afterward sank.'[34] *Camperdown* was 'abandoned and sank in Davis Straits on the 10 October 1878'.[35] Even the famous *Polynia* was 'crushed in Lancaster Sound 11 July 1891'.[36]

All seafaring was hazardous, with a steady flow of deaths and casual-ties from accident, disease and weather, but Arctic whaling seems to have been worse than most other seagoing activities. There were 99 ships lost between 1815 and 1834 alone. Over all, 5.9% of Arctic whal-ing voyages resulted in the whaling ship being lost.[37] Of all seamen, perhaps the Greenlandmen understood ice best, and their surviving words indicate that they took its danger seriously. When stuck in the Arctic they thought mainly of their families and their religion: 'Alas! I may never see you again, for here we are, hard and fast, among the ice above Fury Point... God be with us, He will preserve us, if it be His will.'[38] In many cases God did preserve the Greenlandmen, but it was while they were in real danger that the true voice of the Greenlandmen sounded.

11

ACROSS THE POND

'There are only two types of people in the world: seamen and landsmen.
All the rest, politics, creed, colour, is immaterial'
Thomas Ritchie Archibald

Wherever they have gone, Scots have made contact with the local people. As early as the twelfth century Scotsmen taking part in the Crusades were noted for being 'ferocious among themselves but elsewhere unwarlike... offering... their faith and devotion'.[1] An ability to befriend different peoples appears to be a trait among people from Scotland, manifesting itself in various ways throughout history. Relationships between Scotland and her maritime neighbours were more usually cordial than not, with strong trading links formed between the East Coast ports and the Baltic and North European cities. Scottish names such as Renny, Ochterlony and Fyfe were well known in Scandinavia, with the Clarks becoming Klercks in Sweden and immigrant Scottish Greigs begetting one of Norway's finest composers.

Scottish families headed great dynasties among the port makers in Portugal, Scots and Norwegians formed enduring trade links that blossomed into many marriages, Scots and Irish blood is so close that it is virtually identical. After Waterloo, Parisian families squabbled to have a Highland soldier billeted with them rather than an Englishman or a Prussian, for the Highlander would help with the house and play with the children. The fascination of a short kilt on the sensibilities of the French female may also have been a contributing factor. When the Scots ventured to the New World they took these gregarious qualities with them. Although the Hudson Bay company was run from London, much of its manpower came from Orkney, while the rival North West Company was Highland. Alexander McGillivray, descended from a Jacobite member of Clan Chattan who left Scotland after the 1715, was Chief of the Creek Indians and a major player in international politics. The Cherokee chief in the late 1830s was John Ross, who raised money from his Native American people to aid the Highland poor during the Potato famine of 1847. In 1964 the chief of the Creeks was named McIntosh.

It is a formidable, honourable list, demonstrating the spirit of Robert Burns 'A Man's a Man For a' That'. Scots abroad seem to have been a friendly, if at times a quarrelsome, bunch and the Greenlandmen were no different. They met with two distinct cultures, the indigenous Inuit and the people of Newfoundland, whose ancestors had chosen to settle there. The results of both areas of contact have been expertly written about already, by Dr C. W. Sanger in the case of the Newfoundland sealing industry,[2] and by Dorothy Harley Eber for the Inuit.[3] Dr Sanger's articles detail the 93 voyages of Scottish whalers between 1862 and 1900, and the impact of Scottish whaling on Newfoundland sealing as well as the influence of sealing on the Scottish whaling industry. Dorothy Eber's work reveals the impact of Scottish whalers on the Inuit.

The English explorer Martin Frobisher might have been the first modern European to meet the Inuit that the later whalers came to know so well. Frobisher thought the Inuit were like Tartars, and that their tawny colour implied they were legitimately descended from Noah. As so often with early contact between different cultures there was suspicion and misunderstanding, but the Scottish whalers seemed to have avoided such misadventures. When the whalers first met the Inuit, they found a self-reliant people who lived mainly on the coast and whose food, fuel and clothes were products of their hunting skills. Politically they were tribal, with no concept of a class system but with the eldest man in each family having the major say in their affairs.

The Greenlandmen encountered these people on the Greenland coast, particularly at Godhaven, a Danish settlement on the south west coast of Disco Island, which was a place well known to the whalers. The whaling men would exchange European goods for Inuit clothing here, much as they had done with the islanders in Shetland. 'Some of the natives came aboard at night with barter. They were all very much amused at a phonograph which they heard.'[4] The natives also listened to a melodeon and Alexander Lamb commented that 'some of the native women are good dancers'.[5] William Barron in his *Old Whaling Days* remarked that in 1850 Disco was noted for whales,[6] reinforcing his words with a whaler's rhyme:

> With Riff Koll Hill and Disco dipping,
> There you will see the whale fish skipping.[7]

As whales became scarcer, some Greenlandmen overwintered in the Arctic. Repulse Bay in Hudson Bay became a virtual Scottish colony, but there were other places where the distinct accent of Dundee and the

Doric of Aberdeen and Peterhead mingled with the indigenous language. By the end of the nineteenth century, football fever had struck Scotland, and the Dundee whalers enacted on the ice a prelude of the mighty tussles at Tannadice and Dens Park. They also staged plays and danced. Margaret Penny 'found them dancing reels with the greatest spirit',[8] and wrote that there was music and dancing every night. Again the log of Alexander Lamb provides proof: when 'a boatload of natives came aboard… we started a concert and dance… the natives were very much amused at the Cake Walk'.[9] Men from Peterhead and Dundee hunted with the Inuit throughout the winter. For instance *Xanthus* of Peterhead spent the winter of 1872–3 in Cumberland Gulf, returning with 60 tons of oil in September 1873.[10] The following year *Perseverance* and *Alert* both overwintered at Cumberland Gulf, with *Perseverance* returning with 88 tons of oil.[11]

Some whaling men remained as semi-permanent residents. Peterhead folklore speaks of Frederick Cameron, who was with the Inuit in 1914 and did not speak with a European until 1919, when he first learned of the First World War.[12]

There does not seem to have been any friction between the Greenlandmen and their Inuit hosts, and close relationships were formed on both sides. Whalers hunted with local men and played with local children. Nataraq, an elderly Inuit, recalled an incident of her childhood: 'on one ship there was a man who would tease and make fun and chase me round the deck… this man who was so kind to me must have had children of his own.'[13] Another Inuit, Anirnik, remembered that 'the Inuit and the white people used to have a lot of fun and the relationships… were very close.'[14] Possibly even more revealing was the statement of Joe Curley 'I can't recall any disagreements between the Inuit and the Qallunaat (the white men)… They would help each other out as best they could.'[15]

It was inevitable that the whaling men should become friendly with the Inuit women, with many forming attachments that were more than just transitory. When *Esquimaux* overwintered in Hudson's Bay in 1885 'some of the men took up with the Eskimo women and had them living aboard with them.'[16] Nutaraq had close memories of the whaling men because 'My quallunaaq [white man] father was one of them.'[17]

Less inevitable than sexual relations was the tolerant attitude of the Inuit men, who appear to have accepted the situation quite happily. Perhaps this politeness was natural to a dignified and balanced people who treated the whalers with the same respect that they had long shown to the whales. There was an Inuit saying 'we like the ways whales think', while the Kwakiutl of Alert Bay believed that the whales brought prosperity. In a more direct and possibly more detrimental manner, so too did the Aberdeen and Dundee whalers. The Inuit, however, were more than just accommodating, they also saved lives. For instance, when the Kirkcaldy whaler *Lord Gambier* was sunk in 1862, the local Inuit took in the crew and cared for them for four months.

Snowdrop was another case in point. She was a very small whaler of just 62 tons, owned by Captain Forsyth Grant of Ecclescraig, Montrose, and her career could almost be seen as an epitome of the closing days of Scottish Arctic whaling. She left Dundee in April 1906, but her engines failed in a Davis Strait fog, she was damaged on rocks and while most the crew returned home, others remained in Canada. With *Snowdrop* repaired, Grant recruited Inuits and fished for walrus and seal. The following year an experienced Greenlandman, Captain Brown, took over command, and, after further repairs in St John's, *Snowdrop* killed 205 walrus, 25 bears and 180 seals. They also befriended a sick Inuit named Inea, from near Frobisher Straits, and took him to a hospital.

Next year *Snowdrop* had a sizeable catch of walrus, but was wrecked and disappeared from European knowledge. In 1909 Mr Crawford Noble of Aberdeen chartered a schooner named *Jantina Agatha* and found all save two of the crew still alive. The Inuit of Baffin Island had cared for them for the best part of a year. For a people often close to subsistence level, such actions spoke of true kindness.

While most of the visiting was from East to West, there were occasions when the Inuit reversed the process. One such was when, in 1846, a young boy named Autotook Zininnuck voyaged to Scotland on the Kirkcaldy whaler *Caledonia*. The Kirkcaldy people took Autotook to their heart, and after a winter of learning art, English and, naturally, religion, about eight thousand waved him good-bye when he returned home with a chest full of parting presents the following spring. Other Inuit who visited Leith appear to have been equally popular, giving displays of kayaking in the harbour and being welcomed by the populace. William Penny brought back Eenuoolooapik to Aberdeen in 1839, to a similar reception.

Relationships between the Inuit and the whalers were long-lasting and resulted in an exchange of cultures, from which the Europeans benefited most. While the Inuit gained Christianity, European goods, metal tools and tobacco, the Greenlandmen learned how to hunt in Inuit fashion, snow-navigation, dog-handling and snow-house building. Inuit artefacts began to make their way back to Scotland, with souvenirs such as Inuit carvings and kayaks appearing. Arbroath Museum still has some miniature kayak paddles brought home by a Greenlandman. The Greenlandmen made another impact on the area; Cape Milne and Cape Adams were both named after Dundee whaling masters, while Norrie's Island was named after a Peterhead whaler who died and was buried there. In a strange coincidence his son, George Norrie of *Xanthus*, also died at the whaling and was buried beside his father.[18]

Whaling men had hunted seals for centuries before the Dundee Greenlandmen began to visit Newfoundland, but from 1867 their presence in Britain's oldest colony was an annual event. Since the use of auxiliary steam power, Dundee whaling ships were no longer restricted to a single voyage to the hunting grounds, and since the demise of the bounty system they had no time restrictions. Now they left Dundee in February or March for St John's in Newfoundland, picked up extra men that the whalers knew as 'sweilers' and spent time hunting the seals. The reinforced crews generally numbered around eighty men. When the seal hunting was complete, around the middle of April, the ship would return the sweilers to St John's and sail home to Dundee to refit. In early May they sailed to the Davis Strait for the whale hunting.[19] The Greenlandmen seemed to have a friendly relationship with the sweilers,[20] despite the obvious problems that overcrowding would bring. It is interesting that while whaling spawned many songs, dealing with either the hardships of the trade, the triumphs or the grief felt at parting, sealing was a lot less musically prolific. Seemingly the only song that has survived is 'The Old Polina', which probably alludes to *Polynia*, the 358-ton auxiliary steamer from Dundee that operated from 1861 to 1891.

> We're back again in old St John's where rum and beer are cheap,
> And we'll drink a health to Captain Joy who brought us o'er the
> deep...
> No other ship could make the trip with *Polina* I declare.

Other ships did, in fact make the trip; in 1873 the Customs Collector reported that *Polynia*, with *Ravenscraig*, *Intrepid* and *Tay*, had returned from their annual spring sealing voyage.[21] The famous *Terra Nova* was another regular. Under Captain Fairweather she made the crossing to Newfoundland in 1889, 1890, 1891 and 1893.

The number of seals killed by Dundee vessels alone was immense. In 1859, 2841; in 1863, 11,400; in 1865, 6404; in 1869, 44,424; in 1870

87,768. The sealers killed so many seals that they were a victim of their own success, and in 1875 Dundee and Peterhead, the only two Arctic whaling ports left in Britain, suggested that there should be a close season for seal hunting. Nonetheless, the massacre continued with 86,321 seals slaughtered in 1878, but from a peak of 152,584 in 1881 the trend was downward as the stocks became exhausted.[22]

At times the Newfoundland sealing was as dangerous as the whaling. In 1886 the Dundee whaler *Resolute* was crushed in the ice, with the crew being forced to jump on the pack ice with a seventy-mile trek ahead of them to reach the shore.

For the owners and masters, working from St John's presented both problems and opportunities. Auxiliary-powered whaling ships were freed from the thraldom of the wind, but instead they had to carry their own fuel. In 1877 the master of *Aurora* claimed that he would burn 10 or 12 tons of coal a day for the 15 or 16 days it took to cross the Atlantic. Captain Adams of *Arctic*, a vessel of equal size, said his ship would take 20 days on the crossing, using 19 tons of coal a day, plus another 600 tons for the whaling voyage alone. He would need more for the sealing trips. Captain Adams apparently intended carrying coal with him to St John's, landing it in the port and collecting it for later voyages. This scenario left the Collector of Customs at Dundee with the problem of whether to mark *Arctic* as sailing in ballast, or treating the coal as a cargo and charging dues on it.[23]

Coal was not the only thing that created problems with the Customs for the Dundee whalers. *Arctic* was in trouble again two years later when she carried *Lizzie* across to St John's. *Lizzie* was a five-ton steam launch that the master intended to use to ferry his crew from their berth on one side of the Bay of St John's to the town itself. If the launch were used, the trip would take ten minutes; without *Lizzie* there was a six-mile walk on a rough track. Alexander Stephen, owner of *Arctic*, claimed that *Lizzie* was essential to the sealing business.[24]

Despite these difficulties, the whalers of Dundee and Peterhead seemed to have retained positive images of their time across the Atlantic. The Inuit were regarded as skilful, friendly and knowledgeable, and the Newfoundlanders as hardy seal hunters that the Greenlandmen could work with. With no apparent record of riots, quarrels or even disagreements in Newfoundland or the Arctic, the negative reputation of the Greenlandmen seemed confined to Britain. Much of that reputation was based on their fondness for drink.

12

WHALERS AND DRINK

'By despising all that has preceded us, we teach others
to despise ourselves.'
William Hazlitt

Rum. The word conjures up visions of piracy and debauchery, of a sea-man with a patch over his eye, smoking cannon and gold doubloons. Robert Louis Stevenson used the mystique of rum in his famous *Treasure Island* song, 'Yo-ho-ho and a bottle of rum' while the saying 'Rum, Sodomy and the Lash' has often been used to characterise life in the Royal Navy. While it was probably too cold for sodomy in the whaling ships and it is unlikely that the Greenlandmen would have tolerated the lash, rum there certainly was. Rum is an alcoholic spirit distilled from sugar cane residues, although in some parts of North America the term was used for any alcoholic liquor. It was following the conquest of Ja-maica that rum became common in British ships, replacing brandy as a daily tipple, although beer was also issued. Probably because of its easy availability, rum was considerably cheaper than brandy—in 1849 a gallon of rum cost 1s. 10d., compared to 3s. 3d. for gin, and 5s. 6d. for brandy.

Every journal and book about whaling voyages was seasoned with references to rum, grog or general drinking. It seems that despite the hard work, the scrimshaw, the dancing and the hardships, the Greenlandman's favourite pastime was upending a bottle of something alcoholic. To judge by the stores of a whaling ship, he would have plenty opportunity to indulge.

In 1824 the whale ship *Fairy* shipped three puncheons of rum as stores for the Davis Straits.[1] *Thomas* and *Three Brothers*, sailing the same year, were also permitted to carry three puncheons of rum each, as the owners intended to 'discontinue the usual allowance of beer'.[2] The pre-vious year, *Princess Charlotte*, *Estridge* and *Advice* each carried two puncheons of rum, with the proviso that the rum was not shipped until the vessels were ready to sail.[3] Puncheons seemed to contain varying amounts of rum, with one puncheon measured at 113 gallons and an-other at 101 gallons. In either case, the Greenlandmen appear to have been adequately provisioned for their voyage, particularly as they also carried 12 hogsheads of beer, at 63 gallons to the hogshead, and 5 gallons of strong ale.[4]

When the rum arrived at a whaling port the Collector of Customs ensured that the quantity was correct. Each puncheon appears to be have been ordered for a specific vessel, with *Pilgrim*, Dugald Campbell, master, carrying a puncheon from Jamaica to the McEwan Watson's warehouse at Greenock for *Estridge* of Dundee. When the rum arrived it was found to be one gallon short. The 101-gallon puncheon carried by *Diana*, Mathew Roxburgh master, for *Advice* of Dundee, was also one gallon short.[5] In one occasion the Montrose Collector found his measuring callipers were faulty, which meant that his measurements were imprecise. The callipers were sent to Leith to be corrected.[6] Unless the ships were due to leave immediately, the rum was stored in a warehouse, 'under the joint locks of the officers of the revenue and proprietors'.[7]

The Greenlandmen appeared to drink the rum, and everything else they could get their hands on, at every opportunity. The pre-voyage celebrations of whaling ships were legendary, so that Markham noted that their departure was 'marked by the total incapacity of the crew to perform any duties.'[8] The Mayday festival was also highlighted by drinking whisky and grog, sometimes tempered by tea and coffee.[9] In 1856 Surgeon Trotter of the Fraserburgh whaler *Enterprise* was perhaps a little tongue in cheek when he thought it 'shocking to relate' that when Mr and Mrs Neptune came on board 'both man and wife dearly loved rum'.[10] Sometimes the celebration could turn sour, as in *Hercules* in 1831 when fighting broke out and the captain had to 'thrash among them with a stick'[11] to restore order. The elder Scoresby hints at the predilection of whalers for drinking when he wrote 'our men have behaved very well here and kept themselves sober.'[12]

Drink was part of everyday life on board. As on naval vessels, there was a daily allowance: 'it is half past 11 am. The sailors are getting their grog. This they do every day at the same hour.'[13] Drink was also something to be worked for, as when Trotter noted that the sailors made a seagull pie for the master, hoping for a 'glass of grog, which pleases them above everything else.'[14] The captain would often serve out a tot of rum or grog when a whale was being flensed, with the specktioneers being allowed a double. Scoresby also served out rum if any of his men fell in the icy water when hunting for whales. He suspected that some men deliberately immersed themselves so they could be consoled with a dram.[15]

The Shipmasters: Captain 'Coffee' Tam Robertson, of Newport on Tay, on deck (McManus Galleries, Dundee City Council)

The Men: John Beveridge, a Kirkcaldy whaler (Fife Council Libraries)

*The Men: crew of SS Hope in 1882—a fine collection of beards and headgear
(Aberdeen Heritage)*

But wonderfull to say, just as the greedy Sea was opening its mouth to swallow us – the Ship contrary to all expectations rose upon the bosom of the tumultuous Sea as a feather upon the wave – thus I have often since, around and beneath us was this everlasting Arms, and by those arms we were born ere our danger. But like the Patriarch Jacob, tho he prevailed, yet was made to feel, by the Angel touching the hollow of his thigh, and went halting, the Ship in rising from the trough of the Sea, as the sea spoken of took her she strained herself – sprung a leak – and for 3 more Weeks we were lashed to the pumps night and day, thus few to weeks were we in the most eminent danger –. To detail would be tedious – we arrived at our destination Davis Straits 76 –. Succeeded beyond all other Ships in Catching Whales – Sharks, and Seals – One day after 3 days and nights culling up 3 large fish and pulling them away, another fish was seen – Boats were lowered down, the first Boat came up to her, she was harpooned the Boat I was in was 2d the second a 2d Harpoon, the Whale went to the bottom remained there some time, came up – as soon as she appeared the first Boat threw a Lance which mortaly wounded her, the fish blew Blood and nearly sunk the Boat with the quantity emmitted – the Boat I was in got right in the top of her Back – She reared herself – Shudderd upset the Boat, went down to the ... and died ... 600 fathom deep – the Ice began to close in upon

*The Men: page from the journal of Alexander Alison, who sailed on a whaling
ship as a boy (Private Collection)*

The Men at Work: working on a whale alongside the whaler Eclipse. *Note the birds in the water and the harpoon gun at the bow of the whaling boat (McManus Galleries, Dundee City Council Leisure and Arts)*

The Men at Work: a whale being flensed alongside the Eclipse *(McManus Galleries, Dundee City Council Leisure and Arts)*

The Men at Work: the Dundee whaler Eclipse *and men in pack ice (McManus Galleries, Dundee City Council Leisure and Arts)*

The Men at Leisure: 'Dundee whalers enacted on the ice a prelude of the mighty tussles at Tannadice and Dens Park'—football team from the whaler Active *(McManus Galleries, Dundee City Council Leisure and Arts)*

The Surgeon: John Wanless, surgeon and diarist (McManus Galleries, Dundee City Council Leisure and Arts)

Farewell Dear Scotia: crowds watch the whaler Active *leaving Dundee
(McManus Galleries, Dundee City Council Leisure and Arts)*

The Equipment: the head of a hand-held harpoon, showing the stop-withers

The Equipment: flensing tool, used for stripping blubber from the whale (Scottish Fisheries Museum, Anstruther)

The Equipment: mouth foghorn of William Smith, the Cellardyke harpooner who became a shipmaster (Scottish Fisheries Museum, Anstruther)

Pastimes: the mermaid on this piece of scrimshaw work reveals something of the superstition of the whaling men (Scottish Fisheries Museum, Anstruther)

The End of the Voyage: signpost marking the original location of East Whale Lane, Dundee. It is now a car park

It seems that Dutch vessels also carried liquor on board. When the English trawling fleets were fishing the Dogger Banks, vessels put out from Dutch ports to sell them cheap gin and tobacco. These were known as 'copers' and, although popular with some fishermen, the drink that they sold was often little better than firewater or 'kill-me-deadly' in the parlance of the times. Greenlandmen, with all their fishing associations, were equally prone to temptation. When the crew of *Thomas* sighted a Dutch vessel, some scrambled on board, hoping for gin. With no ready money, and despite the fact that they were sailing into some of the coldest and most hostile seas on the planet, 'the Barter was for any wearing apparel.'[16] The opportunity to obtain drink was obviously more important than any future discomfort.

If reaching for the bottle was habitual for Greenlandmen in the course of an ordinary day, it became something of an obsession in times of duress. Basil Lubbock states in his *Arctic Whalers* that the Greenlandmen believed that discipline ended when a ship was wrecked, and the evidence appears to prove him correct. When *Middleton* sank in the bad season of 1836, six of the crew of *Viewforth* crossed to help but found the hands 'all intoxicated'.[17] It was probably the boredom caused by the long Arctic winter that affected *Emma* in 1859–60, when she overwintered in the ice. 'We had twelve bottles of brandy… some drunk… all kept from quarrelling.'[18] Other ships were also affected: 'There has been a row on board the *Sophia*. The men has took charge of the rum puncheon.'[19]

In 1856 the Dundee vessel *Princess Charlotte* was lost in the ice. When the master decided to blow up the wreck of his ship to get warm clothes for the crew, he realised that she was lying in the wrong position. The crew worked for sixteen hours to get her into position and once the noise and fury had subsided, some of them swarmed aboard and broke into the spirit locker. Dividing three casks of rum into six portions, they sat on the ice for a thirty-hour binge. As each cask held 21 gallons, there is possibly truth in the assertions of the Hull whaler *Truelove* that some of the men were drunk, but it seems to have been *Truelove*'s men who started the fight that broke out.

It was not only the men who drank, the officers also imbibed. When the mate of *Union* of Peterhead was unwell, Trotter wrote that 'it was evident that the poor silly man had drunk too much grog.'[20] More serious was the death of Alexander Fairweather, the master of *Balaena*, in 1896. The log recorded that he 'took ill' with delirium tremens on 25 May while at sea and died six days later.[21] Fairweather was a famous

Dundee whaling name. Alexander Fairweather had sailed *Balaena* to the Antarctic in the 1892 expedition. His brother James, short, stocky and with a neatly pointed beard, had been master of *Aurora* in the Arctic during the 1880s, and at 63 years old, commanded the exploring ship *Discovery* in the hunt for Shackleton in 1916. He lived in Newport in Fife, hard by the Firth of Tay.

Greenlandmen, however, were not alone in succumbing to the pleasures of drink. An estimated 40% of deaths in the Royal Navy between 1793 and 1815 were caused by accidents, and drink was a contributory factor in most. In 1840 Captain Mills of the Dundee, Perth and London Shipping Company was dismissed for persistent drunkenness.'[22] Another Dundee Company, the Dundee Clipper Line, had trouble with drunken seamen in 1892 when there was a fight on board their barque *Arthurstone* in San Francisco. When the crew were refused shore leave, they took their revenge by killing Captain Adam's pet canary. The captain stopped all shore leave, but five men disobeyed orders and left the ship, returning drunk and truculent. They stabbed the mate and assaulted Captain Adam with an iron bar. Seamen from the Leith smacks had a similar reputation for drunken violence when in London. The Wapping Agent for the London and Leith Company spoke of the boys and protected men drinking, quarrelling with local girls and 'insulting every respectable man or woman that passes'.[23]

When the Greenlandmen returned to Dundee they were sailing into a city that had the reputation of being the most drunken in the Empire. Partly that was because the water from the city wells was so polluted that it was safer to drink beer. Although the opening of the Lintrathen Reservoir in the 1870s helped alleviate that problem, the heavy drinking continued. By 1888 it was estimated that Dundee, with 447 officially licensed premises and an unknown number of illegal drinking dens, had the highest percentage of pubs to people in Scotland. With their wages loose in their pockets and a terrible thirst in their throats, seamen swarmed to the taverns of the Overgate, to drink and brawl with the locals. Many did not get that far, but staggered into the pubs of Dock Street, a place shunned by respectable people for its bloodstained doorways and the casualties of the frequent bottle fights. In Dundee, however, the Greenlandmen were well matched in drink by the mill girls. In 1887, of the 201 cases of drunkenness that came before the court, 101 were women.

Despite the undoubted trouble drink could create, there were compensations. Ship masters and owners realised that, without rum, their crews would not function so effectively, so that in 1822 one whaling ship owner applied for a puncheon and a half of rum to be issued duty-free to his vessels.[24] No doubt he would have agreed with the surgeon of *Samuel* of Hull who believed that rum prevented murmuring and discontent among English sailors.[25] Rum was also seen as having beneficial qualities. Margaret Penny mentioned that when a boatload of seamen arrived back at the ship after rowing in sub-zero temperatures they 'soon forgot their hardship in a glass of grog'.[26] Toward the end of the century, when Britain was gripped by temperance debates and the Mission for Deep Sea Fishermen was hounding the spirit copers off the sea, the *Dundee Yearbook* mentioned that the Dundee whaling fleet no longer took alcohol to sea.[27] The slightly derogatory nickname of Captain Thomas Robertson, Coffee Tam, indicates that as late as 1896 the whaling community did not all share the temperance view. Coffee Tam, of Newport on Tay, commanded *Active* during the Dundee Antarctic Expedition.

Given the tensions of dozens of men crowded into a cramped space, it was perhaps inevitable that, with or without alcohol, some crews experienced trouble. When *Emma* overwintered in the Arctic, Albert Whitehouse wrote of the tension: 'Midnight, mutiny on board, all hands falling out on the half deck'.[28] There were quarrels over pastimes such as 'cards and chequers. We ended the night with a fight.'[29] Sometimes a member of the crew squabbled with an officer: 'second mate and one of the 'prentices been fighting.'[30] *Emma* was not unique; officers and men also fought on *Thomas,* and once the Master intervened to stop a fight between 'our second mate and a seaman.'[31] Violence also troubled other whaling vessels.

During the terrible season of 1836, *Middleton* was trapped in the ice off Baffin Island. Whaling ships only carried provisions for a voyage of a few months, with little spare, so the Master ordered that the food should be rationed. Almost at once the crew objected, and the tension grew so that the master considered deserting his ship. By ordering rationing, the master was acting in the best interest of the ship, but when the captain of an Aberdeen vessel intended to eat the 'cook's [pet] duck' the crew took offence 'as the duck was a great favourite.'[32] Even William Penny, one of the most successful of the Aberdeen whaling masters, occasionally had to deal with a restless crew. In one instance some of the crew showed their dislike of the carpenter by 'putting disagreeable things in his food' so that Penny 'had all hands called on deck to reprove them.'[33] As in the case of *Middleton* and *Emma,* Penny's ship had been icebound for some time. Boredom and frustration appear to have been the cause of much of the discontent on board whaling ships.

119

Nevertheless, the majority of voyages were probably free from any major trouble. There would be the usual minor frictions that occur in any small community, but most mentions of the crew in the logbook were purely nominal. In the 1834 log of *Dorothy*, references to the crew consist of phrases such as 'called all hands to make Sail.'[34] This log, like those of *Chieftain* and *North Pole*, are more probably typical of whaling voyages than the more spectacular stories of drunkenness and violence that the press and folklore highlighted. One entry in the logbook of *North Pole* probably typifies most voyages when it says 'Pepol Engaged varriously'.[35] As long as the people were engaged, variously or otherwise, and the drinking was moderate, the whaling ships would be tolerably trouble-free. It was boredom or drink, or a combination on both, that created friction on board.

13

RELIGION AND SUPERSTITION

'Superstition is godless religion, devout impiety'
Joseph Hall: Of the Superstitious

*'God always exists where there is a danger that makes
strong men helpless'*
Terence Wise

If drink and the sea are often linked, then in the past superstition and the sea were almost synonymous. It is difficult to imagine, in this twenty-first century of technology and progress, exactly how much the eighteenth and nineteenth century seamen were at the mercy of nature. No matter how skilled they were as mariners, every time they left the harbour they were dependent on wind and weather. In such conditions, when they could be cut off from the land for weeks or months at a time, it must have been tempting to look for signs and portents in everyday events.

Seamen became notorious for their superstitions, some of which possibly had a rational foundation. Seamen may well have worn gold ear-rings to prevent rheumatism, and also as a protection against drowning, but gold ear-rings would also pay for a dignified burial if the body of a seaman was washed up on shore. The cattle drovers who traversed the lonely paths between the Highlands and Norfolk wore a silver belt buckle for exactly the same reason.

The superstition that banned women from going to sea is perhaps less easy to clarify. It was in the nature of their work that deep-water sailors did not spend much time with their women, so it must have been extremely difficult to maintain a stable relationship with a woman who was only seen for, at best, a few weeks every year. Many seamen would only know the women of the dockside taverns and brothels, and would return to sea carrying disease, which would tend to give a negative impression of womankind. The words of an American whaling song carry this message:

> Our jolly salts have sorry faults
> Concealed beneath their breeches

> They bring disease from overseas
> The scurvy sons-of-bitches.

There is another possible reason. The mediaeval and early modern seaman held great store by the sea god, who was personified as Neptune. There is no doubt that the sea god was feared, for old-time seamen used to offer him sacrifices and incantations at times of bad weather. In an appeal to the god's chivalry, seamen feminised their vessels, calling them 'she'. However, it became unlucky to allow a female on board, as the ship would resent the competition and would retaliate against the crew. However, it is unlikely that the average Greenlandman could trace the origin of his superstition back to its origin; they just knew that it was bad luck to bring a woman on board. Even a captain's wife could be affected, as when Mrs William Scoresby refused to sail for fear of a woman bringing bad luck to the ship.[1] Having said that, at least a dozen whaling masters are recorded as taking their wives to sea with them. No doubt there were others.

After the eighteenth century age of reason, the nineteenth century brought Romanticism, emotion and resurgence in Christianity. Waves of revivalism lashed the nation, new churches were founded and religion became a topic of earnest debate. There were equally intense discussions about the demise of Christianity as people huddled into the expanding industrial urban centres, further from the paternal care of rural landowners and the pastoral scrutiny of ministers. Whaling vessels mirrored these nineteenth century religious disputes, with a contrast between the sincerely Christian, the indifferent, the superstitious and the frankly ignorant.

When Alexander Alison was in Shields he was singled out for conversion:

> An exciseman, as is the custom in all outward bound ships, came on board, to protect the Ships Stores. One day he took me by the Arm, and said My Boy, I have marked something in your looks that tells me that you are different to all the other boys in the ship. He asked me whether I was not religiously disposed, and whether I did not fear God—and many other questions of a similar character. He had heard me like the rest swear and take God's name in vain, he asked me if I had a Bible, and if I read it. He begged of me to leave of swearing, to read my Bible to pray to God… he was amongst the first persons who ever spoke to me personally about my soul, and God, all my information was derived

from hearing, and reading the Bible... I promised to swear
no more till I returned, and that I should read my Bible.

Alison proved to be a particularly devout and strong-willed boy. He
commented that he had: 'much to put up with during the passage out
from the men and my fellow apprentices—abuse and bad treatment all
to provoke me to swear but their Efforts proved useless and vain as far as
that went.' Others of the Greenlandmen needed help with their religion, although the crew of *Thomas* appeared particularly God-fearing.
Wanless wrote that when there were 'religious tracts dealt out... the
watch diligently read them'.[2] A few days later he wrote that 'eight Testaments... and 4 Bibles' were sold 'if we had double the number they
would have all gone.'[3] If anything, *Enterprise* of Fraserburgh was even
more religious, with the sale of '30 bibles and testaments.'[4] Even on
Emma, where there had been trouble with the crew, Whitehouse commented that the men visited chapel and had 'prayers every Sundays.'[5]
Margaret Penny seems to have been particularly impressed with the devotion of her husband's crew, even mentioning the psalms that they
sang—'The 103 psalm & the 64 paraphrase were sung'.[6] She said that it
was usual to have divine service in the afternoon, and mentioned that
the Greenlandmen listened to the 'Word of God' with 'respect and attention'.[7] In 1836 when *Viewforth* of Kirkcaldy was trapped by ice off
Baffin Island, William Elder, the mate, held daily Scripture readings and
remarked that it was 'really pleasant to see how eager the men are for
it.'[8]

Campbell's *Nova Zembla* also appeared to have a religious crew.
'Called at 5 PM, turned out for tea then had prayers.'[9] Alexander Smith
mentioned that after tea there was an assembly 'to read ourselves a les-
son from the Book of Books, which guides us all (or ought to).'[10] The
master of Alison's ship 'was a proffesser of religion. We had Divine
Worship every Sunday, the office duty was performed by the Doctor.'[11]

Even the Reverend Mill mentioned, reluctantly, that three Greenland Captains had bought a copy each of the 'holy Catholic Church.'[12]
The religious interest lasted as late as 1903, when the crew of *Diana*
sang hymns in the 'tween deck.'[13]

Other seamen also seemed to share this interest in religion, for when
the Dundee Perth and London Shipping Company was formed in 1826,
the timetable prohibited 'sailing the company's vessels on the Lords
day.'[14] Nonetheless, there were some that doubted the sincerity of the
whaling men's religious convictions. Mrs Penny negated some of her
earlier words when she said that 'divine service always attended by the

men with great apparent sincerity'.[15] The use of the word 'apparent' may be significant. There was a lack of enthusiasm for anything religious in *Grenville Bay* despite the frequent visits of the Captain to the crew's quarters to read 'some chapters in the Bible.'[16] Thomson dwells at some length on the mockery by Greenlandmen of those few members of the crew who were religious. His messmates spoke more of spending their money on grog, a fiddler and 'a company of lewd women.'[17]

There were times, however, when even the men on Thomson's ship were eager to embrace the Lord. When *Dunscombe* sailed into a storm, the habitually blasphemous whalers pleaded with a Methodist member of the crew to pray for them. As soon as the storm had passed the pleaders dropped their cloak and in a wholly expected *volte-face* they were again 'loading him with irreligious epithets.'[18] Danger, presumably, heightened the significance of religion. When *Dundee* survived an encounter with an iceberg, the crew was 'grateful to a Merciful Providence for such a miraculous deliverance.'[19] On a similar occasion, when *Viewforth* was saved from being crushed by ice, William Elder reported 'it was unanimously proposed by the men that we should all... give thanks to that God who had so mercifuly delivered us.'[20]

Sometimes knowledge of the Bible had a negative effect. When Alexander Alison first arrived at Shields, storm-driven from Yarmouth, the owner of his vessel boarded: 'And without any preface ordered me out of the ship Instantly—and to take what few things I had and in order to pricipitate my removal—he used all the force he had.'

Alison believed that the owner 'thought I was a Jonah and that he had had no luck since I was with him'

Luck was an important factor with the Greenlandmen. Thomson wrote that the Greenlandmen were very superstitious and would try to ship with a lucky captain. He also said that all the officers were followed according to their luck, and the Greenlandmen believed that whales would come to a lucky captain. Markham mentions that the master of *Arctic* habitually carried a lucky penny, 'one of those huge coins in circulation in the reign of George III.'[21] There seemed to be an association between money and luck, perhaps because of the hopes of a prosperous voyage, for when *Balaena* sailed for the Antarctic in 1892, the older women 'put money into the crevices in our rudder head to bring us luck.'[22]

Luck ruled many aspects of the whaler's life. It was lucky to launch a boat bows-first, but unlucky to accept anything passed between the shrouds. While some beliefs were generally held, others seemed specific to a single ship. Captain Markham said that the men of *Arctic* attributed bad luck to different things, 'One day it is put down to a comb... another day it is a small pig.'[23]

Among seamen generally, Friday seems to have been an unlucky day to start a voyage, or any sort of work. When *Camperdown* turned for home, Smith wrote that a Sunday was the luckiest day of the week for sailing, adding that they had sailed on a a Friday the previous year 'which... a good few accounted for their unsuccessful voyages'.[24] Fridays were perhaps originally seen as unlucky because that was the day that Christ was crucified. Some seamen knew it as an 'Egyptian day', and shunned it, as Egyptians, like Finns, were thought to have the power of second sight. The fear of sailing on a Friday delayed the departure of *Perseverance* from Peterhead[25] and *Arctic* from Dundee.[26] Nonetheless, other days might also be unlucky. Campbell mentioned that when his captain hoped to sail from Lerwick on a Tuesday, a Shetland superstition kept them tied up until the Wednesday.[27] Fishermen and whaling men from East Lothian ports believed that Sunday was the best day for sailing, as the better the day the better the catch, but this idea does not seem to have been general in Scotland.

Alexander Smith passed his 24th birthday on board *Camperdown* and, like Thomson, seems to have looked down a little on other members of the crew. He wrote eight pages on superstitions, some of which appear to be general to many ships, others are more unusual. For instance, when *Camperdown* passed the Old Man of Hoy, Smith mentions that the 'Old Man' demanded that the crew should raise their caps 'if he wishes a prosperous voyage.'[28] Smith said that Greenlandmen believed that the fingers of St Peter made the black spot on the gills of the haddock,[29] but fishermen had a similar belief. He also observed that certain animals and birds could be used as weather omens. For instance the sighting of a porpoise or a dolphin was a good omen unless the animal jumped out of the water, which meant a storm.[30] The call of a Great Northern Diver was also a storm warning, for it heralded a southerly gale.

Other observers noted the Greenlandmen's belief in fish and bird folklore. Wanless said that some of the crew thought it a bad omen when a grey crow sat on their yard.[31] Crows, ravens and rooks were often associated with death, possibly because of folk memory with Norse warriors and gods, but probably because of their sombre colour. Burn Murdoch related that whalers believed that sailors that died were reborn as seabirds.[32] William Barron also wrote about animal superstitions of the Greenlandmen, saying that there would be poor whale hunting if a seal thrust its head from the water in front of the ship, but good hunting if the seal was astern. Horseshoes were as powerful on board ship as they were on land, being nailed to the masts in the lower decks. If the shoe did not work, it was removed, placed in the fire and returned to its correct position. On Barron's vessel it was also considered unlucky to shoot a fox and bring the body on board.[33]

While some Greenlandmen were undoubtedly devout, and others adopted Christianity when it suited them, there were a few who turned to older beliefs. There were witches and wise women in the Northern Isles, with Walter Scott mentioning Bessie Miller who could call up a favourable wind for sixpence. Perhaps it was the same woman, described as 'an old wrinkle-faced witch' who offered to tell the course of Thomson's voyage for 'saxpence and a noggin'.[34] The belief that witches had the power to raise unfavourable winds was an ancient one, which had occasioned the famous witchcraft trial at North Berwick in 1592 and was still prevalent in the nineteenth-century whaling vessels.

When *Thomas* ran into unfavourable winds, Wanless commented that some of the crew thought they were bewitched and wanted to throw the garland overboard. Another man burned an article of his own clothing, saying 'burn the bitches'.[35] The ceremony of 'burning the witch' was fairly common on whaling vessels, with a flat stick sprinkled with salt thrust through the ring of the anchor, and the salt then ignited. Salt was a substance frequently used by people who practised witchcraft. However, not only witches were burned. When *Arctic* failed to catch any whales, Captain Markham said that the men burned effigies of two men who were reputed to bring bad luck.[36] Both men had served in ships that had returned clean from previous voyages.

When *Balaena* hit calm weather in 1892, the crew tried playing the bagpipes[37] to call up a favourable wind, and when that failed they threw a black cat overboard. As a boy aboard *Perseverance* in 1885, John Murray was struck for whistling. 'Damn you,' he was told, 'don't we have enough wind now, without whistling for more?'[38] In Eastern England, home of the Hull and Whitby whalers, a woman who whistled was looked at with great disfavour:

> A whistling lass and a crowing hen
> Are good for neither gods nor men.

Sometimes there was a tangible reason for the whaler's fears. Along the West Coast of Greenland, on the rare occasions when the sea was flat calm and the weather clear, the air itself seemed to whistle to the seamen. The sound started on a high note and died away 'to a very low tone'.[39] This sound was most clearly heard in a small boat, close to the water, and seldom on deck. To the Greenlandmen, already working under the burden of many superstitions or the weight of intense religion, this strange sound was just another cross to bear.

Overall, the evidence suggests that the whalers mixed sincere religious beliefs with a broad mixture of superstition that was based on old nautical lore, ancient witchcraft and personal fears. Superstitions, of course, were never confined solely to Greenlandmen. Fishermen, from which stock many originated, held similar beliefs, and Knut Weibust in *Deep Sea Sailors* catalogues a great many superstitions from seamen of various nationalities. Even in the twenty-first century there are some people who believe that the wardroom of *Discovery* is haunted by the ghost of an angry Shackleton or by Charles Bonner, a seaman who fell from the yard. Given the greater sophistication of today's world, and the vast technological and educational advances that have occurred during the last century, Greenlandmen can hardly be blamed for grasping at any straw that might have made their lives safer.

14

WHALERS AND THE LAW

'There's never a law of god or man runs north of Fifty-Three'
Rudyard Kipling, 'The Rhyme of the Three Sealers'

After spending the summer in the Arctic, those whaling ships that were not overwintering slid south. There was still killing to be done, for the whales retreated before the encroaching ice. Barron wrote of dark nights and uncertain weather as the blubber boats cruised the coasts, thrusting into the ragged coves and indentations of Eastern Canada. The work was harder now, because the men were tired, but the whales were larger so the rewards were greater.

Only when the ice threatened to overwhelm them, or the ship was full, did the master point her bow toward Scotland. The decision to return called for nice judgement; too early and there would be less profit, too late and the ship could be caught in the ice.

The ships of the eighteenth and early nineteenth centuries returned in July or August. In 1788 *Tay* returned to Dundee on 7 July,[1] in 1789 she returned on 23 July,[2] while *Dundee* and *Success* returned from the Greenland Whale Fishery on 25 August.[3] In 1809 the dates were similar, with *Jane* and *Horn* returning on 20 July, *Estridge* on the 22nd, Rodney on the 28th and *Mary Ann*, which had sailed out late, on 9 August.[4] By 1860 the ships were returning later, with the screw steamer *Tay* reporting back to Dundee from the Davis Straits on 24 November.[5] In 1880 *Aurora* arrived as early as 28 August,[6] and eight years later *Active* returned on 22 September.[7]

Before the whaling ships could arrive in their home ports, they returned the Orcadians and Shetlanders to their home islands. If there was ever a time when the Greenlandmen earned their reputation for drunken violence, it was then. Walter Scott, a visitor to Lerwick in August 1814, commented that the crews of the nine Greenlandmen that were in harbour added 'much to the liveliness of the scene'.[8] Scott said that the thousand returning Shetland whalermen bought drink for their English messmates. The Englishmen promptly became drunk and began to riot.

128

The Reverend John Mill had little good to say about the whalers. In August 1775 he reported that the Greenlandmen broke into the Custom House to recover some smuggled gin. Mill spoke of the whalers' 'lusts and idols', and said that they 'stick at nothing for gain.'[9] The robbery appeared to have been organised by the original smugglers, who obviously believed that the whalers would act in a lawless manner. In 1789 the *Aberdeen Journal* carried a report that *Thorn*, sloop-of-war was sailing 'from Leith Roads to Bressay Sound, to protect the inhabitants of Lerwick from the ravages and insults of the Greenland whalers.'[10] Although this may seem like overkill, it must be remembered that in mainland Britain it was customary to use the army to police any major crowd. There was no regular police force to stand between the public and either full-time criminals or rioters. Where there was no army, the navy had to be used. With dozens of whaling ships expected at Lerwick, each disembarking up to fifty tough men who had experienced months of hardship in a cramped environment, it was nearly inevitable that there would be some rowdiness.

Observers compared the behaviour of Dutch fishermen with the Greenlandmen. The *Aberdeen Journal* of July 1789 printed a letter stating that the Dutch in Lerwick gave 'no manner of insults' to the townsfolk and suggested that the whalers should behave in 'such a peaceful manner.'[11] Walter Scott labelled the Dutch as 'careful, quiet and economical', and mentioned that when the Greenlandmen arrived, the Dutch retreated to their herring busses for fear of trouble. Scott, the professional novelist and establishment sheriff, related an incident where fifty whalers armed with flensing knives attacked a hundred Dutchmen and chased them into the sea. Despite his strictures, perhaps Scott's words contain a little admiration for the bravado and spirit of the Greenlandmen, in some ways so similar to the reivers of his beloved Borders.

> Here's to the Greenland tar, a fiercer guest,
> Claims a brief hour of riot, not of rest;
> Proves each wild frolic that in wine has birth
> And wakes the land with brawls and boisterous mirth.[12]

A glance at the records of Lerwick Sheriff Court reveals that the brawls and boisterous mirth were sometimes all too evident. There are numerous cases that highlight the actions of Greenlandmen, although it may be significant that the offenders appear to be mainly from English, rather than Scottish, ships. There was an interesting case in 1797 when the inhabitants of Scalloway encouraged the whalers to attack a sheriff's officer who had raised men for the navy.[13] It would seem that not only smugglers manipulated the Greenlandmen for their own ends.

Scott mentioned that Sheriff Erskine used the garrison of veterans in Fort Charlotte as a police force to control the worst excesses of the whalers. An evening patrol in Lerwick picked up any whaling man still on shore. Perhaps justice was a little arbitrary, although Scott wrote that the soldiers at Fort Charlotte stood between the whalers and the destruction of Lerwick. Scott was present when Greenlandmen from the Hull whaler *Augusta* attacked several people including George Hughson, a Lerwick constable.[14] The dispute, like so many, started with something very minor, in this case the theft of a duck, for which Hughson had arrested a Greenlandman on *Augusta*'s outward voyage the previous spring.

Greenlandmen were involved in many more incidents in Shetland. For instance in 1820 some of the crew of *Neptune* were thrown in prison for quarrelling and abusing the peace officers.[15] That same year William Harmon of the whaler *Hope* of London petitioned to be released from prison where he was placed after an alleged assault on officers of the law. Claiming that any assault was due to the effects of liquor, Harmon offered to pay a reasonable fine.[16] There were also petty cases such as the theft of a fur cap in order which was sold to buy drink.[17]

Drink seemed to be a factor in every case, and in the instances where violence spilled out beyond the whaling fraternity, the other party was invariably a figure of authority. Other sheriff court cases vary from Captain Couldry of the Hull whaler *Abram* being accused of slander and not paying his Shetland pilots[18] to a theft of bedclothes.[19]

In 1897 Greenlandmen were still apt to become boisterous. The *Shetland News* of 4 September carries an article entitled 'A Row Among Dundee Whalers', describing an incident when crewmen from *Balaena* fought amongst themselves. The article spoke of their 'deplorable' appearance, with 'blood flowing freely, and their faces bearing evidence of the hardness of each other's fists.' Two of these men were fined £1 and sent home by steamer. Another young seaman from *Balaena* was charged 5 shillings for being drunk and incapable.[20] Despite the reputation of the whalers, a search of the Commissioners of Police Records failed to confirm that the Town Council of Lerwick recruited any Special Constables to help control them. It appears that the behaviour of the native Shetlanders in the winter was worse.[21]

Once they returned from the Greenland ships, the Shetlanders, according to Scott, quietly returned home. They saved their money for dancing, drinking and singing during the long winter season. The

Statistical Account of Scotland 1791–1799 claimed that Shetlanders who sailed with the whalers earned high wages but learned bad habits and wasted their money.[22] Orkney men who returned from the whaling also apparently spent their wages 'in idleness, and often in dissipation'.[23]

If the departure of a whaling ship was emotional, so too was the homecoming, with each port having similar, but still unique, memories. Fraserburgh is barely mentioned as a sealing and whaling port, yet there was a lively, if short lasting, industry from the 'Broch' in the 1850s. There were six ships in total, the first being the 297-ton *Melinka*, commanded by Captain John Stephen. In 1852 *Melinka* was so successful that her crew spoke of stores being thrown over the side to make room for her cargo. There was also *Alexander Harvey*, commanded by Captain Alexander Stephen, the 177-ton *Vulcan*, commanded by Captain Alexander, and the 130-ton *Sovereign,* commanded by Captain Burnett. Bad weather drove *Fortuna* ashore at Fraserburgh, so a Mr Oliphant bought her and renamed her *Lord Saltoun*. Captain John 'Jottie' Stephen commanded her. Lastly there was *Enterprise*, a ship that had a reputation for bad luck and bad catches when she sailed from Peterhead, but at 349 tons she was the largest in the Fraserburgh fleet.

Like the Dundee whalers, Fraserburgh Greenlandmen created a garland from ribbons and wire, but unlike the Dundee men they waited until the ship was returning from their voyage before raising it midway between the mainmast and foremast. When the ship returned to port, and the people crushed into the Castle Green to cheer them, the younger seamen ranged themselves, starboard and port watch, each on their own side of the vessel. At a signal from the master, they raced up the ratlines to seize the garland, with the winner becoming something of a celebrity in the town.

Alexander Trotter said that when *Enterprise* returned to Fraserburgh the men did not wait for leave before going ashore to see their womenfolk and to get drunk.[24] He also wrote of a mass fight between members of the crew,[25] but he held himself aloof. Even after a voyage to the Arctic, he felt he was of a different breed to the Greenlandmen. *Enterprise* retained her reputation as an unlucky ship to the end, being lost in Davis Straits on her fifth trip; her crew was all rescued.

However, many sailors behaved badly after returning from the sea. After the herring season, Anstruther was the scene of drunken brawls by fishermen, and Solway-born Captain William Neilson of *Acamas* mentioned the drunken behaviour of British seamen in South America. In July 1833 there was a minor riot on board the steamship *Dundee* while in Dundee harbour.[26] Seamen tended to settle quarrels on shore, where officers would not interfere.

The Dundee men would be glad to return, hailing the gothic Royal Arch at Shore Terrace, with its clock and towers, as an old friend. Perhaps the arch was raised for the visit of Queen Victoria, but to the Greenlandmen this was the 'Gateway to Nowhere' or the 'Pigeon's Palace'.

There were aspects to the return other than drink and violence. Edmund Charlton, a medical student from Newcastle, found whalers returning to Leith 'a merry careless set',[27] but the arrival was often less pleasant. When *Dee* returned to Aberdeen after being trapped in the ice for a winter, the *Aberdeen Herald* wrote of 'weeping widows' and the grief of parents and friends. There was also great joy from those whose men had survived,[28] with the *Dundee Advertiser* mentioning wives fainting in their arms of their husbands.[29] Even a single death was a tragedy to the relatives involved. In 1868 John McDonald, surgeon of *Tay*, died on the voyage. When the ship passed Broughty Ferry on her return, one of the crew rowed ashore to ask the seamen's missionary to break the news to McDonald's wife.[30]

Despite the evidence of quarrels on some other vessels, the men on board *Dorothy* seemed to trust each other, for the University of Dundee Archives holds a letter signed by six men authorising one David Inglis to collect all their oil money.[31] As the total value exceeded £118, the letter shows their trust in Inglis, and his honesty.

In Fraserburgh, the owners hired watchmen to guard whatever stores of duty-free tobacco and spirits remained on board the whaling ships when they lay in harbour over the winter. One, Andy Greig, was a retired carpenter. When he caught some of the bold Broch youngsters slipping on board, he would dangle them by their feet over the side of the ship and threaten to let them fall. Even so, he was not totally successful, for many a Greenlandman succeeded in smuggling a 'stick' of tobacco ashore and distributing it to his sons, nephews and neighbours. Local youths also found illegal use for the whaling boats. Upturned for the winter, they made splendid shelter for boys playing truant from school. The watchmen had other functions, for in October 1827 the Montrose Union Whale Fishing Company advertised a twenty-guinea reward for information to help discover who had stolen ninety fathoms of towline.[32]

The Customs records at Dundee also contain numerous instances of small-scale smuggling. On the return of *Dorothy* to Dundee in October 1829, Thomas Davidson, the second mate, who had responsibility for the ship's stores, was caught attempting to smuggle six gallons of rum ashore to his lodgings.[33] The Collector of Customs recommended that, as it was Davidson's first offence and he had intended the rum for his private use, a fine would be sufficient punishment.[34] The Magistrates of Dundee were not so merciful and sentenced Davidson to three weeks in jail while arrangements were made for him to be sent on board a Royal Naval man of war. This ruling seems to have been overruled by the Customs in London, for after his incarceration Davidson was released without being forced into the Navy.[35] Davidson was lucky: that same year a Dundee surgeon charged the magistrates 2s. 6d. for examining a seaman named Alexander Robertson and declaring him fit to serve in the Navy.[36]

It had long been the practice for convicted smugglers to be sentenced into the Navy. In 1804 the Lords of the Admiralty ordered that any fisherman found smuggling would be 'impressed notwithstanding any protections with which they might be furnished'. They were to be sent to the 'Sea Fencible Service' and would not be discharged 'on any pretence'. If smuggling was known to have taken place in any particular village, all the fishermen were liable to impressment unless they delivered up the guilty persons.[37] In 1823 the Customhouse in Edinburgh directed that whenever a convicted smuggler was sent on board 'any of His Majesty's Ship's of War in order to be impressed', the commander of the ship was to be given an attested copy of the conviction.[38] The press gang may have ceased scouring the seaports after 1815, but impressment continued as a threat to any seaman who attempted to smuggle.

Davidson's case was referred to as late as 1835, when some deal timber with an excise duty of £8 3s. was seized on *Dorothy*, but the owners stated that second mate Thomas Davidson no longer worked for the company.[39] While the mate of *Dorothy* was being convicted of smuggling, the master was also in trouble. Captain Thomas Davidson was fined £10 for having no cargo manifest for the voyage.[40] With the fine paid, no further proceedings were taken, save that he was fined 5 shillings for having brought a box of cigars, 'segars', without paying duty.[41]

Fishermen were often involved with smuggling, and, in 1854, when George Murray, Acting Tidesman at Broughty Ferry, saw a fishing boat push off from the shore to meet the whaling ship *Heroine* off the Lights of Tay, he became suspicious. As the tide was low, Murray walked across the exposed sands to watch, until the flood tide forced him back onto land. Together with the Custom's boat crew Murray rummaged the fishing boat when it returned at eleven at night, and found quantities of tobacco, which he seized, along with the boat.[42] James Lorimer, a

Broughty Ferry fisherman, was arrested, but the owner of the boat, Alexander Gall, protested that he had no knowledge of the smuggling and asked for his boat back. While Lorimer was fined £3 10s., the boat was eventually released.[43]

James Sturrock, master of *Alexander*, found himself in trouble the following year when William Gilchrist, tide-surveyor at Broughty Ferry, rummaged his vessel on her return from the Davis Straits. Over four pounds of tobacco were found, some in a chamber pot in Sturrock's cabin, with over 14 pounds of tea in a pillow case in his sea berth and 20 pounds of refined sugar in the bed. There were also seven bottles of port, six of sherry and three of brandy around the water closet.[44] Not surprisingly, Sturrock was arrested, and the ship placed in detention.[45] On being fined £100, plus £3 11d. in expenses, by Provost Rough of Dundee,[46] Sturrock appealed, on the grounds that in his eleven years in command of *Alexander* he had never broken any of the Custom laws.[47] On a letter of support from Mr Willingale, the Collector at Dundee, the sentence was reduced to a £50 fine, with a further £5 for the release of *Alexander*.[48] Despite the owners' protest that they had not been involved in the smuggling, the Lords of the Customs insisted that the release fine be paid. The £5, together with one third of Captain Sturrock's £50 fine, was paid to the Customs officers who made the discovery.[49]

Alexander was again in trouble when she returned from the Davis Straits four years later, this time under Captain Nicol. The rummaging officers found that Robert Lonie, the mate, and a seaman named James Pettygrew had hidden tobacco. There were also small quantities of tobacco and tea hidden between decks. Having found the contraband, Mr Smith, the tide-surveyor, was unsure how to proceed, as 37 of the 47 crew had already left the ship. He seized *Alexander* and hinted that the oil money, which could not be paid until the blubber had been melted down, should be withheld. More generous, the Lords of Customs ordered that the ship be released on payment of a £1 fine.[50]

Earlier that year the Customs had rummaged *Narwhal* on her return from the Greenland seal fishery. They seized tobacco from Robert Ogston, mate, tea from Charles Marshall, harpooner, and tea and tobacco from Thomas Webster, spectioneer.[51] Cases such as these were just the day-to-day routine of the Customs; they compare to people returning from the continent with an extra bottle of duty-free hidden in their suitcase.

Taken in context, there is no doubt that the Greenlandmen could be obstreperous while in drink, but no more than most seamen. It was unfortunate for the islanders of Shetland and Orkney that so many whalers arrived at the same time, in a small community that lacked the law enforcement capabilities to deal with trouble. Nonetheless, the islands probably benefited more from the extra employment created by the Greenland ships, and by the money spent in taverns and on ships' stores. Compared to the number of vessels employed in the whaling trade, the number of arrests for even small-scale smuggling are small. Overall, the whaling men do not seem to have been any worse than other seamen when they arrived back home, and their wives, at least, would have been pleased to see them.

15

BACK HOME

'It'll be bricht both day and nicht when the Greenland lads come hame
Wi a ship that's fu' o' oil my lads, and money to our name'
The Bonny Ship *The Diamond*

When the Greenlandmen celebrated in the dockside taverns, exchanged fisticuffs with each other or were united with their families, and tide-surveyors rummaged through the newly arrived ships, the work had not finished. The arrival of the whaling vessels in Dundee was only another stage in the process for ship owners, shipmasters and the customs staff. Until the bounty system ended in 1824, bounty certificates had to be completed and sent away so that the money could be paid. The licence that had been issued for the vessel to proceed on her voyage was sent to their Honours in Edinburgh, together with a certificate stating that the ship had returned, and the oath of the Master that all the crew had been employed in the whale fishery. The Master had to add particulars of any person who had left the vessel, such as members of the crew who had returned home at Shetland. The Master and mate also had to supply a certificate of the cargo and an extract of the logbook from the time the ship left the Tay until her return.[1] Although everything was sworn to by oath, a saying of the time, 'that's worth as much as a Customs oath' reveals the perceived veracity of the procedure.

Occasionally, as the whaling ships probed further afield in their search for prey, the Customs officers were confused. When *Eliza Swan* of Montrose hunted in the Davis Straits in 1798, officials were unsure whether to charge her tonnage duty of 6d. a ton, as was charged for the Greenland Sea and Southern Whale Fishery, or the 1 shilling charged on vessels that traded in America.[2]

On their return, the whaling ships often needed to be repaired and refitted. For instance in 1810, *Friendship* was fitted with a new fore-mast,[3] and when *Arctic* returned in December 1885 she was reported as being 'in a leaking condition', so had be placed in dock even before her cargo was discharged. Such stores as remained on board were removed to the Queen's Warehouse to enable the ordinary patrol to guard *Arctic*.[4]

The crews were also mustered and disbanded, which until 1821 was a duty of the Collector and Comptroller, and thereafter fell to other officers.[5]

Upon arrival the catches were examined and weighed by the Customs staff. In the early days of the whaling industry it seems that the casks were measured by weight, but, following the practice in Leith, from around 1787 the contents were gauged by taking the dimensions of the cask and its contents.[6] At the beginning of the nineteenth century the officers used callipers, but in 1814 asked to use measuring rods instead.[7] The officers would demand explanations for any discrepancies that they found. In 1811 Adam Christopher, master of *Estridge*, was asked to explain why he was two casks short, and said that one cask was staved in the hold and another burst while it was being hoisted out of the hold when the ship was being discharged.[8] When a number of vessels arrived together the Customs officers were often hard-pressed to watch and process them all. In 1814 the Dundee Collector begged for the assistance of six additional tidesmen from another port. His eleven men could not cope with the eight whaling ships that were in the harbour, the two Baltic vessels already unloading and the five more that were expected.[9] A similar situation occurred in October 1821, when fifteen vessels were waiting in the harbour and roadstead.[10]

It was the practice in Dundee for the casks of blubber to be loaded in barges and floated to the boiling houses, rather than be landed on the quay and carted round by land. This procedure meant that the large whaling vessels did not have to come alongside the quay, which was thus freed for other vessels. It also saved the large casks, each containing up to 300 gallons, from being laboriously transported through the narrow alleys around Dundee's unmodernised docks, which would certainly create congestion, particularly if the carts broke down under the weight. In the eighteenth century some Dundee whaling ships discharged their cargo on the beach to the east of the harbour. In 1811 David Brown headed a contingent of owners who requested that they return to this practice. Their Honours in Edinburgh were not so enthusiastic, replying that cargoes could only be landed on the beach in 'cases of obvious necessity'.[11]

By that date there were four copper boilers in Dundee, with two landwaiters gauging the casks that lay either on the quay or in the mud.[12] In 1824 the duty on whale oil and blubber dropped to such an extent that it was no longer worth the Custom Officer's time to gauge the casks individually. Instead the Collector suggested that the casks be unloaded and the Tidesman arrange them in order of size, from the great 400-gallon casks to the smaller 20-gallon size. The landwaiters would then gauge one cask of each size, presuming each cask to be full.[13] The casks were passed at a standard calculation of 126 gallons for a pipe, and 63 for a hogshead. However, Mr J. Herries, a secretary to the Lords Commissioners of the Treasury, warned the Customs Officers to ensure that there was no 'fraudulent introduction of other articles' in the casks.[14]

When the ships arrived at Dundee, a tidesman would take charge of the discharge of her blubber, depending on the availability of the boiler house. The Customhouse calculated that if the importers worked regularly, it would take twenty-two days to unload. After that time they expected the ship owners to pay the wages of the tidesman at 3 shillings a day.[15] There were occasions when whaling ship owners protested that they should not pay the excess amount. For instance, *Thomas* began to discharge her cargo on 7 November 1827, but did not complete the task until 2 January, making 62 days. Rather than working steadily, the owners had only landed a small amount of blubber at a time, as the boilers could not hold the entire cargo. The Dundee Union Whale Fishing Company, who owned *Thomas*, petitioned that they should not pay the tidesman's wages.[16]

There was an occasional discrepancy in the records, as in 1802 when Robert Webster, master of *Estridge*, claimed to have 182 casks, containing 107 tons of blubber, and Alexander Black, the land-surveyor, calculated only 179 casks. Webster claimed that the three-cask difference of three tons and 216 gallons of blubber arose from a simple mistake when the casks were stowed. Black did not believe there was any attempt to defraud the customs, as the tidesmen never left *Estridge* during the unloading. Nevertheless he withheld the bounty payment pending their Honours' decision.[17]

While in Dundee the boiling house did not seem to have any other name, in Kirkcaldy the boiling house became known as the 'naphtha shed'. This building was situated at the western edge of the inner dock at Dysart, with the blubber stored on the upper of the two floors and the actual boiling taking place at ground level.

Not every Dundee tidesman was devoted to his duty. In 1833 Robert Steven, a First Class tidesman who had come from Campbeltown to Dundee ten years previously, left his post on board *Heroine*. Steven pleaded that as it was common practice for one tidesman to supervise the unloading of several whalers, he did not think his absence for a short while would matter.[18] Their Lordships, however, suggested that he should be removed to another port.

In the beginning of the nineteenth century, the whaling ships were not idle in the winter months. Once they had unloaded their whalebone and blubber they sailed on conventional trading voyages. For instance in 1808 the whaling ship *Horn*, under William Adamson, sailed for Quebec.[19] She had already been licensed to carry arms in the whaling trade, and renewed her licence to cross the Atlantic.[20] That same year *Mary Ann* and *Advice* sailed for Merremachie in North America. The same masters, William Duchars and James Webster, had commanded the vessels on their whaling voyages.[21] Sometimes it seemed that trading between whaling voyages was not a good idea, for her winter voyage made *Mary Ann* late for the 1809 whaling season.[22] Her owner must have considered the profits worth the delay, for *Mary Ann* voyaged to Charlotte Town on her return from the whaling, while *Estridge* sailed to New Brunswick, and *Rodney* to Holmstade in Sweden.[23] *Horn*, commanded again by William Adamson, brought back a cargo of timber from Quebec.[24] In 1814, *Calypso* and *Advice* returned from the whaling and sailed immediately to Riga, coming back to Dundee in December.[25] Not only Dundee whalers worked over the winter, in August 1810 *Eliza Swan* of Montrose voyaged to St John's.[26]

By the last decades of the century, Dundee whalers were no longer used for trading voyages. Rather than four or five month voyages to the Greenland Sea, they were leaving Dundee in January and not returning until October or November, when they were unloaded, dismantled and laid up for the winter.[27] Custom officers supervised the unloading of the blubber from the massive iron tanks that had replaced the casks. Usually several of the whaling vessels arrived at the same time, and some vessels had to wait for weeks until the last of their blubber was transferred to the boiling yards.

At the beginning of the nineteenth century, whale fins were also valued, paying around 1s. 9d. duty per hundredweight.[28] As weight was an important factor, the fins were cleaned of any dirt and hair that might add to their dutiable value.[29] The whalebone was also cleaned on arrival. In 1830 Elizabeth Hunter was paid £3 5s. 3d. for cleaning 29 hundredweight of bone. She signed a receipt for the money with a cross.[30]

It was when the whaling ships returned to port that the Customs officers checked the logbooks to ensure that all the bounty regulations had been adhered to. These logbooks are fascinating documents, giving every change of course during the voyage, with bearings and weather reports, and occasional comments about the progress of the fishing. Many of the masters decorated the margins with the drawing of a whale's tail when the hunting was successful. The Scottish Fisheries Museum at Anstruther has such a logbook on display. However, the Custom officers were more interested in accuracy than artwork, so when William Valentine, master of *Horn* submitted a logbook where the tally of whales disagreed with a report originally made, he was asked to explain the difference.[31]

To claim the bounty, logbooks had to report when the vessel had been in sight of land, giving details of what land it was, the bearings from, and distances to the land as well as the soundings taken. They also had to record when any whale or other creature was captured.[32] In 1805 Alexander Young, junior, of the Montrose whaler *Eliza Swan*, was challenged that his logbook did not include soundings and latitudes where his whales were caught. Young explained that it was his first voyage in true command of the vessel, as hitherto his father had been there to supervise. He also said that his crew had only caught seven of the nine fish, with the other two being found dead, while he could not take observations owing to lack of sun, or because he was busy out of the ship and in a boat at the time.[33]

The master of *Eliza Swan* was again in trouble in 1809, when he failed to take bearings when in sight of land on the homeward voyage. He said that he thought there was no need as the pilot was on board.[34] Other Montrose whalers were just as guilty, for in 1814 the master of *London* failed to take bearings when in sight of various places, such as Johnshaven, Fair Isle and Spitzbergen.[35]

Dundee whalers were equally capable of omission. For example, in 1807 Robert Webster, master of *Estridge*, was also taken to account for deficiencies in his logbook. The course of his voyage can nearly be traced by the places he failed to take soundings. On 4 April he was off Cape Elizabeth on the Islands of Good Fortune; on the 13th he found a dead whale and six days later he killed one whale and three seals. *Estridge* was off Old Greenland at 67 degrees north on 12 May, and two days later was south of the Western Isles at 68.36 north, but failed to take soundings. She steered to the south east of the Whale Fish Isles the next day, still without taking soundings, and on the 20th was four miles off Disco Island, without soundings, observations or bearings being taken. On 5 June there were no soundings taken when *Estridge* was eight miles west of Ice Hook, nor were soundings taken when she was south west of North Hook on the 13th. By the 21st *Estridge* was south west of Black

Hook at 71.26 north, but still without soundings, and on the 25th she was back off Disco.[36]

Captain Robert Webster claimed that without the sun he could not take observations, but he gave no reason for not taking soundings. That same season Captain James Webster of *Advice* had a similar catalogue of omissions, but gave more detailed excuses. His reasons for not taking soundings include 4 April 1807: 'no opportunity for Soundings as they were beating to Windward Thro' Bay Ice'; 15 May: 'surrounded by loose ice and ice bergs'; 19 May: 'employed in killing a fish and a great deal of ice round them'.[37] Perhaps the Customs clerks, as they read these entries, could compare their offices with the bleak life up in the high latitudes and allow some license to the Greenlandmen.

There was little charity shown when the Collector knocked on the door of James Ireland, master of *Rodney,* and asked him why he had failed to take soundings when his ship was in sight of Greenland on 12 June 1807. Ireland replied that none of the sounding lines would be long enough to touch bottom, as *Rodney* was between 40 and 50 miles off the land.[38]

Even when the bounty ended, the pressure on the whaling masters was not relaxed. In 1826 there was a clutch of complaints that whaling masters were failing to produce manifests of their cargoes. All nine of the Dundee ships claimed that they saw no need to hand in a manifest as they continued to keep a logbook.[39] The Customhouse in Edinburgh was not sympathetic, declaring that the Leith whalers regularly produced manifests. Although there was no action taken that year, the Collector at Dundee was directed to make sure their whaling masters did likewise in future.[40] There were also pilot dues[41] to erode the profits of the ship-owners, but as the entrance of the Tay was notoriously tricky, with shifting sandbanks, perhaps they thought that was money well spent.

Another source of friction arose later in the century, when ships were making two voyages a year. Vessels that carried cargo were obliged to pay lighthouse dues as they passed out of the Tay, but many of the whaling ships claimed that when they sailed outward they were in ballast. There do not seem to have been any disputes early in the century, with the Minute Books of the Tay Whale Fishing Company recording light dues being paid in 1830,[42] but attitudes seemed to have altered.

When *Polynia* returned from Greenland in April 1872, her master claimed that she had no need to pay the light dues of £5 19s. 8d. as she was in ballast. Her entire trip had only resulted in a catch of 13 or 14 seals.[43] As seal catches from Greenland diminished, more vessels returned with the same claim. In 1873 *Polynia, Intrepid, Ravenscraig* and *Tay* all had light catches from between 5 and 47 sealskins.[44] Later that year their Honours ruled that any vessel 'with even a thimbleful of oil' had to pay light dues.[45]

When the last of the whaling vessels arrived in Dundee, the owners calculated the catch and pored over their profits. The results of the 1872 season, when eleven Dundee vessels were active, will serve as an example. The ships, together with their masters and catches were:

Arctic: Captain Adams, 8000 seals, 80 tons of oil; 15 whales, 210 tons of blubber, 13 tons whalebone.

Erik: Captain John Walker, 7000 seals, 70 tons of oil; 5 whales, 70 tons of blubber, 3 tons of whalebone.

Esquimaux: Captain Yule, 5300 seals, 55 tons of oil; 12 whales, 95 tons of blubber, 5.5 tons whalebone.

Narwhal: Captain McLennan, 4400 seals, 40 tons of oil; 6 whales, 80 tons of blubber, 4.5 tons of whalebone.

Ravenscraig: Captain Allan, 3700 seals, 40 tons of oil; 10 whales, 90 tons of blubber, 4 tons of whalebone.

Camperdown: Captain Gravill, 3200 seals, 39 tons of oil; 25 whales, 60 tons of blubber, 7 tons of whalebone.

Tay: Captain Greig, 3442 seals, 35 tons of oil; 7 whales, 70 tons of blubber, 3 tons of whalebone.

Intrepid: Captain Souter, 2764 seals, 32 tons of oil; 16 whales, 150 tons of blubber, 9.5 tons whalebone.

Diana: Captain Kilgour, 1400 seals, 23 tons of oil.

Victor: Captain Edwards, 1402 seals, 15 tons of oil; 8 whales, 70 tons of blubber, 3.5 tons of whalebone.

Polynia: Captain William Walker, 13 seals; 1 whale, 15 tons of blubber, 1 ton of whalebone.

That year seal oil sold at £39 a ton, making a total of £16,731 for all the ships. The sale of sealskins, at 4s. 6d. each, made £9139 14s. 6d., so the sealing voyages grossed £25, 870 14s. 6d. for the Dundee fleet. Without *Diana*'s presence there were only ten vessels at the whale fishing, but with whalebone at £500, the total amounted to £27,000, with another £42,420 for the oil. The total gross profit from the whaling fleet was £69,420, so added to the sealing, brought in £95,290 14s. 6d.[46] After reviewing their books, and paying their expenses, the shareholders pocketed the profits.

When they had spent much of their pay on carousing, the sore-headed Greenlandmen would roll home to their wives, while the ship masters, ship owners and custom officers disputed exactly how much money had been made. The ships would lie in dock, forlorn in the dreich drizzle of a Scottish winter, and Dundee would continue with her normal routine. The last Dundee whaler sailed to the Arctic in 1913, and in 1920 the last Scottish Arctic whaling company finally closed its books. It had been a long, arduous voyage, marked by great bravery and terrible tragedy, but although it is the ships and whaling masters that have been remembered, it was the hard-drinking, strangely sentimental Greenlandmen who did the actual work. Without them, there would have been no industry.

L' ENVOI

'Having done what men could, they suffered what men must'
Edith Hamilton

Whaling did not end when the last Dundee ship returned from the north. On the contrary, it entered an even more intensive period. If Arctic whaling was no longer profitable, the Antarctic became a new killing ground. Naturally there were Scots involved, from ports without a tradition of whale hunting as well as from the old blubber ports of Leith, Dundee and Lerwick, but if the blood and danger were the same, the rules and techniques had changed. Christian Salvesen may have been based in Leith, but his methods were as Scandinavian as his name. It was in 1908 that Christian Salvesen opened his whaling station in South Georgia, and he remained there until British whaling ceased.

In 1860, when Dundee men hunted with harpoon and small boats, the Norwegian Sven Foyn put the finishing touches to a harpoon that carried a bomb in its nose. He patented his weapon on Christmas Eve, and wrote 'I thank thee O Lord. Thou alone hast done all' in his diary. The Lord is often blamed for the blood-thirst of humanity. It was a German named Hartmann who invented a boiler that extracted sufficient glycerine from dead horses to make high explosive, but a Finn named Nils Kvaerner who converted the boiler into a pressure cooker that could produce whale oil. The old try-works with their copper boilers, which had caused so much worry to the Customs officers in Dundee, were now obsolete. In 1903 a floating factory ship joined the Scandinavian arsenal, and in 1925 came a factory ship with a ramp in her stern up which whales could be hauled using the *Hval Kla*, or grab. There was no longer a need for spurred boots as when the Greenlandmen flensed the ship just above the lunging waves.

With Norwegian ingenuity, whaling was no longer an adventure, it became mechanised slaughter. Foyn's harpoon gun mounted on fast whale-catchers meant that the whalers could catch blue whales that had been able to swim faster than the Dundee blubber boats. Whale oil was no longer needed for fuel, but the whales were caught, slaughtered and minced before being processed into food and margarine. The numbers butchered annually ran into the tens of thousands, until the international community cried 'Enough!' and allowed a semblance of peace to settle on the chilly seas. The last British whaler killed her last whale in 1963.

At present it seems unlikely that commercial whale hunting will return to international respectability, but public opinion is fickle. No doubt, if the dictates of fashion or economics require the produce of the whale, the hunter-killers will again slide out from the ports of the world, ready to hunt the whale.

And how will the ghosts of the Greenlandmen react? They will probably look up from behind the bottle of rum where they have rested for so many decades, and be thankful that their days of hunting are past.

APPENDIX
Selected Crew Lists of Dundee Whalers

Estridge, 1808 season, 312 tons; Adam Christopher, Master

Harpooners: Andrew Elphinston, John Fife, James Mackay, Alexander Fenton, Robert Barclay, James Watt.

Line managers: Thomas Nicoll, Thomas Small, John Fenton, Thomas Law, John Elphinston, David Lorimer.

Boatsteerers: Alex McPherson, John McPherson, Mathew Henry, John Welch, David Malcolm, David Greig.

Common Mariners: Andrew Steedsman, David Sime, James Lorimer, Alexander Avas, George Gibb, David Thoms, Alexander Lyall, James Budges, William Anderson, Alexander Yeaman, Alexander Ramsay, William Ramsay, George Bishop.

FOR 1809 SEASON

Horn,[1] 291 tons; William Valantine, Master

Harpooners: William Adamson, Andrew Chapman, William Brown, Thomas Anderson, Andrew Anderson.

Boatsteerers: Andrew Greig, William Carmichael, William Anderson, John Chalmers, David Kennedy.

Line managers: John Dewars, James Mann, George Kerr, Charles Latto, Thomas Fife.

Common Mariners: John Miller, David Finlay, George Smith, Andrew Manson, Archibald Leitster, John Latto, James Leitster, James Peter.

Rodney, James Ireland, Master

Harpooners: Alexander Mill, Alexander Legerwood, James McKie.

Line managers: William Thoms, John Hull, James Chapman.

Boatsteerers: William Simmers, John Mitchell, Allan Watt.

Common Mariners: Andrew Haggart, William Duncan, James George, Thomas Hill, William Ramsay, Alexander Elder, James Wilson.

Jane, 279 tons; William Christopher, Master[2]

Harpooners: Thomas Aitken, Robert Nicoll, Alex Templeman, Mark Christopher, James Anderson.

Boatsteerers: David Reid, William Stephen, Thomas Hill, Mark Christopher Jr., George Norrie.

Line managers: William Shanks, Rob Lorimer, William Air, James Shatton, James Morrice.

Common mariners: David Trail, Thomas Wilson, Thomas Fyffe, John Whitten, Givan Wallace, Andrew Hebenton, Joseph Jamieson, David Morrice, Alexander Hull, Robert Watson, John Knols, Andrew Adamson.

FOR 1810 SEASON

Calypso, 306 tons; William Christopher, Master

Harpooners: Thomas Aitken, Mark Christopher, Andrew Lyston, Andrew McKenzie, Alexander Norrie.

Boatsteerers: Mark Christopher Jr., Andrew Hebenton, David Trail, Peter Henderson, Thomas Hally, Alexander Hebenton.

Line managers: George Norris, Robert Lorimer, Andrew Adamson, William McLeod, George Adamson, Joseph Jameson.

Common mariners: Anderson Cargill, John Whitton, John Barcly, Alexander Anderson, William Allan, Alexander Hull, David Jack, John Oliphant, Alexander Tyall, Alexander Simpson, Alexander Brown, Alexander Kilgour, Alexander Gray.

Friendship,[4] 304 tons; James Ireland, Master

Harpooners: William Stiven, Alexander Templeman, Alexander Fyall, John Wilson, William Dunian, William Smith.

Boatsteerers: David Reid, William Shanks, James Stratton, Thomas Scott, Andrew Haggart, James Norrie.

Line managers: John West, John Mckenzie, George Bridges, James Cameron, Thomas Chapman, Robert Watson.

Common mariners: David Tailer, William Wilson, Andrew Couper, James Couper, John Shands, Peter Anderson, John Wemyss, John Hall, John Bathie, James Bailie, William Thomson, Thomas Peebles, John Fyall.

Mary Ann, 292 tons; William Deuchars, Master

Harpooners: Alex Thoms, William Jeffreys, Thomas Cunningham, John Ros, Thomas Wilson.

Boatsteerers: Alex MacDougal, George Cameron, John Fairney, James Peebles, Fergus Anderson.

Line managers: John Greig, Robert Webster, John Gowans, George Taylor, James George.

Common mariners: Francis Christie, Thomas Sturrock, David Howie, John Kinnaird, Robert Browne, James Lister, John Doig, John Gofsins, David Adam, John Fisher, Thomas Sime, David Paterson, John Stevenson.

Calypso,[5] 306 tons; William Christopher, Master

Harpooners: Thomas Aitken, Mark Christopher, Andrew Lyston, Andrew Mckenzie, Robert Grant, Alexander Norrie.

Boatsteerers: Mark Christopher Jr., Andrew Hebeton, David Trail, Peter Henderson, Thomas Hally, Alexander Hebenton.

Line managers: George Norrie, Robert Lorimer, Andrew Adamson, William McLeod, George Adamson, Joseph Jameson.

Common mariners: Anderson Cargill, John Whitton, John Barcly, Alex Anderson, William Allan, Alex Hull, David Jack, John Oliphant, Alex Tyall, Alex Simpson, Alexander Brown, Alex Kilgowar, Alex Gray.

Horn,[6] 291 tons; William Valantine, Master

Harpooners: William Adamson, Andrew Chapman, William Brown, Thomas Anderson, Andrew Anderson.

Boatsteerers: John Dewar, David Kennery, James Mann, George Kerr, Charles Latto, Andrew Mail.

Line managers: John Chalmers, William Adamson, George Valentine, Thomas Fife, Andrew Greig.

Common mariners: Alexander Davidson, Peter Thomson, James Findlay, William Patullo, William Yeaman, Robert Peddie, Thomas Thomson, John Moodie, Robert Ferguson, Alex Yeaman, William Graham, David Lawson, David Ramsay.

Rodney, 176 tons; Alex Mills, Master (it seems that Mills was both master and harpooner in this voyage)

Harpooners: Alex Mills, Alex Legerwood, James Mackie.

Boatsteerers: William Lorimer, John Mitchel, James Chapman.

Line managers: William Thoms, William Ramsay, John Fyffe.

Common mariners: John Mckie, David Finlay, Francis Batchellor, William Elder, John Fraizer, James Harley, Alexander Forbes.

Friendship, 304 tons; James Ireland, Master

Harpooners: William Stiven, Alex Templeman, Alex Fyall, John Wilson, William Dunian, William Smith.

Boatsteerers: David Reid, William Shanks, James Stratton, Thomas Scott, Andrew Haggart, James Norrie.

Line managers: John West, John Mckenzie, George Bridges, James Cameron, Thomas Chapman, Robert Watson.

Common mariners: David Tailer, William Wilson, Andrew Couper, James Couper, John Shands, Peter Anderson, John Wemyss, John Hall, John Bathie, James Baillie, William Thomson, Thomas Peebles, John Fyall.

PROTECTION LISTS FOR 1811 VOYAGES

Mary Ann, 292 tons; William Deuchars, Master

Harpooners: Alex Thoms (Dundee), William Jeffreys (Dundee), Thomas Wilson (St Monance), John Roofs (Crail), John Greig (Dundee).

Boatsteerers: William Thoms (Dundee), Robert Webster (Dundee), Matthew McLean (Dundee), John Ferny (Dundee), Geo Cameron (Dundee).

Line managers: Alex McDougall (Dundee), James George (Dundee), Fergus Anderson (Pittenweem), Geo Deuchars (Dundee).

Common mariners: John Randall, John Logie, Alexander Brown, David Philip, Swan Swanston, John Stephinson, David Paterson, David Howie, Francis Chrystal, David Adam, John Cossins, Thomas Donnet, William Miller.

Horn,[7] 291 tons; William Valantine, Master

Harpooners: Andrew Chapman (St Monance), Thomas Anderson (Pittenweem), Andrew Anderson (Dundee), John Chalmers (Dundee), Geo Valentine (Dundee), Thomas Cunningham (Cellardyke).

Boatsteerers: David Henney (Dundee), Andrew Mail (Dundee), William Anderson (Pittenweem), Geo Kerr (Dundee), James Mann (Dundee), William Hunter (North Shields).

Line managers: John Dewar (Dundee), Thomas Fife (Dundee), Alex Davison (Dundee), Robert Peddie (Dundee), David Ramsay (Dundee), William Elder (Dundee).

Common mariners: Andrew Edwards, Robert Trail, James Elder, David Gardner, Lindsay Martin, James Hume, Robert Chisholm, Mathew Lister, William Miller, Stewart Ruxton, Alexander Yeaman, James Findlay, Francis Balbirna, George Adamson, Andrew Sword, James Harley.

Advice,[8] 324 tons; William Adamson, Master

Harpooners: James Anderson (Pittenweem), Alex Donaldson (Easter Anstruther), John Fyall (St Monance), David Easson (St Monance), David Marr (St Monance), Thomas Dowie (St Monance).

Boatsteerers: William Wilson (St Monance), Thomas Fyffe (Dundee), John Kidd (Dundee), Geo Adamson (St Monance), Alex Elder (St Monance), Lanceman Webster (Dundee).

Line managers: Robert Webster (Broughty Ferry), Robert Pattie (Newport), Robert Reekie (St Monance), Lawrence Gaull (Broughty Ferry), David Ogilvie (Dundee), John Bathie.

Common mariners: Robert Davidson, William Christie, Thomas Muir, William Miller, William Mathers, Andrew Trail, James Oliphant, James Robertson, James Felton, Thomas Small (2), John Simpson, Thos Small (1), Robert Scott.

Estridge, 312 tons; Adam Christopher, Master

Harpooners: James Watt (Pittenweem), Andrew Elphinton (Dundee), James Mackie (Dundee), John Fyfe (North Ferry), John McPherson (North Ferry), John Welsh (South Ferry).

Boatsteerers: Thomas Small (North Ferry), Alexander McPherson (Dundee), David Thoms (Dundee), Matthew Hendry (Dundee), David Malcolm (South Shields), David Lorimer (North Ferry).

Line managers: Thomas Nicol (Dundee), Thomas Low (Dundee), Peter Mann (Dundee), Robert Barclay (Dundee), John Warden (Dundee), Thomas Barclay (Dundee) (John Warden and Peter Mann later deserted and were replaced by John McKay and John Morris).

Common mariners: William McLeod, James Bridges, James Horsburgh, Alexander Hutt, Alexander Fyall, Robert Davidson, William Allan, Alex Duncan, Robert Cameron, James Irons, John Thomson, James Smith, David Lorimer, David Swan.

Calypso, 306 tons; William Christopher, Master

Harpooners: Thomas Aitken (St Monance), Andrew Liston (Newhaven), Andrew McKenzie (Dundee), Alex Norrie (North Ferry), Andrew Greig (Woodhaven), John Dixon.

Boatsteerers: Andrew Hebenton (Dundee), Mark Christopher (Dundee), Alexander Hebenton (Dundee), George Morrice (St Monance), George Thoms (Dundee), Joseph Jamison (Dundee).

Line managers: William McLeod (Dundee), George Anderson (North Ferry), David Trail (Dundee), Peter Henderson (Newcastle), Thomas Hally (Newcastle), Alexander Kilgour (Dundee).

Common mariners: Robert Rattray, Samuel Lak, Charles Butchart, George Gibb, James Dall, George Marr, David Simpson, Alex Norrie, John Robertson, James Shepherd, James Nicoll, John Pousty, Peter Gerrard.

1815 SEASON

Friendship, 394 tons; James Ireland, Master

Harpooners: William Smith (Cellardyke), William Shanks (Dundee), Thomas Lett, (Dundee), Ralph Wake (Seaton House), Robert Watson (Cellar Dyke).

Boatsteerers: George Kidd (Dundee), James Ireland (Dundee), George Banks (Dundee), Peter Anderson (Dundee), John Bourel (Dundee), Robert Ritchie (Cellardyke), James Graham (Anstruther).

Line managers: James Morgan (Dundee), Alex Durie (Dundee), Thomas Grant (Dundee), Kenny Anderson (Dundee), Bethrin Ireland (St Andrews), Will Small (Cellardyke).

Common mariners: Thomas Smith (St Monance), Robert Ireland (St Monance), James Fyal (St Monance), James Watson (St Andrews), Thos Miller (St Andrews), James Gibson (St Andrews), Alex Doctor (St Andrews), Thomas Barry (Dundee), James Urquhart (Dundee), James Bell (Dundee), William Young (Dundee), Joseph Low (Dundee), Thomas Webster (Dundee).

Notes to the Text

INTRODUCTION
Notes to pages ix–xi

1 DCA/KRS/AF 32.45, p. 57
2 Gilbert Gourdie (Editor), *The Diary of the Reverend John Mill: Minister of the Parishes of Dunrossness, Sandwick and Cunningbrough in Shetland 1740–1803* (Edinburgh 1889) p. 42, hereafter Gourdie, *Diary of John Mill*

1
THE HISTORICAL BACKGROUND
Notes to pages 1–15

1 Quoted in Donald S. Johnson, *Charting the Sea of Darkness: The Four Voyages of Henry Hudson* (New York, 1993) p. 18, hereafter Johnson, *Charting the Sea*
2 Quoted Johnson, *Charting the Sea*, p. 18
3 *Ibid.*, p. 18
4 William S. Bruce, *Polar Exploration* (London, 1911) pp. 85 and 129, hereafter Bruce, *Polar Exploration*
5 NAS: Privy Council Records: PC5/4, folios 40b & 41a; Edin. 1 February 1625; From the Council to His Majesty...to fish in Greenland.
6 Gap, Finn, *The History of Greenland* (volume II 1700–1728) (London 1987) p. 120
7 NAS Exchequer Records, E508/47/8; September 1750–September 1751; two whale bounties E 508/47/8/1; first whale bounty of Tryal

(Edinburgh Whale Fishing Company) 1750
8 NAS, Leven and Melville Muniments, GD26/13/648/1, 29 November 1756
9 DCA/KRS/CE 70.1.3, 29 March 1754
10 DCA/KRS/CE 70.1.3, 08 April 1757
11 DCA/KRS/CE 0.1.4, 30 January 1760
12 Dr Ches Sanger, *Scottish Geographical Magazine*, Vol. 107, No. 3, 1991, pp. 187-197, 'Changing resources and hunting grounds of Scottish whaling-sealing vessels in the second half of the nineteenth century.'
13 ASUOD/MS 59/2, Minutes of the Tay Fishing Company, hereafter *Tay*

2
THE QUARRY
Notes to pages 16–23

1 Quoted from Tim Severin, *The Brendan Voyage* (London, 1979) p. 240
2 NAS Patents: C3/22 No 96: Robert Bowman, part 1; item 265 in specifications, re Robert Bowman, manufacturer from Leith, using whalebone, 18 October 1806.
3 Dyson, John, *The Hot Arctic* (London 1979) p. 187, hereafter Dyson, *Hot Arctic*
4 The Petition of the Royal Boroughs of Scotland, 17 Dec 1767 in *Convention of Royal Burghs 1759–1779* (Edinburgh 1918)

3

THE BLUBBER BOATS
Notes to pages 24–33

1 'Northern Whale Fishery' in *The Montrose Review*, Friday 5 November, 1830
2 Stamp, T. & C., *Greenland Voyage*, (Whitby, 1983) p. 2
3 Tony Barrow, *The Whaling Trade of North East England* (Sunderland, 2001) p. 21, hereafter Barrow, *Whaling Trade*
4 Knut Weibust, *Deep Sea Sailors: A Study in Marine Ethnology* (Stockholm 1969) p. 431, hereafter Weibust, *Deep Sea Sailors*
5 R. B. Robertson, *Of Whales and Men*, (London, 1956) p. 45, hereafter Robertson, *Whales and Men*
6 ASUOD/MS 57/3/2, *Dorothy Whale Fishing Company and Friendship Whale Fishing Company*, hereafter *Dorothy*
7 *Montrose Review*, December 5 1822
8 DCA/KRS/CE 70.1.4; 25 February 1760
9 ASUOD/MS 59/2, *Tay*
10 DCA/KRS/CE 70.1.6, 20 March 1773
11 DCA/KRS/CE 70.1.6, 20 March 1773
12 DCA/KRS/CE 70.1.9, 22 July 1800
13 DCA/KRS/ Register of Dundee Shipping: CE 70.11.1
14 DCA/KRS/CE 70.1.19, 12 August 1801
15 DCA/KRS/ Register of Dundee Shipping: CE 70.11.2, 26 February 1827
16 DCA/KRS/CE 53.2.15, 4 August 1815
17 DCA/KRS/CE 70.11.2
18 DCA/KRS/CE 70.11.2
19 DCA/KRS/CE 70.11.2
20 DCA/KRS/CE 70.1.6, 26 October 1777
21 DCA/KRS/CE 70.1.5, 10 October 1770
22 DCA/KRS/CE 70.11.1
23 DCA/KRS/CE 70.11.2
24 DCA/KRS/CE 70.11.2
25 DCA/KRS/CE 70.11.2
26 DCA/KRS/CE 70.11.10
27 DCA/KRS/CE 70.11.10
28 DCA/KRS/CE 70.11.10
29 DCA/KRS/CE 70.11.10
30 DCA/KRS/CE 70.11.10
31 DCA/KRS/CE 70.11.13

4

THE GREENLANDMEN
Notes to pages 34–46

1 DCA/KRS/CE 70.1.16; 3 December 1822, p. 50, no. 344
2 ASUOD/ MS 59/1, *Tay*
3 Tom and Cordelia Stamp, *William Scoresby, Arctic Scientist* (Whitby 1975) p. 55, hereafter Stamp and Stamp, *Scoresby*
4 *Dundee Directory, 1809, 1818, 1829, 1834*
5 NAS, E/508/52/8/10, Note contained in Bounty Payments 18.8.1755
6 DCA/KRS/CE 70.1.12, 9 January 1810
7 DCA/KRS/CE 70.1.13, 21 August 1810
8 DCA/KRS/CE 70.1.13, 23 August 1810
9 DCA/KRS/CE 70.1.13, 23 August 1810
10 DCA/KRS/CE 70.1.13, 30 August 1810
11 DCA/KRS/CE 70.1.13, 13 September 1810
12 DCA/KRS/CE 70.1.13, 15 September 1810
13 DCA/KRS/CE 70.1.13, 18 February 1814
14 ASUOD/MS/57/3/3, *Dorothy*
15 ASUOD/MS/57/3/2, *Dorothy*
16 ASUOD/MS/57/3/3, *Dorothy*
17 Letter from Edward Nicoll of

Leamington Spa to the author, 5 November , 2000

18 *Aberdeen Journal,* 1 December 1783

19 *Aberdeen Journal,* 27 December 1790

20 *Edinburgh Courant,* 28 March 1751

21 MDCLA/ Unpublished MS, Hilliard, R.N, *Voyage of SS Narwhal from Dundee to the Greenland Seal Fishery 1859,* hereafter Hilliard, *Narwhal, 1859*

22 Captain A.H. Markham, *A Whaling Cruise to Baffin's Bay and the Gulf of Boothia And an Account of the Rescue of the Crew of Polaris'* (London 1874) p. 170, hereafter Markham, *Whaling Cruise*

23 Barrow, *Whaling Trade,* appendices

24 DCA/KRS/CE 70.2.13, 24 March 1819

25 Markham, *Whaling Cruise,* p. 10

26 DCA/KRS/CE 70.1.12

27 Mentioned in Robertson, *Whales and Men,* p. 26

28 ASUOD/MS 73.26, Ingram Papers

29 MDCLA, Unpublished MS, Alexander J Lamb, *Whaling Log, (Diana, 1903),* 18 July 1903, hereafter *Lamb, Log*

30 Basil Lubbock, *Arctic Whalers* (Glasgow 1937) p. 2, hereafter Lubbock, *Arctic Whalers*

31 Arthur Conan Doyle, 'Life on a Greenland Whaler', *Strand Magazine,* Number 13, January to June 1897, p. 19, hereafter Conan Doyle, 'Greenland Whaler'

32 ASUOD/ MS/53/3/3, *Dorothy*

33 ASUOD/MS/15/28/2, Dr David Lennox, *Working Class Life in Dundee for 25 Years,* table 153

34 David Fraser, (editor), *The Christian Watt Papers,* (Edinburgh 1983) p. 16, hereafter Fraser, *Watt Papers*

35 Gourdie, *Diary of John Mill,* June 1787, p. 76

36 Christopher Thomson, *The Autobiography of an Artisan* (London 1847) p. 118, hereafter Thomson, *Autobiography*

37 Weibust, *Deep Sea Sailors,* p. 203

38 W. G. Burn Murdoch, *From Edinburgh to the Antarctic: An Artist's Notes and Sketches During the Dundee Antarctic Expedition of 1892–93* (London 1894), p. 18, hereafter Burn Murdoch, *Edinburgh to the Antarctic*

39 *Ibid.,* p. 20

40 Burn Murdoch, *Edinburgh to the Antarctic,* p. 69

41 DCA/KRS/CE 70.1.14

42 ASUOD/MS/57/3/3, *Dorothy*

43 Captain Andrew Shewan, *The Great Days of Sail: Reminiscences of a Tea Clipper Captain* (London 1927, 1996) p. 23

44 *Ibid,* p. 36

45 ASUOD/MS/73/26, Ingram Papers, April 1838

46 Walter Scott, 'Diary to Nova Zembla and the Lord knows where' in John Gibson Lockhart, *The Life of Sir Walter Scott,* Volume IV (Edinburgh, 1837–8) p. 201, hereafter Scott, 'Diary'

47 DCA/KRS/CE 70.2.12, 24 March 1818

48 Seymour, Admiral E.H., *My Naval Career and Travels* (London 1911), p. 102, hereafter Seymour, *Career and Travels*

49 Markham, *Whaling Cruise* p. 17

50 *Ibid.,* p. 17

51 Lubbock, *Arctic Whalers,* p. 6

52 *Ibid.,* p. 54

53 Nigel Gatherer, 'The Dundee Whaler' in Nigel Gatherer, *Songs and Ballads of Dundee* (Edinburgh 1986) p. 46, hereafter Gatherer, *Songs*

54 *Ibid.,* p. 52

55 W Gillies Ross, *This Distant and Unsurveyed Country: A Woman's Winter at Baffin Island 1857–1858* (Montreal and Kingston 1997) p. xxii, hereafter Gillies Ross, *Distant and Unsurveyed Country*

56 Derek Flinn, *Travellers in a Bygone Shetland: An Anthology* (Edinburgh 1989) p. 69, hereafter Flinn, *Travellers*

57 James Irvine, *Lerwick: The Birth and Death of an Island Town* (Lerwick 1985) p. 64

58 Gordon Jackson, 'Battle with the Arctic: Montrose Whaling, 1785–1839' in Gordon Jackson and S. G. E. Lythe, *The Port of Montrose: A History of its Harbour, Trade and Shipping* (New York and Tayport 1993) p. 219

59 DCA/KRS/CE 53.1.22, 28 November 1812

60 Burn Murdoch, *Edinburgh to the Antarctic*, p. 5

61 Robertson, *Whales and Men*, p. 145

5

SKETCHES OF SOME WHALING MEN
Notes to pages 47–52

1 DCA/KRS/CE 70.1.2, 9 January 1810

2 DCA/KRS/CE 70.1.12, 24 August 1810

3 DCA/KRS/CE 70.1.14, 18 February 1814

4 DCA/KRS/CE 70.1.14, 16 February 1815

5 CLDCRD, Unpublished MS, Captain Thomas Davidson, *A Journal of a voyage from Dundee toward Davis Strait On Board the Dorothy, 1834,* 18 May 1834, hereafter Davidson, *Journal*

6 CLDCRD, *Ibid.*, 22 September 1834

7 CLDCRD, James Lyle, *Barque North Pole from Leith to Davis Straits, by James Lyle, Master,* 15 April 1835, hereafter Lyle, *North Pole*

8 CLDCRD, Unpublished MS, Anonymous, *Princess Charlotte from Dundee toward Davis Strait, 1853,* 30 April 1853; hereafter Charlotte

9 CLDCRD, Unpublished MS, Mathew Campbell, Surgeon, *Diary of a Voyage to the Davis Straits Aboard the Nova Zembla of Dundee, 1884,* 21 March 1884, hereafter Campbell, *Diary of a Voyage*

10 *East of Fife Record*, 9 April 1875

11 DCA/KRS/CE 70.1.12, 7 February 1809

12 DCA/KRS/CE 70.1.12, 12 February 1810

13 DCA/KRS/CE 70.1.13, 24 August 1810

14 DCA/KRS/CE 70.1.14, 18 February 1814

15 DCA/KRS/CE 70.1.11, 01 February 1808

16 DCA/KRS/CE 70.1.14, 21 September 1814

17 DCA/KRS/CE 70.11.13

18 Letters from James Gibson of Bobcaygeon, Ontario to the author, 25 June 2001 and 23 July 2001

19 DCA/KRS/CE 70.1.8, 15 March 1790

20 DCA/KRS/CE 70.1.9, 30 October 1800

6

WHALERS AT WAR
Notes to pages 53–62

1 Acts of the Parliaments of Scotland., ii, 235, c 20

2 *Extracts from the Records of the Convention of the Royal Burghs of Scotland 1759–1779* (Edinburgh 1917) 26 November 1766

3 *Extracts from Convention of the Royal Burghs of Scotland, 1759–1779* (Edinburgh, 1918) 30 January 1767

4 *Extracts From the Records of the Convention of the Royal Burghs of Scotland, 1738–1759* (Edinburgh 1915), 10 July 1755

5 *Ibid.*, 2 August 1755

6 *Aberdeen Journal* 23 August 1790

7 Christopher Lloyd, *The British Seaman 1200–1860: A Social Survey* (London 1968) p. 168

8   Letter written by Captain W. Essington of *Sarah* to the Mayor of Hull, quoted in Lubbock, *Arctic Whalers* p. 137
9   DCA/KRS/CE 70.1.10, 29 October 1804
10 DCA/KRS/CE 70.1.13, 27 July 1810
11 DCA/KRS/CE 70.1.12, 29 September 1808
12 Act 26th George 3rd Cap. 41
13 DCA/KRS/CE 70.1.9, 12 August 1801
14 DCA/KRS/CE 53.1.20, 17 March 1810
15 DCA/KRS/CE 53.1.20, 17 March 1810
16 DCA/KRS/CE 53.1.20, 27 March 1810
17 DCA/KRS/CE 53.1.21, 4 April 1811
18 DCA/KRS/CE 70.1.12, 10 December 1808
19 DCA/KRS/CE 53.1.22, 11 March 1814
20 DCA/KRS/CE 70.1.12, 8 February 1810
21 DCA/KRS/CE 70.1.14, 15 November 1814
22 DCA/KRS/CE 70.1.11, 15 January 1808
23 DCA/KRS/CE 70.1.14, 23 February 1814
24 DCA/KRS/CE 53.1.23, 1 September 1814
25 DCA/KRS/CE 53.3.2, 29 November 1813
26 DCA/KRS/CE 53.2.15, 26 July 1810
27 DCA/KRS/CE 53.1.24, 23 March 1816
28 DCA/KRS/CE 53.1.20, 28 March 1808
29 DCA/KRS/CE 53.1.16, 28 March 1800
30 Gourdie, *Diary of John Mill*, p. 51
31 *Aberdeen Journal* 11 August 1777
32 *Aberdeen Journal* 31 July 1780
33 Gourdie, *Diary of John Mill*, p. 51 April 1781
34 *Aberdeen Journal* 1 May 1781
35 DCA/KRS/CE 53.1.15, 13 March 1793
36 DCA/KRS/CE 70.1.7, 13 March 1793
37 DCA/KRS/CE 70.1.8, 3 October 1794
38 DCA/KRS/CE 70.1.8, 3 October 1794
39 DCA/KRS/CE 70.1.3, 29 March 1754
40 Gourdie, *Diary of John Mill*, p. 54, 1794
41 DCA/KRS/CE 53.1.20, 31 December 1808
42 DCA/KRS/CE 70.1.10, 10 February 1804
43 DCA/KRS/CE 70.1.10, 11 July 1805
44 DCA/KRS/CE 70.1.12, 21 March 1809
45 DCA/KRS/CE 70.1.12, 20 August 1809
46 DCA/KRS/CE 70.1.12, 22 August 1809
47 DCA/KRS/CE 70.1.12, 16 February 1809
48 DCA/KRS/CE 70.1.12, 24 July 1808
49 DCA/KRS/CE 70.1.12, 2 May 1809
50 DCA/KRS/CE 70.1.12, 9 February 1810
51 DCA/KRS/CE 70.1.12, 9 February 1819
52 *Montrose Review*, 11 August 1813
53 DCA/KRS/CE 53.2.15, 21 Oct 1813; CE 53.1.22, 15 October 1813

7

'FAREWELL DEAR SCOTIA'
Notes to pages 63–75

1   *Aberdeen Journal*, 30 June 1857
2   DCA/KRS/CE 53.2.15, 5 September 1810
3   DCA/KRS/CE 70.2.8, 5 September 1810
4   DCA/KRS/CE 53.1.22, 15 October 1813

5   DCA/KRS/CE 70.1.12, 23
    November 1809

6   DCA/KRS/CE 70.1.13, 5 October
    1810

7   Captain G. W. Clark : *The Last of the
    Whaling Captains* (Glasgow 1986),
    p. 3, hereafter Clark, *Last of the
    Captains*

8   Seymour, *Career and Travels,* p. 104

9   *The Dundee Directory for 1874–75
    including Lochee, Broughty Ferry,
    Newport and the rural districts in the
    vicinity of Dundee* (Dundee 1874) p.
    3

10 ASUOD/MS 59/4 R. Kinnes 'Some
    Ideas and Information on the Whale
    Fisheries in the Arctic Sea', paper
    read to the French Society of
    Broughty Ferry by N. S. Crondance
    1885

11 Burn Murdoch, *Edinburgh to the
    Antarctic,* p. 20

12 Markham, *Whaling Cruise,* p. 21

13 Burn Murdoch, *Edinburgh to the
    Antarctic,* p. 341

14 *Montrose Review,* 28 October 1825

15 MDCLA, Unpublished MS, John
    Wanless, *Journal of a Voyage to
    Baffin Bay Aboard the Ship Thomas
    Commanded by Alex Cooke* (1834), 3
    May 1834, hereafter Wanless,
    Journal

16 Letter from Stephen Wilson of Hebe
    to his wife, March 1821, quoted in
    Lubbock, *Arctic Whalers* p. 219

17 ASUOD/MS/57/3/30, *Dorothy*

18 Thomson, *Autobiography,* p. 152

19 Patrick Shuldham-Shaw and Emily
    B. Lyle, editors, *The Greig–Duncan
    Folk Song Collection,* Volume 1
    (Aberdeen 1981) p. 17

20 Amy Handy *The Golden Age of Sail,*
    New York 1996, illustration on p. 53

21 MDCLA, Hilliard, *Narwhal, 1859,*
    20 March 1859

22 Markham, *Whaling Cruise,* p. 21

23 Innes MacLeod, (Editor), *To the
    Greenland Whaling, Alexander
    Trotter's Journal of the Voyage of the*
    *Enterprise in 1856 from Fraserburgh
    and Lerwick* (Sandwick 1979) 19
    Feb 1856 p. 20, hereafter Trotter,
    Enterprise

24 Scott, 'Diary' p. 72

25 Verse 5 of 'The Old Polina' (possibly
    the Dundee whaling ship *Polynia*)
    1861–c1895, quoted in Gatherer,
    Songs, p. 49

26 Statement by Nutaraq, an aged
    Inuit, quoted in Dorothy Harley
    Eber, *When the Whalers were up
    North; Inuit Memories from the
    Eastern Arctic* (Kingston, Montreal,
    London 1979) p. 8, hereafter Eber,
    Inuit

27 Stamp and Stamp, *Scoresby,* p. 13

28 Mary Jane Whitehouse to her
    husband, Albert Johnston
    Whitehouse, May 1859, from Albert
    Johnston Whitehouse MS Journal
    1859–60 (Hull Museums and Art
    Galleries) 1859/60 quoted in W.
    Gillies Ross, *Arctic Whalers, Icy Seas*
    (Toronto, 1985) p. 155; hereafter
    Whitehouse, *Journal*

29 Dr Robb, head of the English
    Department, Dundee University, to
    the author, November 2000

30 Margaret Penny, *Journal kept by
    William Penny on board the Lady
    Franklin 1st November 1857* 29 May
    1858, in Gillies Ross, *Distant and
    Unsurveyed Country,* p. 21, hereafter
    Penny, *Journal*

31 Clark, *Last of the Captains,* p. 76

32 Fraser, *Watt Papers,* p. 68

33 *Ibid.,* p. 72

34 *Ibid.,* p. 74

35 ASUOD/MS/73/13, Ingram
    papers

36 Fraser, *Watt Papers,* p. 15

37 Fraser, *Watt Papers,* p. 15-16

38 DCA/KRS/CE 53.1.23, 19
    October 1814

39 DCA/KRS/CE 70.1.6, 12 Sept
    1788

40 DCA/KRS/CE 70.1.7, 13 February
    1790

41 DCA/KRS/CE 53.1.20, 30 March 1808
42 DCA/KRS/CE 70.2.26, 31 January 1823
43 DCA/KRS/CE 53.1.24, 4 April 1816
44 DCA/KRS/CE 70.2.5, 9 March 1787
45 DCA/KRS/CE 70.2.25, 2 Sept 1790
46 DCA/KRS/CE 70.1.10, 22 February 1808
47 DCA/KRS/CE 70.2.15, 9 March 1821
48 DCA/KRS/CE 53.1.24, 21 October 1818
49 CLDCRD, *Barque North Pole (from Leith to Davis Straits) left Leith 2/4/ 1836;* by James Lyle, Master, this entry dated 21 March 1837
50 DCA/KRS/CE 70.2.28, 21 January 1825
51 DCA/KRS/CE 70.2.7, 16 May 1800
52 DCA/KRS/CE 53.1.20, 21 February 1810
53 DCA/KRS/CE 53.1.24, 25 March 1816
54 DCA/KRS/CE 70.1.11, 11 February 1808
55 DCA/KRS/CE 70.1.11, 20 February 1808
56 DCA/KRS/CE 53.20.1, 12 February 1808
57 DCA/KRS/CE 53.1.20, 21 February 1810
58 DCA/KRS/CE 53.2.33, p. 84
59 DCA/KRS/CE 70.1.22, 18 March 1833
60 DCA/KRS/CE 70.1.17 1822/23, Letter Book p. 110 number 283, 2/ 11/1823
61 DCA/KRS/CE 70.2.14, 20 March 1820
62 DCA/KRS/CE 70.2.7, 16 July 1806
63 DCA/KRS/CE 53.1.22, 9 April 1814
64 DCA/KRS/CE 53.1.23, 20 October 1814
65 Markham, *Whaling Cruise*, p. 10
66 MDCLA, Wanless, *Journal*, 1 May 1834
67 MDCLA, Wanless, *Journal*, 3 May 1834

8
THE VOYAGE OUT
Notes to pages 76–88

1 DCA/KRS/CE 70.1.14, 24 November 1815
2 MDCLA Wanless, *Journal*, 30 April 1834
3 CLDCRD Campbell, *Diary of a Voyage*, 25 February 1884
4 CLDCRD Lyle, *North Pole*, 21 March 1837
5 MDCLA, Wanless, *Journal*, 30 April 1834
6 Thomson, *Autobiography*, p. 128
7 CLDCRD, Campbell, *Diary of a Voyage*, 26 February 1884
8 MDCLA, Hilliard, *Narwhal, 1859*.
9 Grierson, H. J. C. (Editor) *The Letters of Sir Walter Scott 1812— 1814* (London 1934) 4 August 1814.
10 Scott, 'Diary' p. 167
11 SA/D8/149/5
12 Richard Smith, 'Shetland and the Greenland Whaling Industry, 1780– 1872' in *Northern Scotland: the Journal of the Centre for Scottish Studies* (University of Aberdeen, 1992) p. 69
13 SA/D8/149/5, clause 6
14 Donald Withrington and Ian R. Grant (Editors), *The Statistical Account of Scotland, 1791–1793*, Volume XIX, Orkney and Shetland, (Wakefield 1978) p. 194, hereaftr, *Statistical Account*
15 MDCLA, Wanless, *Journal*, 3 May 1834
16 *Aberdeen Journal* 10 April 1787, reproducing a letter sent from Kirkwall 14 March 1787
17 William Barron, *Old Whaling Days*,

(Hull 1895) p. 178, hereafter Barron, *Whaling*

18 CLDCRD, Unpublished MS, *An Account of a voyage to Greenland aboard the whaler SS Camperdown 1861 by Alexander Smith of Dundee, Chief Engineer*, p. 5, hereafter Smith, *Camperdown*

19 Flinn, *Travellers*, p. 69

20 Gourdie, *Diary of John Mill*, p. 45

21 Thomson, *Autobiography*, p. 124

22 *Ibid.*, p. 124

23 Circular letter to the Captains of the Greenland ships, 24 March 1817, quoted in E. J. Reid Tait (Editor) *The Hjaltland Miscellany*, Volume 1 (Lerwick 1934) p. 74

24 Barron, *Whaling*, p. 78

25 DCA/KRS/CE 53.1.15, 2 February 1795

26 MDCLA, Hilliard, *Narwhal, 1859*, 20 March 1859

27 MDCLA Wanless, *Journal*, 10 June 1834

28 CLDCRD, Campbell, *Diary of a Voyage*, 21 March 1884

29 CLDCRD, Lyle, *North Pole* 13 April 1837 10 am

30 CLDCRD, Smith, *Camperdown*, p. 17

31 CLDCRD, Smith, *Camperdown*, p. 37

32 Thomson, *Autobiography*, p. 118

33 *Ibid.*, p. 121

34 R. P. Gillies, *Tales of a Voyager to the Arctic Ocean* Vol. 1 (London 1826) p. 110

35 Robert Wilson and Thomas Twatt, *Remarks on Board the Ship* Grenville Bay *of Newcastle on Tyne, Kept by Robert Wilson and Thomas Twatt, Seamen on board said ship 1ˢᵗ October 1836–27ᵗʰ April 1837*, quoted in James A. Troup, *The Ice Bound Whalers—The Story of the Dee and Grenville Bay 1836–7* (Stromness 1987) p. 92, hereafter Wilson and Twatt, *Remarks*

36 Burn Murdoch, *Edinburgh to the Antarctic*, p. 341

37 MDCLA, Wanless, *Journal*, 6 May 1834

38 Burn Murdoch, *Edinburgh to the Antarctic*, p. 51

39 *East of Fife Record*, October 29, 1869

40 Trotter, *Enterprise*, 1 July 1856 p. 55

41 Markham, *Whaling Cruise*, p. 10

42 CLDCRD, Unpublished MS, *Barque North Pole (from Leith to Davis Strait) left Leith 2/4/1836—James Lyle, mate*, 15 April 1835

43 MDCLA, Unpublished MS, T. Macklin, *Journal of a Voyage to Davis Strait aboard SS* Narwhal *1874*, 26 May 1874, hereafter Macklin, *Journal*

44 Trotter, *Enterprise*, 12 April 1856, p. 35

45 MDCLA, Wanless, *Journal*, 4 May 1834

46 CLDCRD, Smith, *Camperdown*, p. 24

47 MDCLA, Hilliard, *Narwhal, 1859*, 1 August 1859

48 Fraser, *Watt Papers*, p. 40

49 CLDCRD, Smith, *Camperdown*, p. 51

50 Thomson, *Autobiography*, p. 152

51 MDCLA, Wanless, *Journal*, 29 May 1834

52 MDCLA, Wanless, *Journal*, 3 June 1834

53 Thomson, *Autobiography*, pp. 127-8

54 Markham, *Whaling Cruise*, p. 73

55 Burn Murdoch, *Edinburgh to the Antarctic*, p. 55

56 Markham, *Whaling Cruise*, p. 48

57 Barron, *Whaling*, pages 128 and 129

58 Markham, *Whaling Cruise*, p. 168

59 *Dundee Perth Forfar and Fife's People's Journal*, 8 September 1860

60 FCKDM, Unpublished MS, *Whale Fishing Log of* Chieftain, *Captain William Archibald 1852, (To Davis Strait Whale Fishery)*, 12 March 1852, hereafter Archibald, *Log*

61 Markham, *Whaling Cruise*, p. 79

62 MDCLA, Wanless, *Journal*, 30 April 1834
63 MDCLA, Wanless, *Journal*, 1 May 1834
64 Barron, *Whaling*, p. 116

9
THE HUNT
Notes to pages 89–100

1 FCKDM, Archibald, *Log*, 22 April 1852
2 'Northern Whale Fishery' in the *Montrose Review*, 5 November 1830
3 Markham, *Whaling Cruise*, p. 112
4 DCA/KRS/CE 70.1.34, p. 257, 14 May 1877
5 *East of Fife Record*, 22 October 1869
6 Barron, *Whaling*, p. 4
7 'Northern Whale Fishery' in *Montrose Review*, 5 November 1830
8 Goodsir, R. A. *An Arctic Voyage to Baffin's Bay and Lancaster Sound*, (London, 1850) p. 94, hereafter Goodsir, *Arctic Voyage*
9 MDCLA, Lamb, *Log*, 6 July 1903
10 ASUOD/MS59/1, *Tay*
11 E Keble Chatterton, *Whales and Whaling* (London,1926) p. 72
12 Paul Budker, *Whales and Whaling*, (London 1958) p. 102
13 CLDCRD, *Charlotte*, 18 May 1853
14 CLDCRD Davidson, *Journal*, 21 September 1834
15 FCKDM, Archibald, *Log*, 21 May 1852
16 CLDCRC, Campbell, *Diary of a Voyage*, 19 July 1884
17 'Northern Whale Fishery' in *Montrose Review*, 5 November 1830
18 Conan Doyle, 'Greenland Whaler', p. 21
19 *Ibid.*, p. 21
20 'Arrival of a Peterhead Whaler' in *East of Fife Record*, 26 September 1873
21 Conan Doyle, 'Greenland Whaler', p. 22
22 CLDCRD, Campbell, *Diary of a Voyage*, 2 August 1884
23 DCA/KRS/CE 70.2.7, 16 July 1806
24 DCA/KRS/CE 53.1.23, 12 September 1815
25 DCA/KRS/CE 70.1.11, 2 September 1807
26 DCA/KRS/CE 53.1.21, 24 September 1811
27 'Invention of a New Gun for Shooting Whales' in *East of Fife Record*, 27 February 1874
28 Thomson, *Autobiography*, p. 144
29 'Northern Whale Fishery' in *Montrose Review*, 5 November 1830
30 *Ibid.*, 5 November 1830
31 Goodsir, *Arctic Voyage*, p. 8
32 DCA/KRS/CE 70.1.33, Dundee 7 July 1870
33 ASUOD/MS/59/1, *Tay*
34 CLDCRD, Campbell, *Diary of a Voyage*, 26 May 1884
35 Trotter, *Enterprise*, 9 July 1856 p. 56
36 Trotter, *Enterprise*, 9 June 1856 p. 49
37 MDCLA, Macklin, *Journal*, 29 August 1874
38 SAUSC/MS/15914, Letter from Frederic Augustus Lucas, Director of American Museum of Natural History, to D'Arcy Wentworth Thompson, 26 January 1903
39 SAUSC/MS/15926, Letter from Wentworth Thompson to Lucas, November 1908
40 Clark, *Last of the Captains*, p. 11
41 DCA/KRS/CE 53.1.24, 26 August 1817
42 MDCLA, Wanless, *Journal*, 7 August 1834
43 DCA/KRS/CE 53.1.7, 17 July 1802

10
DANGERS OF THE ICE
Notes to pages 101–108

1 FCKDM, Archibald, *Log*, 11 April 1852
2 *Ibid.*, 24 April 1852

3 Barron, *Whaling*, p. 22
4 MDCLA, Macklin, *Journal*, 2 June 1874
5 David Duncan, *Arctic Regions: Voyage to Davis Straits by David Duncan, master of the ship* Dundee (London 1827) 23 August 1826, hereafter Duncan, *Voyage*
6 Wilson and Twatt, *Remarks*, p. 108
7 Letter from the Master of *St Andrew*, published in *Aberdeen Journal* , 13 October 1830
8 MDCLA, Wanless, *Journal*, 10 June 1834
9 ASUOD/MS/59, *Tay*
10 David Gibb, 'A narrative of the sufferings of the whaler Dee while beset in the ice at Davis straits during the winter of 1836/37 (Aberdeen 1837), 1 January 1837', quoted in James A. Troup, *The Ice Bound Whalers—The Story of the* Dee *and* Grenville Bay *1836/7* (Stromness 1987) p. 131
11 'Missing Whale Ships—return to an order of the Honourable House of Commons, 21 April 1837' B.S.P. 1837, Volume 1, p. 553
12 DCA/KRS/CE 53.2.36.11, 17 January 1837
13 Duncan, *Voyage*, 16 August 1826
14 CLDCRD, Campbell, *Diary of a Voyage*, 27 June 1884
15 Barron, *Whaling*, p. 21
16 FCKDM, Archibald, *Log*, 18 June 1852
17 *Ibid.*, 30 May 1852
18 CLDCRD Davidson, *Journal*, 4 June 1834
19 DCA/KRS/CE 70.1.10, 29 September 1807
20 CLDCRD, Campbell, Diary of a Voyage, 6 May 1884
21 Barron, *Whaling*, p. 64
22 MDCLA, Wanless, *Journal*, 29 May 1834
23 'Loss of another Kirkcaldy Whale-ship' in *East of Fife Record*, 11 October, 1862
24 Barron, *Whaling*, p. 64
25 Bruce, *Polar Exploration*, pages 17–61
26 Barron, *Whaling*, p. 140
27 ASUOD/MS/73/26, Ingram papers
28 'Perilous Position of a Dundee Whaler' in *East of Fife Record*, 15 November 1872
29 DCA/KRS/CE 70.11.13
30 DCA/KRS/CE 70.11.13
31 DCA/KRS/CE 70.11.1
32 DCA/KRS/CE 70.11.1
33 DCA/KRS/CE 70.11.10
34 DCA/KRS/CE 70.11.10
35 DCA/KRS/CE 70.11.10
36 DCA/KRS/CE 70.11.10
37 Gordon Jackson, *The British Whaling Trade* (London 1978) p. 60
38 MDCLA, Macklin, *Journal*, 6 August 1874

11

ACROSS THE POND
Notes to pages 109–114

1 Guilbert de Nogent, quoted in Alan MacQuarrie, *Scotland and the Crusades,* (Edinburgh, John Donald,1997) p. 10
2 (i.) *Scottish Geographical Magazine*, Vol. 107, No. 3, 1991, pp. 187-197, 'Changing resources and hunting grounds of Scottish whaling-sealing vessels in the second half of the nineteenth century.'
(ii.) *Polar Record*, Vol. 20, No. 126, 1980, pp. 231-252, 'The 19th century Newfoundland seal fishery and the influence of Scottish whalers.'
3 Eber, *Inuit*
4 MDCLA, Lamb, *Log*, Sunday 24 May 1903
5 MDCLA, Lamb, *Log*, 28 May 1903
6 Barron, *Whaling*, p. 18
7 Barron, *Whaling*, p. 47
8 Penny, *Journal*, 8 August 1857
9 MDCLA/ MS Lamb, *Log*, 8 September 1903

10 'Arrival of a Peterhead Whaler' in *East of Fife Record*, 26 September 1873

11 'Arrival of a Whaler at Peterhead' in *East of Fife Record*, 21 August 1874

12 Ann Savour (Editor), 'Journal of a Whaling Voyage from Dundee to Davis Strait, 1894' in *Polar Record*, Volume 10 1960–1961, 136

13 Quoted in Eber, *Inuit*, p. 9

14 Quoted in Eber, *Inuit*, p. 98

15 Quoted in Eber, *Inuit*, p. 165

16 Clark, *Last of the Captains*, p. 69

17 Quoted in Eber, *Inuit*, p. 8

18 'Arrival of a Peterhead Whaler' in *East of Fife Record*, 26 September 1873

19 20 DCA/KRS/AF/32/45, p. 57, 3 July 1913

21 Clark, *Last of the Captains*, p. 56

22 DCA/KRS/CE 70.1.34, 11 June 1873

23 DCA/KRS/CE AF 32.45, p. 57

24 DCA/KRS/CE 70.1.35, 30 June 1877

25 DCA/KRS/CE 70.2.35, 7 February 1879

12
WHALERS AND DRINK
Notes to pages 115–120

1 DCA/KRS/CE 70.2.27, 9 March 1824

2 DCA/KRS/CE 70.2.27, 16 February 1824

3 DCA/KRS/CE 70.2.26, 22 February 1823

4 ASUOD/MS/73/26, Ingram Papers 1824

5 DCA/KRS/CE 70.1.13, 11 March 1811

6 DCA/KRS/CE 53.1.20, 30 March 1808

7 DCA/KRS/CE 70.1.13, 11 March 1811

8 Markham, *Whaling Cruise*, p. 17

9 Thomson, *Autobiography*, p. 135

10 Trotter, *Enterprise*, 1 May 1856, p. 40

11 AUL/MS 673, Unpublished MS, Anonymous Journal, 1 May 1831

12 Letter from William Scoresby Senior to his wife, quoted in Stamp and Stamp, *Scoresby* p. 6

13 MDCLA, Wanless, *Journal*, 16 May 1834

14 Trotter, *Enterprise*, 14 march 1856, p. 27

15 'Northern Whale Fishery' in *The Montrose Review*, 5 November 1830

16 MDCLA, Wanless, *Journal*, 16 June 1834

17 SPRI/ MS/ 823/1/2 William Elder, *Memorandum Book*, 15 November 1836, quoted in Ross Gillies, *Arctic Whalers*, p. 70, hereafter Elder, *Memorandum Book*

18 Whitehouse, *Journal*, 26 December 1859, p. 156

19 Whitehouse, *Journal*, 1 May 1860, p. 157

20 Trotter, *Enterprise*, 29 March 1859, p. 32

21 DCA/KRS/CE 70.1.39, 4 August 1896

22 DCA/KRS/GD/DPL/1/1, 18 March 1840

23 Sue Mowat, *The Port of Leith: Its History and Its People* (Edinburgh 1994) p. 321

24 DCA/KRS/CE 70.1.15, 20 January 1822

25 John Sanderson, [surgeon] *Greenland voyage of the Samuel of Hull* (Hull 1790) related in Lubbock, *Arctic Whalers*, p. 129-130

26 Penny, *Journal*, 22 October 1857

27 *Dundee Year Book, Facts and Figures*, (Dundee 1881) p. 12

28 Whitehouse, *Journal*, 31 December 1859, p. 154

29 Whitehouse, *Journal*, 31 Dec 1859, p. 154

30 Whitehouse, *Journal*, p. 164

31 MDCLA, Wanless, *Journal*, 1 August 1834

32 AUL/MS 673, Unpublished MS, Anonymous Journal, 17 July 1831

33 Penny, *Journal*, 14 November 1857
34 CLDCRD, Davidson, *Journal*, 27 May 1834
35 CLDCRD, Lyle, *North Pole*, 15 April 1835

13
RELIGION AND SUPERSTITION
Notes to pages 121–127

1 Stamp and Stamp, *Scoresby*, p. 3
2 MDCLA, Wanless, *Journal*, Sunday 4 May 1834
3 MDCLA, Wanless, *Journal*, 25 May 1834
4 Trotter, *Enterprise*, 14 July 1856, p. 58
5 Whitehouse, *Journal*, 27 May 1860, p. 161
6 Penny, *Journal*, 9 August 1857
7 *Ibid.*, 16 August 1857, p. 36
8 Elder, *Memorandum Book*, Thursday 10 December 1836, p. 73
9 CLDCRD, Campbell, *Diary of a Voyage*, Sunday 13 Feb 1884
10 CLDCRD, Smith, *Camperdown*, p. 23
11 Unpublished MS, Alexander Alison
12 Gourdie, *Diary of John Mill*, p. 42
13 MDCLA/ MS/ Lamb, *Log*, 17 March 1903
14 DCA/GD/DPL 1/1, 19 July 1826
15 Penny, *Journal*, 17 January 1858, p. 133
16 Wilson and Twatt, *Remarks*, p. 92
17 Thomson, *Autobiography*, p. 121
18 *Ibid.*, p. 155
19 Duncan, *Voyage*, 23 February 1827
20 Elder, *Memorandum Book*, Sunday 22 November 1836, p. 74
21 Markham, *Whaling Cruise*, p. 72
22 Burn Murdoch, *Edinburgh to the Antarctic*, p. 19
23 Markham, *Whaling Cruise*, p. 44
24 CLDCRD, Smith, *Camperdown*, p. 54
25 Clark, *Last of the Captains*, p. 21
26 Markham, *Whaling Cruise*, p. 16
27 CLDCRD, Campbell, *Diary of a Voyage*, 28 Feb 1884

28 CLDCRD, Smith, *Camperdown*, p. 56
29 *Ibid.*, p. 57
30 *Ibid.*, p. 57
31 MDCLA, Wanless, *Journal*, 10 April 1833
32 Burn Murdoch, *Edinburgh to the Antarctic*, p. 39
33 Barron, *Whaling*, p. 178
34 Thomson, *Autobiography*, p. 126
35 MDCLA, Wanless, *Journal*, 8 November 1834
36 Markham, *Whaling Cruise*, p. 57
37 Burn Murdoch, *Edinburgh to the Antarctic*, p. 52
38 Clark, *Last of the Captains*, p. 20
39 Barron, *Whaling*, p. 139

14
WHALERS AND THE LAW
Notes to pages 128–135

1 DCA/KRS/CE 70.1.7, 7 July 1788
2 DCA/KRS/CE 70.1.6, 23 July 1789
3 DCA/KRS/CE 70.1.6, 25 August 1789
4 DCA/KRS/CE 70.1.12, 23 November 1809
5 DCA/KRS/CE 70.1.30, 19 January 1860
6 DCA/KRS/CE 70.1.35, 20 December 1880
7 DCA/KRS/CE 70.2.35, 19 October 1880
8 Scott, 'Diary' p. 167
9 Gourdie, *Diary of John Mill*, p. 43
10 *Aberdeen Journal*, 3 August 1789
11 Letter in the *Aberdeen Journal*, 27 July 1789
12 Letter from Sir Walter Scott to the Duke of Buccleuch, written on board the Lighthouse Yacht at Lerwick, August 1814, in Grierson, H. J. C. (Editor), *The Letters of Sir Walter Scott 1812–1814* (London 1934)
13 SA/SC/12/6/1797/54, 12 June 1797

14 SA/SC/12/6/1814/30, 12 June 1814
15 Flinn, *Travellers*, p. 78
16 SA/SC/12/6/1820, 12 June 1820
17 SA/AD/22/11/6
18 SA/SC/12/6/1840/30, 7 April 1840
19 SA/AD/22/2/8/41, 7 March 1864
20 *Shetland Times*, 4 September 1897
21 Brian Smith, Archivist of Shetland, provided this information and searched the records on my behalf.
22 *Statistical Account*, p. 390
23 *Statistical Account* p. 135
24 Trotter, *Enterprise*, 27 July 1856 p. 62
25 Trotter, *Enterprise*, 27 July 1856 p. 62
26 DCA/GD/DPL 1/1, 6 July 1833
27 Quoted in Flinn, *Travellers*, p. 188
28 *Aberdeen Herald*, 5 May 1837
29 *Dundee Advertiser*, 9 May 1834
30 ASUOD/MS 73.26, Ingram Papers, 1868
31 ASUOD/MS/ 57/3/3, *Dorothy*
32 *Montrose Review*, 26 October 1827
33 DCA/KRS/CE 70.1.21, 30 October 1829
34 DCA/KRS/CE 70.1.21, 31 October 1829
35 DCA/KRS/CE 70.1.21, 17 November 1829
36 DCA/KRS/CE 70.1.21, November 1829
37 DCA/KRS/CE 53.4.1, 21 April 1804
38 DCA/KRS/CE 70.2.26, 18 January 1823
39 DCA/KRS/CE 70.1.23, 28 January 1835
40 DCA/KRS/CE 70.1.21, 14 November 1829
41 DCA/KRS/CE 70.1.21, 28 November 1829
42 DCA/KRS/CE 70.1.28, 23 October 1854
43 DCA/KRS/CE 70.1.28, 30 October 1854
44 DCA/KRS/CE 70.1.29, 27 October 1855
45 DCA/KRS/CE 70.1.29, 27 October 1855
46 DCA/KRS/CE 70.1.29, 5 November 1855
47 DCA/KRS/CE 70.1.29, 6 November 1855
48 DCA/KRS/CE 70.1.29, 14 November 1855
49 DCA/KRS/CE 70.1.29, 12 December 1855
50 DCA/KRS/CE 70.1.30, 5 September 1859
51 DCA/KRS/CE 70.1.30, 13 April 1859

15
BACK HOME
Notes to pages 136–143

1   DCA/KRS/CE 70.1.13, 5 October 1810
2   DCA/KRS/CE 53.1.16, 7 August 1798
3   DCA/KRS/CE 70.1.13, 15 October 1810
4   DCA/KRS/CE 70.1.37, 29 December 1885
5   DCA/KRS/CE 70.1.16, 3 July 1821
6   DCA/KRS/CE 70.2.5, 5 October 1787
7   DCA/KRS/CE 70.1.14, 27 May 1814
8   DCA/KRS/CE 70.1.13, 9 October 1811
9   DCA/KRS/CE 70.1.14, 23 August 1814
10 DCA/KRS/CE 70.1.16, 16 October 1821
11 DCA/KRS/CE 70.2.9, 20 August 1811
12 DCA/KRS/CE 70.1.13, 19 July 1811
13 DCA/KRS/CE 70.1.19, 5 October 1825
14 DCA/KRS/CE 70.2.28, 8 August 1825

15 DCA/KRS/CE 70.1.20, 21 January 1828

16 DCA/KRS/CE 70.1.20, 21 January 1828

17 DCA/KRS/CE 70.1.9, 24 August 1802

18 DCA/KRS/CE 70.1.23, 21 November 1833

19 DCA/KRS/CE 70.1.12, 23 July 1808

20 DCA/KRS/CE 70.1.12, 25 July 1808

21 DCA/KRS/CE 70.1.12, 29 July 1808 and 8 August 1808

22 DCA/KRS/CE 70.1.12, 6 April 1809

23 DCA/KRS/CE 70.1.12, 19 August 1809, 21 August 1809, 7 November 1809

24 DCA/KRS/CE 70.1.12, 11 December 1809

25 DCA/KRS/CE 70.1.14, 22 December 1814

26 DCA/KRS/CE 53.1.120, 1 August 1810

27 DCA/KRS/CE 70.1.33, 7 July 1870

28 DCA/KRS/CE 70.2.7, 9 September 1802

29 DCA/KRS/CE 70.2.7, 12 May 1803

30 ASUOD/MS/57/3/2, *Dorothy*

31 DCA/KRS/CE 70.1.14, 13 October 1817

32 Act 26, George III, cap 41 and 10, quoted in DCA/KRS/CE 70.2.7, 16 July 1806

33 DCA/KRS/CE 53.1.18, 17 September 1805

34 DCA/KRS/CE 53.1.20, 30 September 1809

35 DCA/KRS/CE 53.1.23, 30 September 1814

36 DCA/KRS/CE 70.1.10, 16 September 1807

37 DCA/KRS/CE 70.1.10, 29 September 1807

38 DCA/KRS/CE 70.1.10, 10 December 1807

39 DCA/KRS/CE 70.1.19, 7 November 1826

40 DCA/KRS/CE 70.2.24, 9 November 1826

41 ASUOD/MS/57/3/2, *Friendship Whale Fishing Company* (hereafter *Friendship*) account for pilotage, 29 October 1830 £1 1s.

42 ASUOD/MS/57/3/2, *Friendship*

43 DCA/KRS/CE 70.1.34, 15 July 1872

44 DCA/KRS/CE 70.1.34, 11 June 1873

45 DCA/KRS/CE 70.1.34, 21 June 1873

46 'Review of the Dundee Whale and Seal Fishing' in *East of Fife Record*, 29 November 1872

Appendix: Selected Crew Lists of Dundee Whalers

Notes to pages 146–151

1 DCA/KRS/CE 70.1.12, 2 February 1809

2 DCA/KRS/CE 70.1.12, 2 February 1809

3 DCA/KRS/CE 70.1.12, February 1810

4 DCA/KRS/CE 70.1.12, February 1810

5 DCA/KRS/CE 70.1.12, 21 February 1810

6 DCA/KRS/CE CE 70.1.11, July 1809 and February 1810

7 DCA/KRS/CE 70.1.13, 23 August 1810

8 DCA/KRS/CE 70.1.13

BIBLIOGRAPHY

ARCHIVE MATERIAL
PRIMARY SOURCES—UNPUBLISHED

Journals in McManus Gallery, Dundee:

Campbell, Matthew, *Diary of a Voyage to the Davis Straits Aboard the* Nova Zembla *of Dundee, 1884*

Hilliard, R. N., *Voyage of* SS Narwhal *from Dundee to the Greenland Seal Fishery 1859*

Lamb, Alexander J., *Whaling Log* (Diana, 1903)

Macklin, T., *Journal of a Voyage to Davis Strait Aboard* SS Narwhal, *1874*

Wanless, John, *Journal of a Voyage to Baffin Bay Aboard the Ship* Thomas *Commanded by Alex Cooke* (1834)

Journal held in the Department of Manuscripts and Archives, Aberdeen University Library:

Anonymous Journal MS 673 (secondary evidence within the journal indicates that this was written by the surgeon of *Hercules)*

Logbooks and Journals held in the Local Studies Department, Central Library, Dundee:

Anonymous, Princess Charlotte *from Dundee toward Davis Strait, 1853* (unpublished MS 1853)

Anonymous, *Log of* SS St Hilda *from Dundee toward Dives* [sic] *Strait* (unpublished MS 1909)

Davidson, Thomas, *A Journal of a Voyage from Dundee toward Davis Strait on Board the* Dorothy (unpublished MS 1834)

Lyle, James, *Barque* North Pole *from Leith to Davis Straits* (unpublished microfilm, 1835 and 1837)

Smith, Alexander, *An Account of a voyage to Greenland aboard the Whaler* SS Camperdown, *1861, by Alexander Smith of Dundee, Chief Engineer* (unpublished MS 1861)

Stephen, William C., *Log of ketch* Earnest Willie *from Dundee to Davis Strait 1912,* William C. Stephen, master (unpublished MS 1912)

Stephen, William C., *Log of ketch* Earnest Willie *from Dundee to Davis Strait 1913,* William C. Stephen, master (unpublished MS 1913)

Logbook held in Reference & Local Studies Department, War Memorial Library, Kirkcaldy:

Archibald, William, *Whale Fishing Log, 1852* (Chieftain)

University of St Andrews—Special Collections, D'Arcy Wentworth Thompson Collection:

MS 15914—letter from Frederick Augustus Lucas to DWT 26/1/1903
MS15925—letter from Frederick Augustus Lucas to DWT 31/10/1908
MS 15926—letter from DWT to Frederick Augustus Lucas (day obscure) November 1908

University of Dundee Archives:

John P. Ingram papers (MS 73/26)—whaling and sealing
Papers of the Dorothy Whale Fishing Company and Friendship Whale Fishing Company (MS 57/3)
Papers of the Tay Whale Fishing Company, Dundee (MS 59)
Lennox, Dr David, *Working Class Life in Dundee for 25 Years* (MS 15/28/2)

City Archives, Dundee:

Agriculture and Fishery Records
Customs and Excise Records: Dundee, Letter Book, Collector to Board
Customs and Excise Records: Dundee, Letter Book, Board to Collector
Dundee, Perth & London Shipping Company, Directors' Minute Book (GD/DPL 1/1)

Shetland Archives:

Sheriff Court records:
SC 12/6/1797/54 Petition (assault on various people in Scalloway) 8 September 1797
SC 12/6/1814/30 Petition (assault on George Hughson) August 1814
SC 12/6/1820/26 Petition (for release from jail) April 1820
SC 12/6/1840/130 Petition (for pilotage of ship and £200 damages for slander of theft by Captain William Couldry of *Abram* of Hull) 7 April 1840

Procurator Fiscal records:
AD. 22/2/8/41 Precognition: theft of bedclothes
AD 22/11/6 Theft of fur cap

PRIVATE COLLECTION:

Fragments of journal of Alexander Alison

NEWSPAPERS:

Aberdeen Journal
Shetland News
Dundee, Perth, Forfar and Fife People's Journal
East of Fife Record
Dundee Courier

PRIMARY SOURCES—PUBLISHED:

Barron, William, *Old Whaling Days* (Hull 1895)

Burn Murdoch, W.G., *From Edinburgh to the Antarctic: An Artist's Notes and Sketches During the Dundee Antarctic Expedition of 1892–93* (London 1894)

Duncan, David, *Arctic Regions: voyage to Davis' Strait, by David Duncan, master of the ship* Dundee. *Sailed from London 3rd April 1826 and Returned 25th June 1827; Having Been Beset by Ice More Than Eight Months; During Seventy-five Days of Which, the Sun never Rose Above the Horison: With an Account of the Hardships and Dangers Sustained by the Crew, and Many Miraculous Escapes.* (London 1827)

Extracts from the Records of the Convention of the Royal Burghs of Scotland 1738– 1759 (Edinburgh 1915)

Dundee Directory for 1874–75: including Lochee, Broughty Ferry, Newport and the Rural districts in the vicinity of Dundee (Dundee 1874)

Extracts from the Records of the Convention of the Royal Burghs of Scotland 1759– 1779 (Edinburgh 1917)

Fraser, David (Editor), *The Christian Watt Papers* (Edinburgh 1983)

Gillies, R.P., *Tales of a Voyager to the Arctic Ocean* (London 1826)

Grierson, H.J.C., (Editor), *The Letters of Sir Walter Scott 1812–1814* (London 1934)

Innes Macleod (Editor), *To the Greenland Whaling: Alexander Trotter's Journal of the Voyage of the* Enterprise *in 1856 from Fraserburgh and Lerwick* (Sandwick, Shetland 1979)

Kinnes, J., *Paper read to the French Society of Broughty Ferry in 1885* (University of Dundee Archives MS 59/4)

Markham RN, Captain A.H., *A Whaling Cruise to Baffin's Bay and the Gulf of Boothia and an Account of the Rescue of the Crew of the* Polaris (London 1874)

Ross, W. Gillies, *This Distant and Unsurveyed Country: A Woman's Winter at Baffin Island 1857–1858* (Montreal and Kingston 1997)

Scott, Walter, 'Diary to Nova Zembla and the Lord knows where', in Lockhart, John Gibson, *The Life of Sir Walter Scott*, Volume IV (Edinburgh 1837-8)

Scoresby W. (Jr.) FRSE, *An Account of the Arctic Regions, with a History and Description of the Northern Whale-Fishery* (Edinburgh, 1820)

Shuldham-Shaw, Patrick & Lyle, Emily B. (Editors), *The Greig-Duncan Folk Song Collection, Volume 1* (Aberdeen 1981)

Thomson, Christopher, *The Autobiography of an Artisan* (London, 1847)

Troup, James A. (Editor), *The Ice Bound Whalers: The story of the* Dee *and* Grenville Bay *1836/7* (Stromness 1987)

Withrington, Donald J., and Grant, Ian R. (Editors), *The Statistical Account of Scotland 1791–99* Volume XIX Orkney and Shetland (Wakefield 1978)

SECONDARY WORKS—BOOKS:

Anson, Peter F., *Fishermen and Fishing Ways* (London 1932)

Archibald, Malcolm, *Sixpence for the Wind: A Knot of Nautical Folklore* (Latheronwheel, 1999)

Attenborough, Richard, *Life on Earth: A Natural History* (London, 1979)

Beaglehole, J. C., *The Life of Captain James Cook* (London 1974)

Beddard, F. E. *A Book of Whales* (London 1900)

Clark, Captain G. W. *The Last of the Whaling Captains* (Glasgow 1986)

Credland, Arthur G., *Whales and Whaling: The Arctic Fishery* (Hull 1982)

Chatterton, E. Keble, *Whalers and Whaling: The Story of the Whaling Ships up to the Present Day* (London 1925)

Conway, Martin, *No Man's Land: A History of Spitsbergen from its Discovery in 1596 to the Beginning of the Scientific Exploration of the Country* (Cambridge 1906)

Dobson, David, *Scots in the Arctic: Tales of the Whalers* (St Andrews 1996)

Dobson, David, *The Whalers of Dundee 1750–1850* (St Andrews 1995)

Dobson, David, *Scottish Whalers Before 1800* (St Andrews 1992)

Dundee Year Book: Facts & Figures (Dundee 1881)

Dyson, John, *The Hot Arctic* (London 1979)

Falkus, Hugh, *Master of Cape Horn: The Story of a Square-rigger Captain and his World* (London 1982)

Ferguson, David M., *Shipwrecks of North East Scotland 1444–1990* (Aberdeen 1991)

Flinn, Derek, *Travellers in a Bygone Shetland: An Anthology* (Edinburgh 1989)

Francis, Daniel, *Arctic Chase: A History of Whaling in Canada's North* (St John's, Newfoundland 1984)

Frank, Stuart M., 'Scrimshaw—An introduction and an overview AD 800–1960' in Basberg, Bjorn L., Rigstad, Jan, Wexelsa, Einar, *Whaling and History: Perspectives on the Evolution of the Industry* (Sandefjord, Norway 1993)

Fraser, Duncan, *The Smugglers*, Montrose, Standard Press, 1971

Frazer, Sir James, *The Golden Bough: A Study in Magic and Religion*, (London 1922)

Friel, Ian, *The Good Ship: Ships, Shipbuilding and Technology in England 1200–1520* (London, British Museum Press, 1995)

Gad, Finn, *The History of Greenland, Volume II 1700–1782* (London 1987)

Gatherer, Frank, *Songs and Ballads of Dundee* (Edinburgh 1986)

Handy, Amy, *The Golden Age of Sail* (New York 1993)

Hawes, Captain Charles B., *Whales* (Heinemann, London 1924)

Henderson, David S., *Fishing for the Whale: A guide/catalogue to the collection of whaling relics in Dundee museums* (Dundee 1976)

Henderson, James, *The Frigates: An account of the lesser warships of the wars from 1793 to 1815* (Ware, Hertfordshire 1998)

Irvine, James, *Lerwick: The Birth and Death of an Island Town* (Lerwick 1985)

Jackson, Gordon, *The British Whaling Trade* (London 1978)

Jackson, Gordon, 'The Battle with the Arctic: Montrose Whaling, 1785–1839' in Jackson, Gordon and Lythe S.G.E., *The Port of Montrose: A History of its Harbour, Trade and Shipping* (New York and Tayport 1993)

Kemp, Peter, *The Oxford Companion to Ships and the Sea* (Oxford 1976)

Lenman, Bruce, *From Esk to Tweed: Harbours, Ships and Men of the East Coast of Scotland* (London and Glasgow 1975)

Lloyd, Christopher, *The British Seaman 1200–1860: A Social Survey* (London 1968)

Lubbock, Basil, *The Arctic Whalers* (Glasgow 1937, 1955)

Lythe, S.G.E; *Gourlays of Dundee; the Rise and Fall of a Scottish Shipbuilding Firm* (Dundee 1964)

MacQuarrie, Alan, *Scotland and the Crusades* (Edinburgh 1997) p. 10

Mackintosh, W. R., *Around the Orkney Peat-Fires, being Sketches of Notable Orcadians, Smuggling Anecdotes, Stories of the Press-Gang and Witch and Other Stories* (Kirkwall, 1893, seventh edition 1967)

McGowran, Thomas, *Newhaven-on-Forth: Port of Grace* (John Donald, Edinburgh 1985)

Mielche, Hakon, *There She Blows!* (London 1952)

Murray, Ian, *The Whalers* (Dundee 1959)

Payne, Fred, *Whaling and Whitby* (Whitby, undated)

Robertson, R.B., *Of Whales and Men* (London 1956)

Robertson, Una A., *Mariners' Meal Times and Other Daily details of Life on Board a Sailing Warship* (Dundee 1979)

Ross, W. Gillies, *Arctic Whalers, Icy Seas* (Toronto 1985)

Savours, Ann, *The Voyages of the* Discovery: *The Illustrated History of Scott's Ships* (London, Virgin Books, 1992)

Severin, Tim, *The Brendan Voyage* (London 1979)

Seymour, Admiral E.H., *My Naval Career and Travels* (London 1911)

Shafe, Michael (compiler), *University Education in Dundee 1881–1981: A Pictorial History* (Dundee 1982)

Shewan, Captain Andrew, *The Great Days of Sail: Reminiscences of a Tea Clipper Captain* (London 1927, 1996)

Scheffer, Victor B., *The Year of the Whale* (New York 1969)

Schei, Liv Kjorsvik, & Moberg, Gunnie, *The Shetland Story* (London 1988)

Smith, Robert, *The Whale Hunters* (Edinburgh 1993)

Stamp, Tom & Cordelia, *William Scoresby: Arctic Scientist* (Whitby 1975)

Szasz, Ferenc Morton, *Scots in the North American West 1790–1917* (Norman, 2000)

Tait, E. J. Reid, (Editor), *The Hjaltland Miscellany*, Volume One (Lerwick 1934)

The Three Voyages of Martin Frobisher—in Search of a Passage to Cathia and India by the North-west, A.D. 1576–78. Reprinted from the 1578 first edition of Hakluyt's *Voyages*, with selections from manuscript documents in the British Museum and State Paper Office. (London, printed by H. Bynnyman, 1867.)

Thomson, George Malcolm, *The North West Passage* (London, 1975)

Veriick, A. Hyatt, *The Real Story of the Whalers* (New York and London 1916)

Watson, Harry D., *Kilrenny and Cellardyke: 800 Years of History* (Edinburgh 1986)

Williams, Heathcote, *Whale Nation* (Jonathan Cape, London 1988)

Weibust, Knut, *Deep Sea Sailors: A Study in Maritime Ethnology* (Stockholm 1969)

Whatley, Christopher A., Swinfen, David B., Smith, Annette M., *The Life and Times of Dundee* (Edinburgh 1993)

Wise, Terence, *To Catch a Whale* (Fakenham, 1970)

SECONDARY WORKS—ARTICLES IN PERIODICALS:

Duncan, W.R.H., 'Aberdeen and the Early Development of the Whaling Industry 1750–1800' in *Northern Scotland: The Journal of the Centre for Scottish Studies, University of Aberdeen* Volume 3, number 1, 1977–78, pp. 47-59

Smith, Richard, 'Shetland and the Greenland Whaling Industry 1780–1872' in *Northern Scotland: The Journal of the Centre for Scottish Studies, University of Aberdeen* Volume 12, 1992, pp. 67-87

SECONDARY WORKS—THESES:

Archibald, Malcolm, *A Wild and Rough Lot: An Investigation into the character and behaviour of British Arctic whalers, 1780 to 1910* (unpublished dissertation, University of Dundee, 2001)

Sanger, C.W., *The Origins of the Scottish Northern Whale Fishery* (unpublished Ph.D. Thesis, University of Dundee, 1985)

Index

172